BECOMING A SUSTAINABLE RUNNER

A Guide to Running for Life, Community, and Planet

Tina Muir
Zoë Rom

HUMAN KINETICS

Library of Congress Cataloging-in-Publication Data

Names: Muir, Tina, 1988- author. | Rom, Zoë, 1993- author.
Title: Becoming a sustainable runner : a guide to running for life, community, and planet / Tina Muir, Zoë Rom.
Description: Champaign, IL : Human Kinetics, [2024] | Includes bibliographical references and index.
Identifiers: LCCN 2023004504 (print) | LCCN 2023004505 (ebook) | ISBN 9781718214033 (paperback) | ISBN 9781718214040 (epub) | ISBN 9781718214057 (pdf)
Subjects: LCSH: Runners (Sports)--Conduct of life. | Running--Psychological aspects. | Social participation. | Community life. | Environmental responsibility. | BISAC: SPORTS & RECREATION / Running & Jogging | NATURE / Environmental Conservation & Protection
Classification: LCC GV1061 .M85 2024 (print) | LCC GV1061 (ebook) | DDC 796.42092--dc23/eng/20230213
LC record available at https://lccn.loc.gov/2023004504
LC ebook record available at https://lccn.loc.gov/2023004505

ISBN: 978-1-7182-1403-3 (print)

The web addresses cited in this text were current as of January 2023, unless otherwise noted.

Senior Acquisitions Editor: Michelle Earle; **Developmental Editor**: Laura Pulliam; **Managing Editor**: Shawn Donnelly; **Copyeditor**: Lisa Himes; **Indexer**: Zinger Indexing; **Permissions Manager**: Laurel Mitchell; **Graphic Designer**: Denise Lowry; **Cover Designer**: Keri Evans; **Cover Design Specialist**: Susan Rothermel Allen; **Photograph (cover)**: tonywithasony; **Photographs (interior)**: © Human Kinetics, unless otherwise noted; **Photo Asset Manager**: Laura Fitch; **Photo Production Manager**: Jason Allen; **Senior Art Manager**: Kelly Hendren; **Printer**: Versa Press

Human Kinetics books are available at special discounts for bulk purchase. Special editions or book excerpts can also be created to specification. For details, contact the Special Sales Manager at Human Kinetics.

Printed in the United States of America   10 9 8 7 6 5 4 3 2 1

The paper in this book is certified under a sustainable forestry program.

Human Kinetics
1607 N. Market Street
Champaign, IL 61820
USA

United States and International
Website: **US.HumanKinetics.com**
Email: info@hkusa.com
Phone: 1-800-747-4457

Canada
Website: **Canada.HumanKinetics.com**
Email: info@hkcanada.com

E8685

To everyone working to make a difference

CONTENTS

PART III SUSTAIN YOUR PLANET

FOREWORD

Why do I run? There have been so many answers to this question, and it's one I constantly check in with myself about. Being a runner isn't just one identity that we have or run with. The moment we choose to run sparks from some goal, action, or commitment, prioritizing our well-being, a tradition, a ceremony, an opportunity to heal, to engage with the community. I've been running for 25 years, and I ran because my family did. I see running as a deep bond. I put so much time, effort, and love into the miles I run—just as much as running gives back to me. It's become a beautiful reciprocal relationship. For as many ups, celebratory moments, and accomplishments as there are, there have been many downs, challenges, pain, and hurt. For me and for many people I know, running is the longest relationship we've ever been in.

Younger Jordan thought running was only about fitness, winning, running fast, and getting those medals. There was a lot of joy in it but a lot of pressure I put on myself to keep this family tradition of running going. I didn't want to disappoint anyone. This perspective was challenged. My running transitioned from a focus on family to Native representation to running for the love of running (as I healed from an eating disorder) to running in prayer (as it intersected with my advocacy) to now, being a new mom and learning this new body of mine. This was a journey of growing, adapting, and working through what I thought it meant to be a runner and the identity by which many have known me for all of my life—Jordan the runner. I'm still running but have found a deeper purpose. I was finding my *why*. Over time, my advocacy (in climate justice; for equality, equity, diversity, inclusion, accessibility, safety, and affordability in the running industry; and for missing and murdered Indigenous women, girls, and relatives) has challenged others around me about what it means to be a runner. It challenges the stereotypical image of what a runner looks like and what they do. It connected me with so many runners who weren't the typical runners I was used to being around. It expanded my community; it exposed me to different perspectives and lived experiences and challenged me in what I thought I knew. And the opportunity to grow and learn is something I embrace.

A big part of what I advocate for is a thriving future for the next generations to come, for my son. That means a healthy planet and for everyone to be safe, to be heard, to thrive, and to be unapologetically themselves. This is where we can work toward living in kinship with the lands and with each other. As a runner, I've struggled with this relationship when the running industry is wasteful and contributes to the damage of a healthy planet—with not knowing what reasonable solutions we can take to still enjoy the love of running without guilt while ensuring it's not damaging to our bodies, the lands, and the health of our sacred ecosystems.

I think running is supposed to evolve as we evolve. This book, *Becoming a Sustainable Runner*, has so much to offer in sustaining the love, passion, training, fueling, pacing, advocacy, well-being, community building, and protection of the planet. It's a beautiful resource that provides different perspectives, lived experiences, and supportive advice; challenges your mind; and eases you in a direction that allows your mind to grow. There is no one right way to be a runner. And what Tina and Zoë share fully supports you in your journey as you find your *why*. I felt validated by what I read. There was much that resonated with me. I learned something new. I have a list of reminders from this book that I will put into practice as I continue running. I'm excited to experience where this running kinship will grow.

Jordan Marie Whetstone
Founder of Rising Hearts
Runner, Organizer, and Athlete Advocate

ACKNOWLEDGMENTS

It feels so strange to write this. Acknowledgments have always been one of my favorite sections of books—something I looked forward to reading. I often wondered what it would be like to write one, thanking those people who helped bring a book to life. Yet now that I am here, it is stressful!

First, I would like to thank my coauthor and friend, Zoë, who tirelessly and passionately fought for needed change in the running space while we worked through this messy process of book writing. Both of us were already stretched thin (yes, at times we abandoned our own advice), yet we still believed in the power of this book. Thank you for your commitment and dedication to making this world a better place, Zoë.

To the friends who read chapters of this book to make it better and to the friends who helped change the trajectory of my future through your important feedback and advice: Elizabeth Inpyn, Chris Mosier, Cat Morris, Maria Vargas, Alli Worthington, Christine Yu, Chris McClung, Sanjay Rawal, Mike Nishi, Ryan Montgomery, Sid Baptista, Brogan Graham, Knox Robinson, Jon Phillips, Lucie Hanes, Ryan Eckel, Matt Taylor, Simran Jeet Singh, Guy Winch, Christine Burke, and Jon Corne.

Thank you to Mary and David Picucci, Holly Fox, Ashley Maschmann, Lisa Houston, and Margie Thornton for the love you give to our girls and your help with child care, which gave me the freedom to write.

To my Running for Real team, not only for your hard work and dedication to the work we are doing but also for supporting me in the writing of this book: Sally Pontarelli, Jeremy Noessel, Kat MacKay, Kelsey Wang, Louise Murphy, and Sandy Gutierrez.

To my coaches and mentors who helped me become the best human being I could be along my journey to become the best runner I could be. Without your conscious choice to put your ego aside and do what was truly best for me as a sustainable runner and human, I never would have been in this moment right now: Brad Plummer, Evie Serventi, and Drew Watts.

To Mum, Dad, Jess, Jenny, Jackie, and Viv for loving me no matter what and for never judging my, at times, turbulent relationship with running—when I first started and had no idea what I was doing, when I was an awkward teenager who nearly quit the sport for good, when you encouraged me to follow my dreams of running in the United States, and when I struggled with my identity as a professional runner who felt that was all she had to give. And especially when I gave it all up to begin my next chapter as a mother yet still found my way back to the sport. I love you all.

To my husband, Steve, for supporting me in my dreams in the past and present. Your encouragement and love mean so much. You are my rock—my steady support system who always grounds me and reminds me of who I am. You always inspire me to keep following my heart and doing the right thing. I learned that from you. I recognize all the extra stress you took on when watching the girls for the many hours I worked this past year. Thank you for always nudging me to keep going.

To my sweet little girls: You have no idea what this book means, and if either of you choose to run someday, I hope it is with joy as the primary goal. Regardless of what you choose to do with your time, as long as you do it authentically yourselves, that's truly all I care about. I love you and Daddy, always.

—Tina Muir

I'm so grateful to my coauthor, friend, and mentor, Tina, for bringing me into this project and believing unwaveringly in our message and environmental values. I used to think that pushing for justice was an inherently lonely pursuit. But working with Tina, and all the sources who helped us bring this book together, proved me wrong. Striving for a more just and equitable world has connected me more deeply and authentically with a vibrant community of fellow athletes, activists, writers, and thinkers. We're now enmeshed in a network of like-minded folks who are dedicating their lives to this important work, and I'm grateful for the opportunity this book has opened to deepen those connections with my environment and with the people working tirelessly to steward it. We're never alone in this work, and following your values will bring you closer to others than you've ever imagined.

I'd like to thank my partner, T.J. David, for his unwavering support as I spent a lot of late nights and early mornings trying to bang out first drafts. His emotional support, in addition to providing feedback and lots of in-office dinners, made this book possible. I'd like to thank my coach, friend, and mentor, David Roche, for always helping me work through the moments when writing a book felt impossible or like the worst idea I've ever had. David, thanks for believing in me and always pushing me to be my best! Another huge shoutout to Kylee Van Horn for not only providing invaluable insights on nutrition but for always being there for me when I was struggling in the writing process. Kylee, you're the fiercest friend and best running partner a gal could ask for. Your love is both tough and unconditional and is exactly what I need! Thank you for dispensing it liberally on so many dog hikes and long runs. I'd like to thank my friend, fellow environmental writer, and *Trail Runner* coeditor, Nick Triolo, for support and guidance in the writing and publishing journey. Nick, your commitment to using sport and storytelling as the bridge to our natural world has moved me for years—and I can't wait to read your book! Thanks also to writer and friend Peter Bromka for fielding all my insecure text messages in the process of getting this book done. Friends, thanks for believing in me even when I didn't! I owe every one of you a six-pack.

—Zoë Rom

To the friends and contributors in these pages who provided us with their insights, wisdom, and words: Addie Bracy, Trent Stellingwerff, Kriste Peoples, Jordan Marie Brings Three White Horses Whetstone, Megan Flanagan, Jason Fitzgerald, Drew Watts, Dr. Margo Mountjoy, Reshma Saujani, Mishka Shubaly, Brittany Charboneau, Jennifer L. Gaudiani, Renee McGregor, Joshua Potts, Aaron Potts, Chris Mosier, Maria Solis Belizaire, Mirna Valerio, Verna Volker, Joe McConaughy, Yassine Diboun, Matthew Huff, Kyle Robidoux, Stephanie Ormond, Lucy Bartholomew, Clare Gallagher, Ryan Holiday, Vic Thasiah, Dakota Jones, Fernanda Maciel, Shelley Villalobos, Corey Simpson, Jess Rogers, Jad Finck, Bennett Grimes, Kylee Van Horn, Emily Olsen, Peter Newton, Mariah Foley, Brené Brown, and Steve Magness.

Thank you to the team at Human Kinetics, especially Michelle Earle and Laura Pulliam, for your guidance and belief in what this book could be. Thank you to Neely Spence Gracey for connecting us, allowing this project to happen in the first place.

—*Tina Muir and Zoë Rom*

INTRODUCTION

Brace yourselves, because this book is going to ask a lot of you.

It's going to ask you to reconsider daily decisions and fundamental values. It's going to ask you to set big goals, fall short—and keep trying. It's going to ask you to do things that are unpopular, hard, and maybe even impossible. It's going to ask you to show up, day after day, and put imperfect action and progress above superficial rhetoric and finger pointing. This book is going to ask a lot of you because it's necessary and oh so worth it.

Running and climate action have a lot in common. You have to be willing to work hard in service of something without knowing exactly what the results will be. You'll need to look deep inside yourself for the motivation to keep going, even when it feels downright impossible. You'll need to learn to take care of yourself so that you can stay in it for the long haul.

You don't need to be an elite athlete. Heck, you don't need to ever sign up for a race. You won't need to forgo cheese or chain yourself to a tree. This book doesn't presume to tell you what to do. It's not going to tell you to stop flying, driving, or buying new running shoes, because environmental stewardship isn't a checklist or a purity test. Climate action isn't pass/fail, and your authors are here to help break you out of a bad-faith binary that seeks to diminish the impact you can have on your world. They're not asking for perfection; they want to *empower*. They want to give you a framework to better navigate the questions that feel relevant to you and your community—because climate action requires falling in love with our world, and love is messy, vulnerable, and imperfect.

In running, as in climate action, the most sustainable pace is not all-out, all the time. That doesn't mean you aren't giving your best. Far from it. It just means you're setting yourself up to give your best in the long run. Tina and Zoë used to believe that the "best" way to run was to go for it with every fiber of their being, to burn a hole in the horizon with narrowed eyes, and to grit their teeth to push so hard that they collapsed at the finish (of the race, yes, but also every hard run and workout). But you know what that did? For Zoë, it led down a path of perfectionism, disconnection, and burnout. For Tina, it led to her quitting the sport. By the time she reached that breaking point, she despised running and was ready to leave it forever.

Thankfully, after years of downtime and two children later, Tina came back to the sport with a new approach to running: one with joy as the goal. This approach does not mean you have to sacrifice the challenge of competing or running as fast as you can. It turns out that, despite what some Pinterest image of "no pain, no gain" will tell you, easing out of the pain cave just a little can leave you in a beautiful place where you get to push yourself but also revel in the challenge. You can soak in your surroundings and that moment in time, all while experiencing immense gratitude for what your body can do (and will continue to do) as you go through your imperfectly perfect running journey.

This applies to the climate movement too. Being good enough is, in fact, *enough*. This book is not going to say that you should replace every single plastic item you own with reusable straws, eco-friendly bags, and moss carpet (yes, that is real!). That doesn't help anyone, and it means we keep on purchasing unnecessarily. And checking the invisible box of awareness, but never addressing our consumerism addiction, is not what this book is recommending; we *do* need to reduce the amount of items we are purchasing, regardless of their materials. But what this book is saying is it does not need to be an extreme.

You don't need to trade in your car for a solar-powered boat (a la Greta Thunberg). You don't need to perfect your TED Talk or stump speech for your next town hall. But you do need to connect honestly and authentically with friends, family, and community members about the climate issues and actions that resonate with you.

You don't need to buy rain barrels and live in a cabin off the grid. You don't have to sail across the rough seas of the Atlantic on a solar-powered boat for two weeks to get to your next race. But could you cycle to work most days (again, not shooting for perfection here) instead of making your car the default? You don't need to quit your job to join an organic farming commune or burn all the money in your wallet. But you can invest, spend, and donate money in a way that's more in line with your environmental values.

The point is, with everything, if we shoot for perfection, not only are we going to fail but we are also going to be miserable every single day we try.

The goal of this book is to take the pressure off you. To show you that there is another, more authentic way to run—one that does not mean you are shaking with nerves at the start line of a race but instead feel excited butterflies to go out there and play. To show you that to be a good community member does not mean being on the board of everything and speaking up on behalf of every challenge affecting your community. To show you that being an environmental advocate does not mean throwing everything you know about your life in the trash can to live in a yurt.

It means holding those who have contributed most of the global emissions accountable. It means saying no to the pressure of saying yes to the things you have absolutely no desire to do (except taxes; we will always have to do our taxes!). It means giving yourself the freedom to live the life you always wanted to live.

Your journey through this book will take you through three major sections. You will begin by developing and deepening your relationship to running to make it a healthy, reliable, lifelong friend who is always in your corner. Next, you will solidify your role in shaping the running communities you engage in and will find meaningful ways to give back in a way that feels right for you. Finally, you will work on revitalizing the way you view our physical world, making it easy to make responsible and environmentally conscious choices in line with your heart and spirit.

As with everything, it is going to be hard. There will be big ups and massive downs, but when we are in it together, we can make big change a reality. So go after what matters most to you.

Let's get started.

PART I | SUSTAIN YOUR RUNNER'S MIND AND BODY

1 Play the Long Game

Running is a lot like life, only smaller.

Many of us are drawn to running because it offers a safe and small-scale opportunity to experience the numerous difficulties and challenges that we encounter in life. It can be a low-stakes way to practice how we respond to setbacks and adversity. It gives us the ability to stretch our discomfort muscle.

When Zoë and her partner, T.J., started their endurance coaching business, they decided to call it Microcosm Coaching to convey the consistent reminder that running is a relatively safe way to work through the challenges that life presents. A microcosm is a community, place, or situation that encapsulates in miniature the characteristics of something larger. Through wins and losses, regressions, and plateaus, running provides a way to practice our core values of courage, community, and self-compassion on a smaller playing field before applying them to the bigger problems that have the potential to knock us to our knees. Tough moments, sadness, and grief are as much a part of life as happiness, joy, and excitement.

Divorces happen, we get passed over for an anticipated promotion, or something reverts us back to a traumatic childhood event. Those moments hit us hard, especially if we are not used to handling adversity. Running can teach us how to navigate all of life's twists and turns and realize that we are able to survive and even thrive in moments that may at first seem impossible. Things will go wrong, but things will also go right. Either way, we can pivot and grow. We have done hard things before, and we will again.

Running teaches us how to work through setbacks and plateaus. While much of life is spent in relative comfort, the trajectory of success is never a straight line, in relationships, in careers, or in personal growth. The problem is, we live in a world that tells us progress and growth should be fast, fun, and easy. If we are not able to achieve what we set out to do on our first try—oh, and make it look effortless—then we are doing something wrong. At times it can feel like we might as well not even bother, because everyone else is progressing and growing much faster than we are. From the track, to the trails, to the office, what could we possibly contribute to the conversation when everyone else's answers sound so intelligent and eloquent, and their wins seem to come so easy?

Running helps us overcome those feelings of imposter syndrome, helping us embrace the slow, measured growth over long periods of time. Through running we learn that improvement takes time. Sure, there will be breakthrough moments that leave us hungry for more—but most of the time, progress in running (like in life) is slow and we learn to embrace and look forward to the process rather than the outcome. It may take a while to learn that lesson, but when we "get it," everything in life levels up.

Elite athletes might spend years trying to shave a few seconds off a PR. Musicians may pull hundreds, if not thousands, of all-nighters honing their music, trying to get noticed. No matter what the goal or undertaking, progress is rarely the rapid upward trajectory depicted on social media. While overnight success might be the narrative we are pitched, it is rare. Ask anyone you admire how they got to where they did and they will tell you about the years of effort, sacrifice, and heartache they put into what they have crafted. According to Michael Gervais, a high-performance psychologist, we can only control three things: our craft, our body, and our mind. That leaves a lot up to chance and often means that we cannot force our way into success.

> Playing the long game, becoming a sustainable runner, means taking a different approach to training. One that emphasizes long-term growth aimed at reaching your potential over the outcome of any specific event.

What does it look like to play the long game? In our experiences as coaches, there are some athletes who play the long game—and some who don't. Playing the long game, becoming a sustainable runner, means taking a different approach to training. One that emphasizes long-term growth aimed at reaching your potential over the outcome of any specific event. Training with a short term-approach is like living paycheck to paycheck. It works until it doesn't. Runners can string along inconsistent training until we need to make a big withdrawal from that account—and then when we overdraft, the result is injury or burnout.

Believing in your long-term potential as a runner is one of the bravest things you can do. Putting too much emphasis on one race or even a single race season is selling yourself short, and counterintuitively, it can be a way of protecting yourself from the vulnerability required to reach your potential. When we are unable to appreciate the small steps taken along the way, we realize that the achievement doesn't feel as good as we hoped, so we set our sights higher. And repeat. That instinct isn't bad; it's human nature, but getting caught up in it means a bumpy road of self-worth pitfalls and fitness regressions.

Sound familiar? You are not alone. We have been to that place, and there is a high likelihood we will end up there again. We live in a world that encourages that kind of thinking. Let's take back our story and choose a different path. It's time to explore how.

Separate Self-Worth and Outcomes

How can we strive toward ambitious running goals while fostering a healthy sense of self-worth? It's okay to want a certain outcome and work hard to make it happen. There are very few runners who are able to train for a race with zero expectations for the finish. We are runners; we commit to our sport, we sacrifice for our running, and we have others who sacrifice for us too. We can't spend all those hours in our heads without wondering what race day will look like. But where we get into trouble is when we have a tombstone-engraved outlook toward one race, instead of seeing it as a single page in the book we are writing about our lives.

Zoë's Thoughts

I used to place a huge part of my self-worth on the outcomes of trail running races. After winning my first trail race, a low-key local 10K, that small taste of success and the feedback I got from others spurred me on. So, I ran a marathon. Then an ultramarathon. Then an even longer ultramarathon. The bigger the event, the more praise I'd get. And the more fear I'd feel leading up to it.

I would experience crushing anxiety in the days and weeks before the race, afraid of the outcome. I was unable to train intentionally or sustainably because I needed to beat the competition to reinforce my sense of self-worth. When I couldn't sleep, I'd peruse my competitor's race results, looking for evidence that I didn't measure up. I believed I needed that pressure to perform well at races and if I loosened my grip, I wouldn't be able to keep up. That insecurity was my edge, right? I bought into a counterfeit idea of mental toughness that hinged on my ability to push through pain—mental and physical. I thought that if I let up and accepted myself, I'd lose a competitive advantage.

When race day finally rolled around, the quality of competition was diminished by my focus on preserving my self-esteem. Though I also enjoyed many of these races, the result—no matter what it was—mattered most of all, beyond a sense of fun, meaning, or community. During the race, all I could think about was getting to the finish line, and what my race time would mean to myself, about myself.

Playing defense against my own sense of self-worth was a poor way to race and an even worse way to live. Each time I was passed by a fellow runner, it felt like a personal affront—a referendum on who I was as an athlete and person. I'd think, "I'm not good enough to be here. Of course I'm getting passed; I don't know why I even try." These negative thoughts would cause me to spiral and disengage from the competition, leading to poor performance and feeling emotionally drained and detached.

But once I started to work with a coach, I began the difficult process of untangling my self-worth from competitive outcomes. It took a season of two tough DNFs for me to reframe my outlook. Running became an exercise in self-compassion rather than a negative self-assessment. Being able to train with a more positive perspective made it less psychologically demanding and stressful, enabling me to increase my volume, run more consistently, and walk away from bad training days or race days without disparaging myself. I learned that facing a bad day frees you up to have a lot more good days.

For runners who like to compete, perceived inadequacy can show up in a variety of ways. Some runners might overinvest in competition to prove self-worth, which can lead to overtraining or burnout from high-volume and intense competition. It could also lead to the opposite. Some runners who too closely tie competitive outcomes to their self-worth might avoid competition they would otherwise enjoy because each group track workout or trail race compels them to question their self-worth.

If you view any negative outcome as a failure and it becomes detrimental to your self-worth, you might inadvertently avoid future situations that could put you in failure's path personally, professionally, and athletically. Giving ourselves the grace to fail and fall short is fundamental to the process of improving at anything—whether it's running, public speaking, or underwater basket weaving. Holding unhealthy expectations about outcomes, particularly ones closely tied to how we view our place in this world, undermines the process of growing and progressing.

Runners who aren't focused on pursuing long-term growth and progress will often sign up for the first event that excites them, and leapfrog from goal to goal without pausing to consider how each pit stop affects their long-term growth and progress. Runners without a sustainable approach might launch full boar into training, then end up injured or burnt-out by the time their marathon or trail race rolls around. It might take weeks or even months of insanity-inducing frustration while their body heals from an injury before they dive right back into an unsustainable level of training. Then they rinse and repeat.

When we aren't invested in the long term, we may find it hard to motivate ourselves without an event on the schedule. Our training might be overly focused on the demands of race day to the detriment of our long-term growth as a runner and human. We may try to cram in more long runs or vert (vertical elevation gain) than is helpful or healthy because we are fixated on overcoming our perceived biggest weakness. We may even reach the point where we find ways to sneak in additional training or ignore our plan, claiming innocence and inadvertent mistakes, when we know deep down it was intentional. Any setback feels like a catastrophe. The smallest steps backward make us spiral into serious regression without a consistent base of training to lean on. We might tell ourselves that once we achieve the next outcome, we will stop these behaviors, but they can become addictive and difficult to stop.

Keep Running in Context

We have been trained to think that we need to put more pressure on ourselves to get out the door, and to get those big goals as soon as possible. We end up in a short-term, "gotta get it done" mindset. We see athletes at the top of their game talking about digging deep, finding a way no matter the obstacle. We conclude that if we don't reach our goals, it is our own laziness and lack of willpower that let us down. Corporate CEOs tell us they hustled hard to score the corner office, and if we don't achieve what we want, we didn't try hard enough. We need to commit, give it our all, and prove that we want it enough. No regrets.

Except, there often are regrets. Looking back on these moments, we wonder why that one small, local race felt like a life-or-death situation; why an attempt at a personal best made us feel like we could throw up; and why we barely slept the night before a race we had run six times before, because we feared we might "fail" this year. Why did we get so worked up when it was just a run? Would our 80-year-old selves really care if we ran a few minutes outside of what we intended? Would our 80-year-old selves even remember that race at all? Unlikely.

Instead of simply appreciating the fact we have the opportunity and privilege to be able to race and challenge ourselves, our mind got stuck in the past with versions of "Why did I?" or anxious about the future with "What if?" We realize we didn't even enjoy the race where we ran our personal best and didn't celebrate our first postsurgery run. We were too busy burning a hole into the horizon as we looked toward a fitter, faster version of ourselves.

Tina, and her husband, Steve, "smiling" after her first marathon, but feeling disappointed because expectations of what the race was meant to be did not match what happened (and it hurt!).

We think we need the negative self-talk of that angry football coach or drill sergeant from the movies to yell at us in our minds. Without that, we will lose all our motivation. Olympians hold themselves to high standards and they get what they want. We may not have the talent to be Olympians, but the message is clear. If we want something, we better be ready to work harder than ever to get it.

Our lack of self-compassion, combined with the cruel labels we give ourselves—*useless, weak, slow, not a real runner, a failure*—make us inclined to give up or give in. Many of us have internalized cultural messages that we must be self-critical, and we shame ourselves into working more, pushing harder. However, the opposite is true. We need positive self-talk to reach our potential. The research unanimously agrees that using compassionate language is the way to go. A 2011 review of literature looking at the relationship between self-talk and performance concluded that positive self-talk interventions proactively affected behavior change (Tod, Hardy, and Oliver 2011).

When considering the impact negative self-talk has on individuals, it is important to start with the difference between *guilt* and *shame*. Guilt is typically understood as "I *did* bad," while shame is "I *am* bad." Rather than motivating positive behavioral changes, shame does the opposite. Internalizing and dwelling on feelings like "I am not good enough" causes us to engage in less healthy behaviors and patterns around food, substance use, and exercise.

The runs where we simply appreciate being out there are the seasons of life when we are most at peace. When we are in love with the purity of the sport, we focus on the process, the experiences, the freedom, and the social connections it brings. We feel the most constricted, strained, and disappointed with our performances when we are only thinking about the outcome. Negative self-talk and self-imposed pressure are cheap and fallible shortcuts to success. It may work once, or even a couple of times, but it'll soon take over and undermine any chance of long-term growth and fulfillment.

Despite what we may see on Instagram, the top performers who achieve the greatest results are able to disconnect from the outcome and focus on their growth along the way. While they may display the importance of commitment and possess a level of grit to be able to dig deep, the real secret is that they love the journey toward mastery.

Tina's Thoughts

In September 2006, I boarded a plane from London to Detroit to go to Ferris State University on a full scholarship. While I knew life would be different, the day I arrived, my world was flipped upside down. I desperately wanted to regain control of my life, and running became my means to do so.

Running evolved from being one small part of my life to becoming my life. I went from running solo every day to being surrounded by 50 extremely dedicated, hardworking, laser-focused teammates. I went from having no idea about what pace I was running to monitoring every rep, every mile, every step. I went from asking myself, "What do I feel like running today?" to wrapping my brain around multiple hard sessions each week with zero rest days. I went from no planned races to 27 races in a year. It was thrilling, overwhelming, and terrifying at the same time. For the first time, I was asked, "How bad do you want it?" And I wanted it bad.

I was so unconvinced of my own self-worth, I felt I had to run well to prove I was worthy of being there. I began to believe all I had to offer the world was my running ability. Refusing to wear heels to celebrate a birthday for fear of rolling my ankle, needing to be in bed by 9 p.m. every night (even though insomnia had fully taken hold by this point!), and spending my free time reading about how to be a better runner. I even broke up with my boyfriend to focus on my running.

While sacrifice was needed to reach my potential, I began to foster an unhealthy relationship with running that would ultimately lead to my quitting the sport. From the outside, everything appeared to be coming together. The training blocks I had been building added up to a level of fitness I had never known. I was motivated to complete the supplemental activities that would keep me healthy. Other than my persistent insomnia, I rested my body and lived like a professional athlete.

In my sophomore year of college, I stunned everyone, including myself, when I finished 12th at the Division II National Cross Country Championships. After a disastrous indoor track National Championships in the spring of 2007 due to a minor injury and a major meltdown, I went on to finish fourth in the 5K at the outdoor track National Championships. It felt like a fairy tale. My mind began to fill with the excitement of what I would achieve in the next three years. I was transitioning from enjoying the experience of improving as a runner into someone who was living for the next dream before the current one had been completed.

I shifted from extremely committed to obsessed. In my junior year, that unsustainable relationship pulled my life apart. I ended up in a bad injury cycle with one setback after the next. A glute strain should have been an indication to take my intensity down a notch, but I didn't see it that way. Soon after, I ended up with a blood blister on the ball of my foot after a race. Rather than resting, I kept on running, even though I was unable to put any weight on the ball of my foot. A few days and many miles later, a stress reaction required several weeks off to heal. Upon my return to training, I pushed too hard running some hills and ended up with a calf strain, requiring a full month off.

Each time, I didn't learn a thing. I lied to myself and blamed bad luck, Michigan weather, other people. Anything but myself. All I could think about was getting back as quickly as I could. Most runners heed these warnings, but 20-year-old Tina was doing the equivalent of sticking her fingers in her ears and singing, "Lalalala."

I began to unravel. Feeling isolated and angry, I avoided practice and my teammates. I slipped into a depression from the loneliness. It was too painful to see others doing the one thing I wanted to do. I knew I was letting down my teammates and modeling bad behavior for the younger athletes, but I couldn't face the vulnerability required to do anything about it.

Running came ahead of everything, even my relationships with the people I loved most in the world, and because of it, I was miserable.

While running can be important to us and might take precedence for short periods, it is not sustainable to prioritize it all the time. The universe will find a way to nudge us toward a sense of balance. Whether we take the hint and rediscover joy is up to us. We convince ourselves that once we achieve our big, scary goal, we will be confident in who we are and able to look around to take in our imagined (or real) mountaintop view. In the meantime, we need to get it done. We wake up thinking about running and fall asleep dreaming about how good that moment will feel. This is no time to smell roses; we have work to do.

This mindset isn't exclusive to elites. While one runner's long-term goals may seem unimaginable to another, running is relative. Some runners might achieve big successes relatively early in their running career. Some runners may surpass the training and recovery regimens of professional runners to set a new marathon PR, overinvesting in recovery hacks and gimmicks to hedge their bets. Ability and performance are less relevant; what matters is our relationship to our sport and how much that outcome means to us.

Olympic 800-meter runners and first-time marathoners might shake with the same level of fear and trepidation on the start line. The fear of messing up, letting someone down, or failing is so intense, so real.

While we may genuinely feel the pressure and insistence of this goal, the world has a strange and wonderful way of presenting us with the perfect opportunity when the time is right. In order for that to happen, we have to let go and not squeeze so tight. For the results to fall into place, we must connect on a deeper level. Focusing on a distant goal and external validation robs runners of enjoying the here and the now, one of the true gifts running provides. It is only when we learn that running is something we do, something we learn to enjoy, something that makes us better people, that we realize we can't fix an *internal* problem with an *external* goal or solution, no matter what level we reach or what we accomplish.

Running can take over our identity. We know it is happening when it feels like it is the one thing that sets us apart from everyone around us or when we wish that everyone we meet is a runner so we can talk about running. When seeing another runner out on a jaunt sparks envy. Soon we find we are spending our free time researching, learning, listening, and counting down the hours until the next time we can get out for a run.

When our confidence is tied too tightly to our identity as a runner, both internal and external conflict occurs, and tension ensues. It is why we race one another in a group practice when there is nothing to win. It is why we struggle to be supportive of friends who are succeeding when we are facing a setback. It is why we make judgments about what others are doing, when we know we have made the same mistakes in the past. That doesn't make us a terrible human being; it simply means we are hurting. We know something is off within us, but we haven't quite found the courage to look ourselves in the eye to figure out what.

Human beings have many identities based on attributes assigned at birth and experiences picked up throughout life. We identify with running, using it as a way to describe what it is we enjoy doing with our time, but it leaves us vulnerable when we believe being a runner is who we are. Running can be an expression of us, but it is not our sole defining feature.

This is not to say that anyone who pushes themselves is doomed to fail or lose themselves. It is not that we should never strive to test our limits; in fact, quite the opposite. Finding a way to push ourselves mentally, emotionally, or physically every day is one of the best ways to thrive. These are adventures and learning opportunities that will help us grow and evolve.

Successful athletes tend to play the long game. They'll organize their race schedules and training so that they're never doing too much, but they're almost never doing too little, either.

Successful athletes tend to play the long game. They'll organize their race schedules and training so that they're never doing too much, but they're almost never doing too little, either. Although they'll train more in some months than in others, they maintain a healthy base throughout the year so that they don't have to rush training or ramp up dramatically to get ready for an objective. Or they can jump into an unexpected opportunity knowing they are not in peak shape but can give it a go. As the saying goes, the best way to get ready is to stay ready. It appears on the outside that these runners are living a full and joyful life, making the most of every opportunity that comes their way. We might envy them and wonder how they do it. How are they so successful when they seem so carefree? The answer is right there; their carefree attitude is what allows them to make the most of every race they enter . . . even if they aren't in peak shape. Ironically, the lack of expectations on performance helps them to perform!

Although it's normal for training volume to oscillate throughout the year—in fact, any coach would recommend down weeks every four to six weeks to minimize chronic and acute stresses accumulated in training—athletes playing the long game will emphasize sustainable, consistent training without significant time away (though injuries or health might get in the way). Keeping a "just enough" level of training is in fact enough. Feeling the need to push to the max and overexert every season will take a lot of the joy out of the sport and potentially limit your number of years as a runner.

Find Your *Why*

Being interested in specific goals and outcomes is great, as long as that's not the only motivation you have. Runners who are intrinsically motivated (driven from within) tend to endure, whereas runners who are extrinsically motivated (driven by something outside themselves) tend to jump from passion to passion when things get hard.

Courtesy of T.J. David.

Zoë finding a way to get the most out of her *why*—connecting her love for the outdoors and her favorite activity.

Intrinsically motivated runners will persevere through injury, setbacks, plateaus, and once-in-a-lifetime global pandemics that cancel running events worldwide. If the pandemic taught us anything, it's that sweatpants are excellent and that folks who train when they don't have a race on their schedule tend to advance the furthest.

Sometimes slumps and setbacks emerge when we are no longer able to connect our daily runs to our overall purpose, in training or life. We might think, "What is the point of this if I'm just going to fall short of my goal anyway? It's not like I'm a professional—I'm just jogging in circles around town when I could be eating a delicious brunch like everyone else!"

Something that can help motivate us to lace up day after day is taking time to figure out our *why*. Your *why* is the deeper connection behind your running and the source of renewable energy that keeps you putting one foot in front of

What's Your *Why*?

Put your phone on Do Not Disturb, go to a quiet place, and give yourself the opportunity to figure it out. Spend 10 to 15 minutes reflecting on your best running moments—times when you felt motivated or connected to what you were doing. Zoë often found she was most motivated in life and training when she was able to connect her daily routine to her love of the environment and passion for environmental justice. A five-mile (8 km) jog around the neighborhood might not seem epic, but for Zoë, it was a chance to connect with her environment and experience the natural world. And even on cold and snowy days when she would prefer to be curled up with a good book by the fire, that love of the natural world gets her out the door. Tina noticed her favorite running memories all involved other runners. Running was a way to connect on a deep, emotional level and create memories together. She noticed a race on the agenda wasn't motivating as something to dig deep toward, but it was an opportunity to surround herself with like-hearted people. As you reflect on favorite memories and moments, here are some prompts and questions to help you sort through your memories, examine your core values, and reconnect with your inner child who found pure joy in those moments.

What do your best running moments have in common?

When you don't have a specific goal on the calendar, what gets you out the door?

If races ceased to exist, would you still run? Why?

If you couldn't post about your runs on social media, upload them to Strava, or otherwise share your results, what would keep you going?

What do you feel passionate about?

When you look back on how you spend your time, what activities make you feel the best or the worst?

What brings you joy?

the other, even when your acute motivation is waning. Anyone who's going to tackle a 5K, a 100-miler, or even their morning jog should start with identifying their *why*. It can keep your running goals and expectations in check and guide your day-to-day decisions about training.

Your *why* can and will shift over time, and that's okay, even beneficial! You're a growing and evolving person, and what motivates and connects you to running can shift and evolve too. That doesn't make it any less authentic.

Your *why* doesn't need to inspire or make sense to anyone but yourself. It doesn't have to be a sexy, inspirational idea or world-changing principle—just something that makes you feel like you and that nudges you along in life and in training. Sometimes it can feel like everyone around you has a deep, meaningful, and eloquent *why* that makes you feel like yours is insignificant and shallow. Remind yourself that your strengths are your own. You are you. Follow your personal journey, not someone else's.

It could be that you like getting outside. Or that it's important to prioritize your physical or mental health. Maybe your *why* is the community and connections that running forges.

It's important to differentiate between your *why* and your goals. Your *why* may help inform your goals, and your goals may be a way to express your *why*, but they aren't the same thing. Goals should not be your primary focus, and ideally your *why* should help you engage with your long-term goals more meaningfully and sustainably.

In her book *Mental Training for Ultrarunning*, author and mental performance expert Addie Bracy says, "Having a *why* is essential. It's a foundational skill, and every athlete should start with *why*. When you wholeheartedly believe in what you're doing, and why you're doing it, your wellspring of determination becomes even deeper and more abundant" (p. 14).

Celebrate Successes

Running provides an arena to experience failure, and gives us an opportunity to learn how to celebrate and own our successes with humility. This can be particularly challenging for female athletes. In a culture that tells us it's impolite to claim success, athletics can be a way to explore how we discuss and relate to our achievements.

Reshma Saujani, founder of Girls Who Code and Moms First, has spent years asking people all around the world to consider the way society raises girls compared to boys and how that influences them for life. While joining Tina on the *Running for Real* podcast, Saujani said, "We (females) never really learn how to be brave, and that means that we do learn how to give up before we even try because we gravitate toward things that we're good at. We get addicted to that perfection; we get addicted to people being like, 'That's so great; you're such a good girl,' and the consequences of that are enormous on every aspect of our life." Not only does this have detrimental effects on our mental health, but it also means we miss out on lessons of leadership. Saujani reminds us that, "If we're waiting to be perfect to lead, if we're waiting to be perfect to live, we're never going to close the leadership gap."

The people-pleasing side of us, especially for women, can prevent us from saying no to activities that we don't want to do, and it stops us from asking for what we do want. Running can become a way to get past that. When we commit to a big goal as a runner, we have to be able to ask for support from our loved ones and be prepared to put our own needs first.

When we have worked hard toward a running goal and achieved it, we are more likely to speak up about our experience and how it changed us. Seeing the pride and excitement others have for us can be a powerful reminder that it is okay to share the successes in our lives. Doing so can inspire others to consider what they are capable of, potentially unlocking a greater purpose in their lives too.

Embrace Imperfection

Perfectionism is the enemy of sustainability. "Perfectionism is not the same thing as striving to be your best. Perfectionism is the belief that if we live perfect, look perfect, and act perfect, we can minimize or avoid the pain of blame, judgement, and shame. It's a shield. It's a twenty-ton shield that we lug around thinking it will protect us when, in fact, it's the thing that's really preventing us from flight," says Dr. Brené Brown, a research professor and bestselling author of *The Gifts of Imperfection* (2010).

It's tempting to get hung up on nailing perfect splits or jogging laps around the parking lot so that your weekly mileage is exactly 50. We have been there, again and again. More often than not, though, an attachment to perfection holds us back more than it propels us forward. Do you ever find yourself dragging your feet before a run? Or struggling with anxiety before a race or workout? You might be struggling with perfectionism.

Never let perfection be the enemy of progress. To quote coach, author, and exercise physiologist Steve Magness, "Don't aim to be consistently great. Aim to be great at being consistent." A lot of imperfect days mean much more than a few perfect days. And for many of us, the pressure of striving for "perfection" is a way to escape the vulnerability inherent in being flawed athletes and humans who are trying our best.

Often, some of our best runs are the least perfect. It's the marathon where you fell short of your goal but were able to finish strong. It's the 5K you blew up in but made a new friend in the process. It's the ultra where you spilled your energy gel on your shorts but tapped into an unknown resilience.

Don't be afraid to get your feet wet in a river crossing, to fall on your butt pushing the pace downhill, or to reach out to that friend you've always wanted to run with. The pursuit of perfection (which doesn't exist) will distract you from the many joys of finding a sustainable path for your running journey.

Zoë's Thoughts

When I first started writing, I often put pressure on myself that everything I wrote had to be the best thing I had ever written. That pressure to be perfect and write perfectly was unsustainable. Instead of motivating me to practice more often and hone my craft, I would spend hours staring at a blinking cursor on a blank screen, paralyzed. The fear of producing something less than perfect prevented me from putting pen to paper at all.

Often, I would struggle with similar thoughts about my running. The night before races or big workouts, I would lie awake thinking, "What if I mess up? What if I don't do it right?"

Then, as often is the case, my coach, David Roche, gave me a bit of timely advice: "Get out there, and give yourself permission to have an imperfect workout."

It felt like a huge weight had been lifted. That simple reframing, making the goal to embrace imperfection rather than to strive for perfection, changed everything. I went into races and workouts much more relaxed, less afraid to make mistakes, but excited to problem solve as things came up. Running became a lot more fun that day. And what's more, I got faster too.

Now I do the same thing in my writing. Rather than applying an arbitrary pressure to get it perfect on the first try, my goal is simply to write—to experiment boldly with words on the page without trying to force them to be something they're not. In allowing myself to write crappy first drafts, my final drafts got a lot better in the process. Sometimes the perfectionism monster in me still tells me my first draft has to be perfect, like during the writing of this book, but now I know better. I know how to take the pressure off and to expect my first attempt to need work. We can't expect to nail everything the first time we try. That would make life a whole lot less interesting!

We know the internal pressures we put on ourselves are a detriment to our running. We have seen others do it, we have done it, and we have that pit-in-the-stomach feeling sometimes that we are doing it again. Even so, it can be difficult to escape, especially when those habits and patterns have been practiced for decades. It takes a huge amount of courage to step away from behaviors that do not serve us. We hope the upcoming chapters will make that easier, but we feel it is important to recognize that this work is not easy. We too struggle with putting pressure on our performances, promising ourselves we will be happy once we reach the next goal (writing a book perhaps!), and are recovering perfectionists. Wherever you are in your journey, know you are not alone; we are out here struggling with you.

ACTION STEPS

- Learn how to sit in the discomfort of failure. To what behaviors do you revert to get away from those feelings of discomfort—blame, avoidance, distraction? What can you learn to make sure you never feel like this again?

- Find ways to emphasize long-term growth in your approach. Short-term focus does not make for a sustainable, lifelong runner.

- Progress is never linear, no matter how it appears. There are few true overnight successes; ask someone you admire about their journey to this moment.

- Give yourself the grace to fail and fall short. It is a critical part of your growth as a human being.

- Running can be one of your identities, but it should not be the only one. If it is, it is time to step back and reassess your relationship to the sport.

- When reading the thoughts and experiences of others, especially elite athletes, keep in mind that the top performers love the journey toward mastery; they're not the ones most concerned with their performance.

- If you have been a people pleaser, pay attention to those behaviors. Are you saying yes because you want to, because it is important to you, or because you feel you should?

- When you have successes, speak up about them! Tell your family and friends; they will be excited to celebrate with you.

- Look at your schedule and be honest with yourself. Is it too much?

- Consider "just enough" training—doing enough training to be able to jump in a race if needed but not be at peak year-round.

- If you think you are heading toward burnout, step back before it is too late. Reconsider the stresses you have in life. Is it too much for one person?

- Find your *why* using the exercise in this chapter.

- Stop comparing your goals and your *why* to other runners. It is yours only.

2 | Bolster Your Confidence

You just finished your long run. Crushed it. Basking in that post–long run glow, you remember that it wasn't always this easy. You used to wonder after just a couple of miles, *Am I seriously going to make it another 10?* Your brain would go into hyperdrive. *I can't do this.* But you did, and now you are going further than ever. You know to break the run into smaller sections. *Just make it past that mailbox. Just make it past that maple tree. One chunk at a time. Get it to 90 minutes. Let's shoot for two hours. Hey! Only 60 minutes to go.* And then you did it. You completed a distance that not too long ago would have been unimaginable.

Beaming, you sit down on the ground, chugging water you have been looking forward to for 45 minutes, your fatigued legs thankful for the break. As you gulp the sun-warmed water, you log on to social media to celebrate.

I DID IT!

Except the first thing you see is another runner who also ran long this morning and started around the same time as you did. Their 24 miles trumps your 20. And how did they rack up so much vert?

All the energy, momentum, and pride leaves your body as your postrun elation fades into a low-hum of anxiety. Not only is that other runner fast, but they're a dang good writer too. *Okay, you Glennon Doyle knock-off. Did you rip this right from Brené Brown's magnetic fridge poetry set?* But it sure makes your semicohesive ramblings pale in comparison. *Dang it. I only have 12 likes? Did I seriously skip brunch for this?* You are left deflated, disheartened, and not so much of a rock star anymore. Maybe you will celebrate when you can run 24 miles in four hours. And so we move the line and keep chasing the dangling carrot; the day we feel content will never come.

Why does their achievement make ours any less valid?

It doesn't, but we all know the physical reaction we experience at moments like this. We have all felt it. In everything we do, there is always someone better, stronger, or more deserving. It always hits us like a physical punch in the gut, but we can learn to sit with those emotions, rather than numbing them or pushing them away. These aren't quick fixes or simple hacks; they require the deep work and growth that can change every area of our lives, not just our relationship to running. Let's dive in!

Avoid Self-Sabotage

Believing we are enough sounds simple, but it also seems like the kind of woo-woo advice that doesn't change actually anything. Really, it is both: simple to do and useful for combating feelings of insecurity, but ineffective unless we go deeper. First, let's work through why we struggle with feeling like we're not enough.

British anthropologist Robin Dunbar claimed that early hunter-gatherer societies tended to live in groups of 150, which is known as Dunbar's number theory (BBC 2019) and has a lot of supporting research. Other research has yielded different findings, with one study stating that 291 was the approximate network size (McCarty et al. 2001). Regardless of the actual number, our brains simply aren't built to handle the amount of social information we're bombarded with today.

While it can be tough to imagine now, we were not always witnessing everyone else's strengths and successes multiple times a day. In those hunter-gatherer societies, we would have had strengths within our tribe that we were known for being skilled in. We would have embraced that strength and used it to support the tribe and strengthen our group survival. Today, we look at our strengths and compare them to millions of other people with millions of other circumstances. It can make us feel we are not good at anything, that we fade away into the background, that we don't even matter.

> We live in a culture of near-constant not-enoughness. We log onto apps and see that how we train, eat, parent, work, dress, and even live is somehow "not enough."

We live in a culture of near-constant not-enoughness. We log onto apps and see that how we train, eat, parent, work, dress, and even live is somehow "not enough." Unhelpfully, these apps also provide us with detailed data and analytics on the specific ways we're not enough. With social media, peers' training data is placed directly into our hands. *How did their easy runs get so fast? Would I be faster if I pushed the pace on easy days?*

Postrun, we log into Strava, the most popular social media app for runners and cyclists around the world, and scroll through our feed. It's easy to believe that everyone around us is training harder and more. Ugh, now we feel slow, so we log out and head to Instagram for some inspiration. But instead of seeing an uplifting story that makes us feel empowered, we see a stream of posts from peers that make us feel worse. *Am I the only person without a six-pack?* Some friends are running through the Grand Canyon just days after they were running along the beach in California, while we're on the same old loop we have been running for years. We see others climbing Mount Kilimanjaro, when our vacation was to our parents' lake cabin an hour away. We see a humble brag about a friend's dream job. Someone else moves into a huge, custom home while we sit on our old, worn-out sofa. We see families welcoming new babies while we struggle with infertility. We feel trapped in our boring job or a city we don't love because we have to make ends meet.

Some of the mistakes runners make in training and racing come from a place of believing they are not enough. Many people feel they need to be hard on themselves to obtain certain outcomes. *If I accept myself where I'm at right now, what will motivate me to get out the door and go for a run or get to the gym? Can I still improve if I accept myself for who I am?*

As runners, we are used to motivating ourselves. We often get up early to fit in a run before we leave for a family event. We do hill repeats near our vacation spot to make the most of the hilly surroundings. But sometimes, what starts out as healthy motivation can turn into a detrimental drive to define ourselves by outcomes. We might desire a specific race goal or athletic achievement so much that we feel like we're nothing without it. We obsess over it, cling to it. If the race or training run goes well, it feels really good. But that feeling is fleeting. It may pass more quickly than it came, and we are left seeking larger and more lasting accomplishments.

Counterintuitively, such an approach tends to have worse outcomes. With a narrow and hyper-specific focus on results, we make poor decisions about our training and succumb to the temptation that more is better, because at least it is productive. We might push our long run a few miles further, run five miles more than last week over the three on our schedule. A few days later, a minor injury pops up. We feel guilty about a run over the weekend being shorter and slower than intended, so we skip a rest day and push the pace on Monday, knowing we have another workout the next day.

> When we are married to a specific time goal or finish position at our next race, we might make increasingly worse decisions to try to protect the outcome we're envisioning, rather than adapting to circumstances as they unfold.

When we are married to a specific time goal or finish position at our next race, we might make increasingly harmful decisions to try to protect the outcome we're envisioning, rather than adapting to circumstances as they unfold. If we keep hitting a wall at mile 20 of a marathon, rather than pausing to assess our nutrition, we might think, *I don't have time to stop and take a gel; I have to keep going to meet my time goal. Go big or go home!* We continue pushing the pace; our fuzzy logic tells us that the quicker we get to the finish line, the quicker we can fuel up. Of course, this strategy rarely works. Our goal race time slips out of our grasp. Rather than easing up to make the best of a bad situation and switching our focus to enjoyment, we deem ourselves total and utter failures and spiral into a hole of self-pity.

This self-sabotage is common among goal-driven athletes. "I've also seen scenarios where athletes who attached too much worth to an event actually self-handicapped themselves and essentially took themselves out of it before they had the chance to fail," says Addie Bracy. "It's a form of self-preservation where an athlete can say, 'Well, I didn't go all in, and that's why I fell short.' When there is so much at stake, these athletes subconsciously make the decision to give themselves

Courtesy of Gameface Media.

Self-sabotage can derail a race quickly. Ignoring the warning signs led to a panic attack midrace for Tina in 2015.

an out or fall back on an excuse because the idea of going all in and falling short seems unbearable." Rather than pivoting to respond to actual events as they unfold, we make decisions tied to a nonexistent outcome because our ego depends on it. Instead of loosening our grip, adjusting our goals, and taking that dang gel, we give up, unable to be fully present in the race as it unfolds, already planning which race we will sign up for next to redeem ourselves.

Spending time in this virtual hall of mirrors can distort our perceptions of self that directly affect our training and alter the way we view ourselves as a valued human being. Social media, and media in general, thrives on generating a feeling of inadequacy that drives us to spend more money and more time online to build up our self-esteem and sense of self. Though it's easy to imagine we're immune to this kind of thinking, it's the philosophy that drives a billion-dollar ad industry that leverages our attention and insecurity. It's no coincidence that advertisements touting clothes, makeup, supplements, and other material goods are interspersed between images of our peers who seem to already have these things.

We can comprehend on a logical level that more money, success, travel, and friendships do not make us happier. We can understand that joy is available to us in any moment and that we only have to look to find it. Yet we find it hard when feelings of insecurity bubble up inside us.

"If we don't think we're enough, we show up at a deficit to whatever it is we're attempting to do. Before we've even begun, we're running in opposition to ourselves. That not only depletes morale and performance, it can also leave us more open to injury if we're not fully invested," says Kriste Peoples, a trail runner and mindfulness and meditation coach. "It can also look like getting easily overwhelmed and shutting down at the first sign of struggle, or lowering our expectations, withdrawal, and refusal to do the hard things."

The more we focus on that feeling of lack, the less likely we are to make careful and intentional decisions. That same feeling of somehow not being enough can drive much of our decision-making in life and in training if we're not careful. But we can fight back with a radical tool: unconditional self-acceptance.

Learn Self-Acceptance

Self-acceptance is acceptance of all of an individual's attributes, positive or negative (Morgado et al. 2014). Self-acceptance enables us to appropriately evaluate our efficient and inefficient features and accept any negative aspects as parts of our personality. It can feel relentlessly optimistic, especially to those of us who have been raised to be hypercritical of the world or to look out for what can go wrong. But the truth is, optimism isn't a predetermined, set trait. It can be developed and cultivated just like unconditional self-acceptance. Even if it feels unnatural at first, we can all learn to love and treat ourselves with respect.

Many of us struggle with this concept, thinking, *How the heck am I supposed to accept the negative parts of myself? I understand I am supposed to love the good parts of me and practice gratitude, but I want to change the negative parts of me, right? Why would I accept them?*

Because accepting them is step one toward a fulfilled and meaningful life. All those people on social media who love who they are, and are comfortable in their own skin, practice unconditional self-acceptance. That is the only way to get there. We cannot be comfortable with who we are while only loving the good parts of ourselves.

> We cannot be comfortable with who we are while only loving the good parts of ourselves.

Those of us with low self-acceptance might try to boost our sense of self with achievements and accolades, which can manifest as increased self-one-upmanship. We might sign up for a marathon, hoping that the temporary rush of achievement will quiet the deeper sense of insufficiency but telling ourselves we simply love being able to race. We may even feel better, albeit temporarily. Coming out of the other side of the COVID-19 pandemic, many of us signed up for race after race. Rather than learning from experience that there is more to running than finish lines and medals, we jumped right back in, almost as if we were trying to make up for the time we missed with more race photos and more events.

Once the immediate postevent glow fades and the "likes" stop rolling in, those same feelings of insufficiency start to creep back. Instead of seeing that our premise was flawed, we assume the problem was with the level of achievement—not the process itself. *Hmm . . . if running a marathon isn't enough, maybe an ultramarathon will do the trick!*

Unfortunately, this is a temporary fix for a deeper problem. When we finally hobble away from the finish line, clutching our belt buckle or emergency blanket, we feel the same sense of "What next?" that we felt before the endeavor. When will it ever be enough? Do we have to destroy ourselves to the point of no return before we realize that races are never going to fill the void? While running and racing bring a myriad of positive mental and physical health benefits, using running to mask a problematic sense of self-worth will force us to chase increasingly bigger feats and to be constantly obsessed with lowering our personal records, still feeling like we are never enough.

Contrary to popular belief, self-acceptance is different from self-esteem. Self-esteem ties self-worth and value to achievements and outcomes and will fluctuate over time. Our self-esteem feels secure when work is great, when our family situation is stable, when we PR'd recently, and when things are generally going well. However, this can break down when our world is uncertain. When we lose a job, end a relationship, or fail to finish and see a *DNF* next to our name on the results, our self-esteem can suffer.

Self-acceptance, or a deep belief in our innate worth regardless of achievements and outcomes, can counter the roller coaster of self-esteem. Embracing all parts of ourselves doesn't mean we stand in the mirror naked each morning and stare lovingly at our bodies. We don't have to blindly adore all parts of ourselves; it means recognizing and accepting, rather than carrying shame or fear about our deepest characteristics.

Bracy believes you can both accept where you are and hope to grow. "So instead of thinking of it as 'bettering yourself,' I like to think of it as committing to personal values such as the desire to grow, learn more, work hard, etc. When you look at it that way, you're not seeking this destination of a future version of yourself but instead committing to a certain way of being and doing each day that still should ultimately lead to improvement and fulfillment," says Bracy.

We need to approach goals from a place of wanting to do well but not needing or expecting it to protect our egos. "When you attach your self-worth to an event, your ego is at stake. That's a lot of power to give to a race or an event. One outcome of removing that pressure that I have seen in athletes is that they are actually more willing to take risks or go bigger than they were before. Athletes that don't attach self-worth to an outcome also tend to have more sustainable careers or seasons and typically perform better. When you're taking a 'loss' as a sign that you're not enough, you can't see it for what it is—a chance to improve. Those with a healthy athletic identity are able to dissect the disappointing races and learn where they can do better next time," says Bracy. Not only can you still progress as a person and athlete when you accept yourself unconditionally, but it may actually help you improve more quickly and for a longer period of time.

Anyone who runs enough to, say, pick up a book about how to sustain *more running* likely attaches part of their identity to running. That's not a bad thing! It is okay to love the part of ourselves that is committed to running and be fascinated by the way our body moves through space. Acknowledging that identity helps us commit to the work that running requires and helps us relate to our goals in ways that are productive. Our athletic identities can help us find community, build relationships, seek resources, and stay engaged in the daily process that running requires.

For many of us, our closest friends are also runners. Running gives us the opportunity or reason to travel to parts of the country or the world we might otherwise never visit. Being a runner teaches us how to work through hard situations—life skills that have helped us endure tough phases. There is no doubt about it; beyond the physical and mental health benefits, identifying as runners has given us a lot.

The pitfalls emerge when we conflate our worth with our identity. We might start to think, *If I could just get my marathon time under four hours, then I'll be happy.* Or *Once I finish an ultra, I'll finally feel fulfilled.* Assigning so much worth

Zoë's Thoughts

When I first started writing professionally, I lived for my next big byline. Dreaming of my name in print, I spent hours every day researching, pitching, and writing stories for all kinds of magazines. As every new writer soon learns, getting started means enduring a lot of rejection. And get rejected I did. Every rejection email from an editor felt like a personal attack rather than reasonable feedback on my approach. It didn't help that I was depending on this work for a paycheck either. I ended up fearing the outcome that paid my rent and dictated my self-esteem!

Because my identity was so closely tied to being a writer, my sole focus was on upholding that identity rather than improving my ability and approach. I wasn't able to see the weak spots in my craft because I was blinded by the need to prove that I already *was* something, rather than embracing the process of improving. Seeing other writers and journalists succeed when I had not also felt like a personal affront, rather than a reasonable outcome of someone else's hard work. When your ego is tied to a certain outcome, everything feels like a zero-sum game. *Their win is my loss*, I thought. As I pushed increasingly hard to validate my self-worth through work, I became constrained creatively and some of my best ideas laid dormant and went ignored.

It took many months of rejection letters before I was able to understand that as long as I tied my identity to an outcome that I only had partial control over, I was going to be miserable and produce low-quality work. Once I separated my identity from the work, I was able to get vulnerable, take chances, and really dig into stories that I was passionate about or that challenged me.

Now, I'm a pro at getting rejected. It just takes years and years of practice. But was it worth it? The proof is in your hands, dear reader.

to an event outcome, one that we don't fully control, leaves us devastated when we don't get the result we want. It's not just a bad race; *we* are bad.

We understand that all of this may sound hollow coming from two runners who have written a book and competed at the elite level. But unfortunately, hitching self-esteem to accomplishments is actually something conventionally successful people do. We know that relationship all too well. Those who have had a taste of success can have even lower self-esteem. How can that be?

Runners might especially appreciate the concept of the hedonic treadmill, partially because of the running metaphor, but mostly because it's an experience many of us identify with. The hedonic treadmill is the idea that our happiness is calibrated to a baseline, no matter what we do or what happens to us. When we finally win that race, get that promotion, or land that book deal, our happiness will temporarily spike, but will quickly return to a set point. We then readjust our expectations to match the status quo of our experience and then need even more stimulus or accomplishment to maintain the same level of happiness. The higher up you go on the ladder of accomplishment, the smaller the improvements and the harder it becomes to feel pride in what you do; what was once considered a success soon becomes a terrible day. While it is easy to look at elite runners and think, *Well, if*

I achieved what you did, I would be so happy, the reality is, you wouldn't. If you could run at the level of an average elite, you wouldn't think, *Yep, I have made it; this is the best.* You would be looking to Olympians or UTMB (Ultra-Trail du Mont-Blanc) winners, believing that you would be satisfied if you were *that* level. If you went on to reach that level, you would want to medal or set a course record. As our logical brains know, running is relative, so we are never going to be content and satisfied if we view our running with this conditional approach.

So, how can we step off the hedonic treadmill?

While hedonic adaptation may not be something we can escape entirely, our happiness levels are not set in stone. There are ways to recalibrate our baseline. Since hedonic adaptation occurs partly because of the repetition of experiences, such as running one 5K PR after the next or gradually rising through the ranks at the office, one way to reset our baseline is to mix things up. Instead of focusing on lowering that 5K time again and again, sign up for a marathon. If the fun and spark of road running starts to fade, head to the trails for a new challenge.

Gratitude can be a powerful antidote to feeling stuck on the hedonic treadmill. Paying attention to what you are experiencing in the moment, and savoring the enjoyment of a specific experience beyond its outcome, can attach meaning to different aspects of an activity. Rather than trying to exceed 20 miles on a four-hour trail run, refusing to "waste time" by taking a break, stop at a particularly beautiful point along the course and stand there for a few minutes, experiencing each of the five senses in that moment. Take a mental snapshot to be able to return to later. Once you can do it standing still, work on doing it while running.

Reverse engineer situations where you can prioritize finding gratitude in the moment over the outcome. If marathon PRs aren't bringing the same level of satisfaction they once did or you're experiencing a performance plateau, try a 50K with dramatic scenery. If running has become all about getting from point A to point B, try focusing on adventure, whether that's on the trails or taking a break from competition. Trail running can be easier to take breaks, refuel, and focus on the experience, not the results. The added challenge of racing on variable, tumultuous terrain adds to the fascinating complexity. Or instead of focusing on where you want to be in your professional career, take a few moments to identify and write down what you are grateful for in your current role. This doesn't mean you can't keep striving toward that promotion or a PR—just don't let those feelings of insufficiency dictate the process.

Kriste Peoples also recommends cultivating a mindfulness practice to bring awareness to areas you find challenging to appreciate: "Without judgment or agenda, mindfulness helps us be present, not ruminating in the past nor straining toward the future. That means we have more access to our power in present time; we're not in resistance to what we fear might go wrong. When we're paying attention, mindfulness plays nicely into all that we do."

Self-acceptance, just like running or any other discipline, is a habit—a practice that must be cultivated over time with care. Work on orienting your mindset toward one of *being* rather than *doing.* "Self-acceptance also means allowing yourself to simply *be* perfectly imperfect," says Peoples.

Practice Self-Compassion

A huge part of being a creative is learning how to deal with rejection. For every piece of writing that we have published or podcast that we have launched, there are many other ideas that fell flat and never saw the light of day. Similarly, our running careers have been built on setbacks and falling short. Failure is inevitable in an athletic life, and the most successful athletes—and writers for that matter—

Zoë's Thoughts

A big chunk of my running career was built on failure. In 2018, I DNF'd the Leadville Trail 100, a historic 100-mile race through Colorado's Collegiate Peaks. It was the longest and most competitive race I'd ever attempted, and I failed.

At mile 86, I was done. Wrapped in a space blanket, shivering and sobbing on the side of the trail at 11,000 feet, my day was over. I couldn't walk, much less run, another step. My pacer, tasked with convincing me to keep moving at all costs, had to call Lake County Search and Rescue to evacuate me from the trail.

Laying in the dust, I watched what felt like hundreds of feet run, shuffle, and walk past me on their way to the finish line—the place I desperately wanted to be but was not going to reach (not that day, anyway). If I had energy left to feel anything other than cold, tired, and sore, I might've felt embarrassed and ashamed that I was failing in such a public way.

Going into the race, a friend told me that no matter what, I better not DNF because according to him, "Once you quit once, it makes it easier to quit every single time. Once you quit, you become a quitter."

Here's the thing: Nothing could be further from the truth. After I was treated for dehydration and hypothermia (quite the combo!), my friends and family who I'd been afraid of letting down were actually proud of me. They admired me for putting myself out there and giving my best shot at something really hard—even though my very best on that particular day wasn't the peak of my capabilities.

On that day, quitting was the right decision for my long-term health and well-being. Moving forward (literally) was no longer a possibility, and having the self-compassion to validate my decision allowed me to move past that failure and learn from it, rather than beat myself up over the outcome.

After a few hours of fitful sleep, my crew took me out to get breakfast pizza. We celebrated, laughing and hugging, like I had finished the race. But still exhausted, I fell asleep face-first in a veggie supreme.

Despite falling short of my goal, who I was hadn't changed. I was the same brave athlete with big dreams who put herself out there. I hadn't "become a quitter." I was someone who made a good decision in tough circumstances and was gentle enough with myself to grow in the process. I learned that love is unconditional, and the people I had the good fortune to be surrounded by that day (and many days after) loved and supported me not because of the things I achieved but because I was courageous and human and flawed—and lovable nonetheless. I learned that outcomes, good or bad, aren't who you are. Successes and failures don't define you. But how you respond to them absolutely does.

are the folks who persevere and learn from failure the quickest. There's a middle way, between overidentifying with a setback (*I am a failure!*) and moving through it too quickly and not absorbing its lesson (*On to the next thing!*). Everyone has experienced setbacks. We've all felt the uncomfortable, physiological symptoms like increased heart rate, upset stomach, and tight chest that accompany missed opportunities. The worst trick that shame and failure play on us is convincing us that we're alone in this feeling. It's just not true. Between the two of us, we've accrued enough failures and setbacks to have doubled the length of this book. We'll spare you the laundry list, but know that you're not alone, even when it feels that way.

Ditch the Comparisons

One of the biggest barriers to practicing self-acceptance is the unprecedented availability of comparison. Without even getting up from the couch, we can compare ourselves digitally across a variety of platforms, which means we can go from perfectly happy to feeling insecure and inadequate in a matter of seconds.

Scrolling through Instagram may offer all the proof we need that our lives are insufficiently glamorous, the drab background of our daily runs thrown into sharp contrast by the dramatic landscapes our peers seem to be running through. Our houses may feel small, our families dysfunctional, and lives generally less exciting in comparison. "In the context of training and racing, this issue almost always boils down to spending too much time comparing yourself to others. In this kind of situation, I would almost always return to values. For example, someone may not feel like they are enough because they aren't training as much as someone else. The trap is that they are focused on only one value or commitment (working hard and improving as an athlete)," says Bracy.

"But maybe one of the reasons they don't train as much is because they are a parent and a partner. Maybe they are very committed to a career that they love. When you look at it holistically from that perspective you can see that the person is investing in several different values. And that the time spent away from training is spent engaging with something else important rather than as not doing enough or being enough."

We can start by paying attention to how and when we engage with social media and to what feelings come up as we start scrolling. When we notice our attention starting to linger on a post, sit with it and try to name the feelings that arise. Envy? Insufficiency? Sadness?

Instead of letting those feelings draw us into hours of more self-deprecating scrolling, we could initiate a new thought process. Perhaps the image of a training partner at the finish line with their shiny new PR prompts feelings of inadequacy. Instead of letting a vortex of feelings overtake and misguide your next actions, think (or say out loud), *I'm happy for my friend. Someone else's success is not my defeat. There is plenty of good to go around!* It might feel awkward and forced at first, especially if we are struggling with insecurity, but with practice and work on the concepts we are discussing in this book, it will become clear that there is abundance. Supporting others, even if it doesn't feel genuine at first, will change your entire mindset around success. While yes, there are only three spots for an age group award, when we have a rough day on the race course, we may befriend a new runner who is considering dropping out. Our support and encouragement could make them believe that they can do hard things. Our kindness in helping them could be the difference between a one-off race and becoming a lifelong member of the community. Sometimes there are road maps to joy in places we never expected.

If someone's summit selfie prompts discomfort, remember that many people turn to social media to validate themselves, not to put others down. (If we do stumble upon the rare breed of online persona who genuinely delights in putting others down, we have permission to gleefully unfollow them.) The person to whom we're comparing our boring, summit-free Saturday morning might be struggling with the same desire to boost their sense of self. In fact, they probably are.

A good place to start is by working toward a scenario in which running is part of us, but not all of us. Think about what you love and admire in other people. Write down what you respect, appreciate, and admire in them. Chances are, very little of that list has to do with what someone has accomplished and everything to do with who that person *is*. Why would you hold yourself to a different and more arbitrary standard? If someone else did that same practice, what would they love, respect, admire, and appreciate about you? Probably a lot more than just your accomplishments.

We are enough, just as we are—simply for being. Untangling our identity from our accomplishments is something that can take years. For both of us, when we have successfully let go of accomplishments being our identity in one area, it shows up in another part of our lives. As soon as we stop placing all our self-worth on our athletic accomplishments, the temptation to do the same thing with professional success comes knocking. The bottom line is this: It's an ongoing process. Moving past feelings of not-enoughness in our brain can feel like we are constantly being judged by an unwelcome houseguest who won't leave—until we do the work to check the foundation. That is exactly why this text is giving you the tools to do it. But that doesn't mean it will be easy!

ACTION STEPS

- Continue to work on accepting yourself for who you are: the good, bad, and everything in between.

- Ask yourself why you signed up for a race so close on the heels of your last one. Could you be trying to fill a void that can't be filled with accomplishments?

- Remember that self-acceptance does not mean loving every tiny detail about yourself; it is understanding that perfectly imperfect is okay.

- Step off the hedonic treadmill and change things up by signing up for something totally different.

- If you get in the mindset of trying to maximize your distance, stop midrun to take a mental picture and feel gratitude for the ability to run at all.

- Write down what you are grateful for in an area you are currently struggling. There is hidden appreciation you have forgotten of late.

- Sit in your failures and try to understand what didn't work, but also recognize that failure is a part of life.

- Pay attention to how and when you engage with social media, notice the feelings that come up when you pause on a post, and reframe your thinking to consider what you are not seeing. Their accomplishments do not take away anything from who you are.

- Write down what you respect, appreciate, and admire in other people. Why hold yourself to a different and arbitrary standard?

3 | Clear Out the Clutter

The race starts in a few short hours. We tell ourselves we are ready, we're going to crush this, and it's going to be so much fun. But then . . . we aren't. We don't. It isn't. Why did we think we could do this anyway? Maybe a shoelace incident or an unplanned trip to the portable toilet derails a 5K PR. Maybe a thunderstorm or heat wave messes up a perfectly planned 50K. When we are dedicated and have big dreams, we expect them to come to fruition just as we planned. We find it hard to accept factors outside of our control could create less-than-ideal conditions, but we also didn't take all the other life factors into account when we set up our dream race in our minds. Instead, we call ourselves a failure and wonder why we bother at all. In reality, a few lifestyle changes or pushing back a few months to work through a major life change could have made all the difference between an average day and our dream day.

Maybe expectations didn't align with reality. We write the story of our race-day expectations long before we get to the start line. It happens to all of us; everyone from elites to back-of-the-pack runners fall prey to overly rosy expectations. Sometimes we hope for the best at a time when we are not set up for success. We don't take into account the stress we are working through in other parts of our lives or other concerns holding space in our heads. It all adds up, taking away from our performance.

Sometimes the reverse happens. The dreaded early-morning alarm after an awful night's sleep unexpectedly leads to a top-notch speed workout. The hour-long slog in the rain reveals a deep reservoir of mental toughness we didn't know we had. That run felt surprisingly good. A weight has been lifted, we feel accomplished, and we are suddenly reminded of how beautiful life is. Positivity and love floods our brain. This was just what we needed.

Courtesy of T.J. David.

Zoë and her partner, T.J., shortly after a DNF (did not finish) at Western States. Trusting the process, even when it's hard.

So, what's the difference between a good run and a bad run? The space between our ears. Our opinion about every single run is determined by the expectations we have placed on it. More than pace or any other metric, our attitude affects the way we view our experiences. It all comes down to losing the connection between our body and our mind. Obviously, we want our runs to be enjoyable; few of us get off on gutting out every single mile. Some runs will be cut short, some will be a start-to-finish struggle, and some we'll spend wishing we were on the couch instead. We appreciate the perspective and gratitude a bad run can give us. We may go through days or even weeks of bad runs, but we trust the good ones will return.

But here's the thing: When our minds are living in the past or future, jumbled with running certain paces, or when our brains are jammed with all the other things we "need to do," it transforms running from a release into another duty that adds to our cumulative fatigue. Once we attach our perfectionism to an act that humans have participated in for thousands of years, we can no longer appreciate the run for what it is. We need less stress, not more. When we rely solely on external validation as our reason to run, we lose who we are in the process. When we stop achieving and improving, we might start to doubt that running is for us and find a reason to step away because we can't see a way forward.

If we are dictated by our attitudes, by the space between our ears, how can we possibly run with a mindset of appreciation and gratitude? The reality is, we do too much. All of us. There is no denying that there are countless tasks, life challenges, and setbacks that come our way. Add in unhealthy doses of comparison, unrealistic life expectations, and an inability to be with ourselves for more than a few seconds, and it is no wonder we feel frazzled and fed up a lot of the time. In this chapter, you are going to find ways to clear out some unnecessary stress floating around in your head, while considering how you can fit running into your life during big life changes. We can't change everything, but we can commit to giving ourselves the same respect we give to everyone else. Time to start now.

Acknowledge Stressors

How often do you go to bed at night feeling accomplished, knowing that you did everything on your to-do list and all that you hoped you would?

Almost never? Us too.

Even after an all-time long run, doing three loads of laundry, getting the kids to bed on time, calling Mom, and finding a few minutes to clean the bathroom before guests arrive, we still go to bed feeling we should have done just one more thing. Better get up early tomorrow and take care of it.

Who cares if we are tired? That's life; get on with it. That feeling of deep fatigue can even feel validating—like a proxy for all the hard work. It seems everyone else is cramming more into their morning than we get done in a day, so how dare we complain? Sometimes we don't even have time, or the energy, to complain. Even if we know we get a lot done, it still feels like there is so much more to do and that we are falling behind. We're somehow simultaneously exhausted, overdrawn, and underaccomplished.

It bothers us deeply that our to-do lists never get completed and seem to grow longer with each passing day. During brief moments of waiting in line at the store or walking up the stairs, we find ourselves mindlessly scrolling social media, perusing a catalog of others' successes and seemingly easy wins. We see the accomplishments of everyone else while we sit on hold with the insurance company. Again. Or we see others relaxed and carefree on vacation, which reminds us we should have already researched and booked our next vacation. Better add that to the list. It feels like we are destined to be spinning on someone else's hamster wheel, and we don't have the willpower or organization skills to figure out how to get our lives together.

This is especially true when we are working through major life events like going through a divorce, losing a loved one, moving, or having a baby. Stressful moments can paralyze us and take over every element of our lives. We might try to convince ourselves that we are the exception, that we can handle more than everyone else when we are going through a major life change, but the stress of a life shift puts a major strain on our bodies and minds. And that is before we add the day-to-day stressors of life in the 21st century.

If you are going through any of the following life events (or something similar), training for a goal race should not and cannot be a priority:

- Starting a new job
- Moving to or looking for a new house
- Processing a divorce

- Separating from a partner
- Experiencing a family member going through a health crisis
- Losing a family member or close friend
- Becoming unemployed
- Becoming incarcerated or a loved one being incarcerated
- Becoming pregnant
- Losing a pregnancy

Running can help to process emotions during a major life change, but it is not the time to set a big goal and expect to knock it out of the park. While some folks might feel inclined to bang out a hard run to avoid feeling tough emotions, that's actually not a great idea—mentally or physically. While it may feel cathartic in the moment, it just adds more stress to your system and does very little to address the underlying causes.

When we can't give our body and mind the mental energy to perform their best, it will only lead to more frustration and disappointment when we cannot follow through with our intentions. If it is helpful to set a big, challenging goal, allow a year to accomplish it. Be honest when setting expectations. Why is now a good time to set this goal? What might we be losing if our focus is on this goal? How does this goal align with our core values? Make sure we're not just subbing an aggressive running goal in place of doing hard, internal work that's often required for true and sustainable personal growth.

While running can be helpful in many ways, it's not a panacea. Would we benefit from reaching out to a mental health professional in the same way that we would contact a physical therapist if something felt off physically?

If our mood continues to be unstable, or we experience physical symptoms that could be related to overtraining (see chapter 5), this is a sign to back off. This is a time to give ourselves grace and understanding if days or even weeks of training are missed. When we take the long view and prioritize consistency, there's always space to take a couple extra rest days to prioritize our mental health. Running should be a tool to help, not another obligation.

> When we take the long view and prioritize consistency, there's always space to take a couple extra rest days to prioritize our mental health.

Think about what you would tell a friend who is going through a major life change. What would you say if they told you they were going to train really hard over the next few months for a big goal race? You'd probably gently advise against it. Why give that advice to them and something different to yourself? What makes you any less worthy of kind words and compassion?

As Jordan Marie Whetstone, founder of the advocacy group Rising Hearts, says, "When times are busy, I am feeling overwhelmed, and life changes are happening—I have shifted my way of thinking towards health and wellness. I constantly ask myself or leave visible notes with, 'How are you doing? How are you feeling?' and allow myself to take a moment to respond. That usually leads to adapting my running to sometimes needing a day off or running less than what I was hoping to do. Before I tried this new way of self-awareness, I used to force myself to run and work out, and would feel awful. It led to not loving running in those moments. It helped me realize that running will always be there for me and that I am no good to running if my mind, body, and heart are not in a good place."

Take Back Your Life

The day-to-day challenges of life can be suffocating and can affect our mental health. At times we may almost wish for a major life change to pull us out of the monotony. In many ways, this is more difficult to recognize and accept. Paperwork will keep requiring our signatures; our homes will always need to be cleaned. And if we don't do these tasks, no one will. We understand how major life stressors can affect our lives, but these day-to-day things—well, that's life. There will always be another load of laundry to fold, another email to send, and another walk for the dog. These are constants in our lives, and using them as an excuse means we will never get anything done.

Parenting young children, caring for older parents, connecting with struggling friends, making career changes, getting promotions, having difficulties with a family member, doing taxes, and many more situations can cause major stress. We know we are overwhelmed and overextended when we feel like we can't keep up, when it feels like we are drowning in things we need to do. During these periods, running should be adjusted accordingly. Our body and mind are connected; stress is stress. Even if our physical body is able to function when we are engulfed by life stressors, our mental health may suffer. We might have trouble sleeping or maintaining our quality of life as we sink deeper into anxiety, depression, or other mental health struggles. Like many running injuries, mental health struggles often do not pop up out of the blue but rather fester and cultivate unaddressed for far too long.

Feeling tired on runs or running slower often accompanies periods of stressful life situations, but if we feel like we want to hammer out a run to release some tension, that is okay too—but approach with caution. Will overdoing it set us back because of stress, injury, or under-recovery? It might not be the best way to prioritize mental health and long-term athletic well-being, as good as it may feel in the moment. Even if we're feeling some mental relief on the run, there's still an amount of cortisol (stress hormone) that's released. So we should have some nonphysical tools for stress relief too. Fitness is cumulative. Each day, month, and year builds upon the last. We do not go back to factory settings at the beginning of each training block, we build upon previous training segments. As long as we are doing our best for this period of life, that is all we can ever ask. Sometimes, forcing a run can set us back, whereas prioritizing rest and recovery might help us move forward.

If it feels like life is never going to calm down, and having a race to work toward improves your quality of life, there is potential to train for one. Trent Stellingwerff, director of performance solutions and applied sport research at the Canadian Sport Institute, works with CEOs and executives who have especially stressful jobs. Trent emphasizes that it is important to consider energy constraints as well as time constraints when we are planning our training. Consider the cost-benefit analysis for each decision. The time constraint element is relatively low for runners, even elite athletes, because our bodies can handle only so much impact from the pounding. For most runners, the energy constraint is what gets us into trouble. If we do not take time to put energy back into our bodies, every function is at risk for breakdown or slowdown.

For runners who have busy lives or especially demanding jobs, Stellingwerff suggests selecting a 10- to 12-week block with the most flexibility and time to fit in hard training for a race. A conversation with family is imperative because we may need to drop other commitments for a few months to gain an additional four to five hours a week beyond regular training to prepare for an upcoming race. It is important to select only one of these blocks each year to prevent strain in family relationships and burnout as a human. This additional designated time can be used to catch up on sleep, integrate elements of therapy or strength training as rehab or prehab, and engage in other self-care methods to support the energy constraint component. This method essentially involves periodizing efforts around a busy work schedule.

Maintain a Positive Perspective

Sometimes, we may not feel like running at all, and that's okay too. A 10-minute run is a great way to assess if a run is what we need or if a rest day is in order. Try the 10-minute rule: Set out with the goal of only going out for 10 minutes. When 10 minutes is up, keep going if it feels good, or head home knowing you listened to your body. The best run is one that feels good. You don't need to finish feeling wiped out or to even work up a sweat for the run to "count."

Some days it's all we can do to barely squeeze in a run. Sometimes it's between a kid's soccer practice and choir, on a lunch break between meetings, or zipping out the door during an elderly parent's nap. There is nothing wrong with cramming in a run on a busy day, but we can't expect personal bests or to feel amazing (although if we do, fantastic!). We have to accept that we are doing the best we can for our current life situation. And our best is always enough.

Beating ourselves up about missed days, bad days, and less committed periods will only add to the stress, putting us further from where we want to be. When we try to force training in busy periods, we end up with one of the five body breakdowns, which we will learn about in chapter 5, and maybe a mental-health breakdown to go with it. If backing off means skipping hard days and replacing them with easy runs, do it. And no, do not try to make them up later that week. Let them go!

> Beating ourselves up about missed days, bad days, and less committed periods will only add to the stress, putting us further from where we want to be.

As runners we often convince ourselves that running is our downtime, and maybe it is. Running can be our peace and tranquility or our time to socialize with friends while doing this activity together. For runners, there are few things better than spending a few quiet miles by ourselves after a hectic day or sharing the activity with people who love it as much as we do. It is good for our bodies, minds,

Tina's Thoughts

While writing this book, with two young kids under four and a business to run, I knew my time was limited. Getting up at 4:45 a.m. most mornings to get in a 60-minute run was not only part of my training but also part of my mental health strategy. I needed that time out in nature—time to be quiet and move my body—knowing that when I returned to the house, the day would be hectic and primarily about my family's needs. During the fall of 2021, I signed up for three races, something I had never done before. Thanks to a supportive husband, fitting in the training was not a problem.

The energy expenditure element, however, was a problem. While part of me wanted to get really fit and give the races my very best, I recognized that this was not the stage of life to do so. All I could do was focus on getting to the races in a healthy state. Trying to run a personal best or even shoot for a specific time would only add unnecessary pressure that would put me at further risk of injury or burnout. It was tough to see other runners training hard, while feeling like I was slacking off, but I reminded myself that there would be plenty of races to train hard for in the future (if I wanted to, of course). This one season of simply running for the joy of the training could teach me just as much as the seasons when I pushed my limits. Those lessons can be applied to future phases and will help me maintain perspective on what running brings to my life. My previous elite running life was all about the end result: what I got at the finish line. Now, my running life is about a sense of adventure; it's a more enjoyable way to approach the sport, and I'm one step closer to becoming a lifelong sustainable runner. My mental and physical health is not tied up in maximizing performance. Running is adding to my health rather than taking away from it.

and hearts, as long as we take other time for ourselves as well. In assessing your relationship with running, be honest. Has it become just one more way to "get stuff done"? Does it check the box of staying fit or keeping weight down? Has it become another way to demonstrate our value and productivity? It's okay for running to meet different needs during different times in your life, but if running becomes just another way to avoid sitting still (because when productivity is king, stillness is the enemy), then it might be time for a break.

We run because we enjoy it, but it is also for our long-term health and for the benefit of our loved ones (with our improved moods!). It is okay to also crave some time to do "normal" things like going out for dinner with a friend or taking a few days' retreat for ourselves.

Whetstone emphasizes this point through her advocacy work combined with her running. "I have really looked at running as more than just trying to get a fast time or reach my goals. It's about running for something more than me—with a deeper purpose, to give back to those who can't run or are no longer here, and to create an intentional space and time in how I connect with the lands I run with. It's me being less dependent on the watch when it's not needed, it's more running at a slower pace, more runs on the trails or different routes to see new things, and organizing more community runs to have that community connection. This is what brings more joy to my running, and a better, healthier relationship."

Reach Out

Stepping back from your role as the assistant coach at your kids' soccer club mid-season or refusing to go on any more work trips may not be an option; however, during hectic periods there are other ways to combine social engagements and life tasks. You could ask a friend to come to the store with you to get groceries or drive with you across town to go to the bank. We all know how it feels to be stretched thin, and a friend will empathize and listen to your frustrations. Text your group of friends to see if anyone wants to squeeze in a dog walk, or ask a pal if they want a buddy for their morning run. When our impulse is to retreat into ourselves, that can be a sign to reach out. Our family and friends often want to spend time with us because they miss us and it reduces feelings of loneliness for both parties—loneliness that affects our physical and mental health. It does not have to be a three-course meal together; focus on creating connection. Shoot for real-life interactions instead of online whenever possible, but if time and space are an issue, pick up the phone. Some connection, even mediated by technology, is better than none.

When we forget to send a friend a comforting message on the morning of her first chemo treatment, or we don't check in with our sister on her first day back at work, we are losing the strong connection to people we care about deeply. It might be time to take a step back from other obligations, or we risk shutting those people out. Other warning signs of doing too much are making mistakes, getting easily frustrated at ourselves or others, and missing occasions that are important to us. If we have always given thoughtful gifts or remembered birthdays of family and friends, but have recently been missing or forgetting them, chances are we are taking on too much. That is not to say you should feel more guilt; instead ask yourself if those gestures are truly important to you or if you just felt obligated. If they are important, consider what you can do to change your behavior. When we start to make decisions that are out of alignment with our values, it can indicate we're no longer making the best decisions.

> When we start to make decisions that are out of alignment with our values, it can indicate we're no longer making the best decisions for ourselves.

Whetstone believes our emotions signal when we are doing too much, and we can only realize it if we stop for a moment to listen. "I can tell I'm doing too much when my mind and body are just constantly exhausted. When my brain can't really think, I am feeling more emotional, feeling overwhelmed, and once the anxiety attacks start to happen—that's my biggest tell to say, 'Jordan, what are you doing and what are you going to do about it?'"

Being snappy with or taking anger out on loved ones is another indication we are not addressing an internal conflict. We will always take frustrations out on those closest to us, but when it happens multiple times a day, or we regularly feel guilt or shame about our actions, we are not handling the accumulation of stressors well and need to make a change. While nothing is easy to cut, and we may feel like we can't let go of anything, our loved ones are almost always willing to help. This is especially true if they know they can help us to decrease our stress level.

Could you lean on friends to help? Could you hire someone to look after your kids a few hours a week? What could you eliminate from your schedule? Could you sign up for a massage or yoga class to de-stress? Remember, just as we want to give our best to our loved ones, they also love us and want the best for us. We are going to be a better parent, child, sibling, friend, and person if we also look after ourselves. It can feel counterintuitive; we don't have time to do all we need to, let alone add something else to our schedule, but we will be happier if we make time for ourselves each day, even if it is just a five-minute voice memo exchange with a friend. And seeing us happier will make our loved ones happier too.

Be Less Busy

Busyness can distract us from our true goals. When we are so focused on keeping everyone else happy, preoccupied with all the things we think we need to do, we sacrifice memories we could have created, we lose childlike joy, and we halt flow. Busyness can blind us to small joys in open parts of the day: a butterfly drifting down the street, the full moon rising over a distant ridgeline. Downtime is not wasted time but time to process, recover, and then continue our effective completion of tasks. Trying to fill every second with "productivity" can distract us from what actually matters or distract us from small moments of joy.

Once we recognize that being busy is holding us back from what we want the most in life, we can work up the courage to say no. While we can't pass on every task (hello, taxes!), we can be more intentional about how and why we engage. Am I doing this because I actually have to, or because I don't want to let someone else down? Am I doing this because I want to, or because I feel obligated? Showing ourselves respect might feel awkward at times, but it feels much better than saying yes to everything and always feeling fried.

Meditate to Be Present

Running feels good when we're present, and being present feels good when we're running. When we appreciate our runs, ride their ups and downs, and stop obsessing over results, it can transform the rest of our life too. But being present isn't that easy. Whether it's thinking back to the day before, agonizing over an email we sent or a meeting we attended, or simply looking ahead to lunch, it's hard to be fully present. To truly become present in our lives, we have to get away from the noise—put down our phones, computers, and iPads, even if time alone with our thoughts may feel like the last thing we want to do. When we fear quiet time will make us worry and overthink, that is a giant warning that solitude is exactly what we need.

Finding time to sit with our thoughts and feelings is also integral to self-compassion and personal growth. We often stare, mouths (almost) gaping at the powerful, strong humans we see daily on social media or in our daily lives. They seem to know exactly who they are and are proud to show it. We feel envy and wonder, *How did they get there? I wish I had that self-confidence!* Here is the beautiful truth: We can have that self-confidence, but getting there, as with

Sandy Gutierrez

Time to be still can be hard to prioritize, but even a few minutes once a day can make a difference.

everything meaningful in life, requires work. It means getting to know who we are by cutting out distractions and spending dedicated time on ourselves.

We know that stillness is mental practice that takes work, and it is much easier to go into autopilot, bouncing around from thought to thought. While the mention of meditation may conjure a picture in your mind of a bearded man sitting cross-legged on a mountaintop for hours, that's not what it needs to be. Meditation isn't about immediately transcending to a different plane or completely turning off our thoughts. It is a daily practice that connects body and mind and can be a powerful tool to slow down our thoughts by focusing our attention on a single, simple action, such as paying attention to each individual breath.

Meditation is a tool that helps us learn how to observe our thoughts without judgment. It is a way of building awareness and gaining a healthy perspective on ourselves. It has been proven that meditation can improve physical relaxation, help individuals cope with illness, reduce anxiety, and improve overall health (Chen et al. 2012). In a study by Basso and colleagues (Basso et al. 2019), after eight weeks, just 13 minutes of meditation per day decreased negative mood state and enhanced attention, working memory, and recognition memory, as well as decreasing anxiety. Meditation has become so valued, NBA players incorporate it into their training. Michael Jordan and Kobe Bryant enlisted the help of meditation coach George Mumford to help them get "flow ready" and "in the zone" (Effron 2016). There are plenty of apps, such as Ten Percent Happier, Calm, and Headspace, that encourage us to meditate for 10, 5, or even 1 minute a day and can guide those new to the practice.

Once we are still, we become more receptive to being present and mindful through the simple act of paying attention to our body in the moment. But don't start thinking it will be smooth sailing once you set the habit; it will still require an intentional decision each day. As runners we know this feeling. Hearing the alarm go off early on a weekend morning, we argue with ourselves that we could use an extra rest day, while knowing we'll feel better if we run. We can use the same approach to get out the door for a run or to sit down on the floor to meditate. Just like expecting a perfect running performance, expecting perfection within our meditation only sets us up for disappointment, and we may decide it doesn't work and give up. And, like heading out the door for our runs, we won't regret the time spent in mindfulness practice either. No matter how focused or unfocused the session, we come out the other side feeling better than when we started.

Meditation for Runners Who Hate Sitting Still

Maybe you want to meditate to feel less stressed, more present, or more focused, or you've heard of the running performance benefits. Maybe you want to grow your self-awareness or build better relationships. There are plenty of reasons to dive into a meditation practice, but it is surprising how difficult it can be to follow through.

"It's so easy for us to get pulled into a comparison cycle with other runners. Meditation is private and non-competitive," says Katie Arnold, a writer and the winner of the 2018 Leadville Trail 100. "You can't qualify it. No one wins at it. You can sit for 30 years and still be a beginner. I love this as a counterbalance to my competitive side as a trail runner."

Getting started might be the hardest part, particularly for those of us who feel uncomfortable or downright itchy when forced to sit with our thoughts and feelings. Like many folks, your brain might feel like a crowded street corner on a good day, and on fire the rougher days. The idea of simply sitting—and *being*—can be totally scary.

"Many of us have this image of sitting pretzel-style, blissed out on a cushion, unperturbed by life," says Kriste Peoples, a trail runner and meditation instructor. "But starting a practice doesn't look like that at all. Meditating doesn't mean you'll automatically be free of stress or challenging emotions."

Peoples emphasizes that runners shouldn't expect to feel immediate peace or instant enlightenment. "What tends to happen is we realize how hard it can be to sit still, how difficult it is to quiet a mind that's being constantly pulled in every direction by distracting thoughts or feelings."

It's called a practice for a reason. Just like training, it's going to take work and a whole lot of patience and discipline to make progress. If you want to commit to a regular practice, a few times a week is a good place to start. Like running, frequency is strongly correlated with results. Try to set aside 10 to 15 minutes to sit in a quiet place without disruption or with minimal distractions. And, actually, meditating is pretty simple. Just sit, and practice. Close your eyes, tune into your breath without forcing it, and let your brain do its thing. Also, you can meditate just about anywhere. The position doesn't matter as much as making sure that you're comfortable and relaxed, not holding any tension in the body.

Arnold likes to meditate before her runs as a way of opening her mind. Peoples likes to meditate just about everywhere, sitting, or even walking outside.

"The point is not to be without thoughts, but to not get attached to the thoughts as they arise. I like to imagine them like clouds—I see them come, and let them pass," says Arnold. She recommends counting and connecting with breath to avoid overidentifying with or dwelling on thoughts. "It's impossible to be bad at meditation. Whatever is there when you sit down—anger, impatience, etc.—is exactly

(continued)

Meditation for Runners Who Hate Sitting Still *(continued)*

right. You are just there to meet it."

Again, there is no such thing as good or bad meditation. This part is particularly sticky for the Strava-inclined among us who may be a little too dependent on kudos, gold stars, and carrots. There is no such thing as meditation failure, just awareness and nonawareness.

Endurance athletes may be inclined to shoot for a long session right off the bat, but Peoples cautions against this approach and advises newbies to start with shorter sessions that feel good and are not stressful, maybe just a minute or two. She also recommends starting slowly and not signing up for a multiday retreat off the couch. "If you're hoping to establish a practice, it's not unlike running in that you start from where you are and you build a practice that works for you."

Running requires the same physical motion over and over. Meditation is doing mental reps; we have trained our minds to wander, just as we have trained our legs to run long distances. Think of meditation as adding speedwork to our training. It will take a little while to get used to the new variation, but once we get going, we improve a little more each day.

The mental and physical rest period allows us to experience what is happening in our body, which we may not recognize in our conscious mind. We notice where tension and emotion are sitting in our body. Meditation can teach us how to process insecurities and criticism mindfully and neutrally with more self-compassion and self-awareness. We will feel more fulfilled if we learn what to work on and improve, while also celebrating and appreciating the process (however imperfect).

All growth opportunities make up our individual story. While others warn us about their mistakes and the tough parts of their own running quest, it doesn't mean we won't experience the same mistakes ourselves. We know the pitfalls exist, but we all have our own path to follow, which is one of the most beautiful parts of the sport we love; it is full of twists and turns, stops and starts, ups and downs. Much like any one run, there is a lot of variability, and all we can do is adapt the best we can. It is not always easy, but it makes one heck of an adventure.

Reduce Technology Use

We are our own worst critics. Our second worst critic? Our GPS watches. Many a running career has been lost to the swirling vortex of activity logging apps. While there are proven benefits to the accountability and community these platforms can offer, they can also suck people further down the rabbit hole of insecurity.

Pay attention to your mindset as you log in to these apps, and observe how you feel when you exit out. How we engage with these feedback systems can alter our feelings about our lived experience in ways that aren't healthy or productive. Many runners, consciously or not, will run faster or turn out higher volume training weeks—not because it's good or productive but to get a Strava segment or display their training triumph online. While Strava is working to further develop and foster their online community, and help runners develop a healthier relationship to achievement, it is still important to examine our relationship to activity apps. If we walk away from these platforms feeling worse than when we opened them, it might be time to explore other features or step away.

Similarly, there might be individuals or entire online communities that are unhealthy for us. It's not uncommon for relationships to start with casual or even friendly competition but devolve into mean-spirited one-upmanship as egos battle. Likewise, some teams, running groups, or other communities might form based on a healthy premise but unintentionally foment strains of inadequacy. While people *usually* don't put others down intentionally or maliciously, those who struggle with their own self-worth are more likely to demean others—even friends or teammates. We have been that person too. We all have.

If we find ourselves in a community or a relationship that habitually undermines our self-worth, it is time to step away and get some air. It doesn't mean forever, or that it was a bad community or relationship, but as our needs and esteem evolve, so will how we relate to others.

Society tells us the more technology we have, the better off we are. If we look up from our phone in any social situation nowadays, it is rare to find anyone not looking down at a personal device. But is it adding to our lives, or taking away from them? One study found that just one hour of screen time resulted in a decrease in psychological well-being among teens (Twenge et al. 2018). Most of us spend much more than one hour a day on screens, so what does that mean for our mental health?

When we are connected to a device, rather than noticing the different calls of birds or paying attention to how our body feels as we run, we let our GPS watches tell us what to feel. We are so out of touch with our body that we struggle to function without electronics. Running may be a sport that requires little equipment, but we have become very reliant on technology and, in particular, GPS watches. Many runners love numbers, love tracking, and love to know exactly where they are at. GPS watches are a helpful tool to monitor training, but they can quickly and covertly turn into an addiction that pushes us beyond our means, especially during periods of high stress. During challenging periods of life, our bodies will adjust accordingly to protect us. If we let go of the pace expectations set by GPS watches, our body will consider all that it is currently dealing with and do the best it can for that day. And doing our best is all we can ever ask for.

This doesn't mean you should stop wearing a tracking watch, but try to avoid looking at your watch at all during runs. Feel free to geek out over stats afterward (although if you can refrain, your mental health would probably be better off), but knowing your pace during easy runs is unnecessary. Monitoring pace ranges can be helpful for newer runners but leaves runners woefully inept to know what a pace feels like. We need to be able to understand how we're actually feeling, not how our watch is telling us we should feel. Relying on our watch causes us to discount other variables like how much sleep we have had, the food we have eaten (or not), stress in our lives, and weather conditions that can have a big impact on our speed.

Having a healthy relationship to our GPS watch can mean turning off the beeping and displaying only distance and time on the main screen. Our body appreciates being able to judge what feels right and then settle in there. Internally, we are always trying to maintain a constant, steady environment, or homeostasis. We often end up surprising ourselves with just how much better we feel and faster we run when we are not staring down at our wrists and letting the psychological impact of what we see affect us. We end up panicking when we see a pace faster than we expect on our watch, waiting for the moment it catches up to us. Maybe we were ready all along to run that pace, but our GPS watch messed with our heads. Besides, runners have gotten by just fine for thousands of years without GPS watches!

In this chapter, we are challenging you to change or discard many of the things runners hold dear—what we genuinely believe helps us to achieve the goals we want. It may seem overwhelming and intimidating, and maybe you're tempted to shut the book altogether. Trust us, though: This work will change your life and make you happier, healthier, and filled with more joy. And we all need a little more joy. Read on.

ACTION STEPS

- When you are expending energy on controlling things that cannot be controlled, step back and take a few deep breaths.
- Consider how major life events and transitions affect your mental and physical health. Is now the right time for a goal race?
- For runners who have busy lives or especially demanding jobs, select a 10- to 12-week block with the most flexibility and time to fit in hard training for a race. Commit, then prioritize family and friends after the race.
- It's okay to take a break from running or take extra days off during stressful times. Let missed days go; you do not need to make them up.
- Be aware of signs you are overdoing it. If you feel tightness in your stomach or chest as you read this, you know it is true for you. See what you can remove from your plate.
- Downtime is not wasted but is a chance to process, recover, and then continue your effective completion of tasks.
- Sleep in if your body needs it. Yes, a few items on your to-do list might not get done, but those you get done later will be done more efficiently and effectively (freeing up more time).
- Say no if it is not a *hell yes!* Some life things need to be done. But be honest with yourself: Do you need to say yes, or are you doing it to avoid discomfort?
- Add meditation to your day or week. Even if it starts as a one-minute practice every day, it is better to start small rather than unrealistic. Try an app like Ten Percent Happier, Calm, or Headspace if you need support.
- Turn off the beeping alerts on your GPS watch, and change the screen to distance and time only on workout days. You will learn to pace yourself if you practice running by feel.

4 Focus on Sustainable Strength

It's tempting to believe that many life and training woes can be solved by simply running more. But part of being a runner means doing what we have to do to keep running. And sometimes that means not *only* running. An increasing amount of research confirms what many runners know to be true: Adding strength training to our routine can help us run more sustainably. Running, broken down to its most essential elements, is a repetitive motion. For our bodies to adapt to that repeated impact, we need to be strong in all planes of motion.

Strength in each plane may not be the most obvious component of running, but research shows stronger athletes are healthier, are more resilient, and can train more sustainably (Lauersen et al. 2014). We don't need to be a powerlifter; a little strength training goes a long way. "Strength training can help runners with injury prevention, running more efficiently, and becoming a more well-rounded athlete, versus just being a runner, and feeling like an overall badass!" says Megan Flanagan, a certified personal trainer, strength, and running coach.

Here is where it gets confusing, though. *Strength training* is a wide-ranging umbrella term, encapsulating everything from push-ups to plyometrics. This chapter will dive into the specific strategies and routines that are most effective for runners, assuming our goal is to improve running, stay healthy, and train sustainably—not necessarily get ripped six-pack abs.

Improve Your Running With Strength Training

Research shows that strength training improves strength, running economy, power, and performance for runners.

According to a study by the *British Journal of Sports Medicine*, up to 90 percent of runners will face injury in a given year, but strength training can help prevent acute and chronic injury. Strength training, when done properly, helps bones, muscles, and tendons become more durable, efficient, and injury resistant. A 2018 article in the journal *Sports Medicine* also indicates that strength work improves running economy, reducing the energy needed to run a certain pace (Blagrove et. al. 2018).

For runners, one of the most important components of strength is the ability of joints and tissues to absorb the forces created from thousands of foot strikes every time we run.

"Strength training toughens up connective tissues and improves strength, giving runners 'armor' that helps guard against the impact forces of running," says Jason Fitzgerald, a Denver-based strength and running coach. For runners, one of the most important components of strength is the ability of joints and tissues to absorb the forces created from thousands of foot strikes every time we run. This can be something subtle like a collapsing arch that causes foot or lower leg pain or something more pronounced like a hip drop and lateral weight shift that causes hip and pelvis problems. Additionally, a weakness in one area can often result in pain or injury somewhere else entirely, which leads us down a path of "chasing pain." This can be frustrating and time-consuming and can ultimately hinder our running plans.

Strength training to address such issues can help us run stronger and faster, which will also make running more enjoyable. It is best to find a nearby professional to help identify potential problems before they sideline us. (Or we can record ourselves running from behind by zooming in on the feet and ankles, and make another recording that looks at the hips.) We still recommend working with a professional to make suggestions, but knowing where our body is vulnerable will help determine where best to spend our time.

Some of the biggest gains from strength training, aside from injury prevention, are in running economy, or how efficient we are at using a given amount of oxygen. "Strength work also improves running economy by helping athletes use less energy to run at the same pace," says Fitzgerald. "Weightlifting is often called 'coordination training under resistance' and by subtly improving the inter- and intramuscular coordination of your leg muscles, you become a far more efficient runner." As both a strength and conditioning and running coach, Fitzgerald works with athletes to make sure their strength training supports their running goals.

For most of us, the amount of running our body can handle is limited by time or injury risk. Strength training is a time- and energy-efficient way to optimize our training without simply stacking on the miles. In our own training, we've put our hands to the injury fire more than a couple of times. Sometimes, an injury or a training plateau is just the kick in the pants we've needed to reemphasize the strength training part of our running program. It is normal for motivation to fluctuate, and it is okay to have periods in which we do not strength train at all, but be aware of what this can do in terms of risk of injury or limiting potential performance. Ideally, we do not want to wait until we have a problem to begin a strength training regimen, but sometimes our running future flashing before our eyes can be the nudge we need to get back on track. A little bit of strength training goes a long way and is an important part of a sustainable running career.

And don't worry about bulking up. The type of lifting that produces a Dwayne "The Rock" Johnson–type physique requires special lifting techniques (and an almost unbelievable amount of fish-based protein). It's really hard to add significant muscle mass when you're prioritizing running, and real bulking requires high-volume lifting (e.g., bench-pressing two times our bodyweight) and significant dietary shifts (consuming far more protein than needed by most endurance athletes). Whatever body composition changes occur when you're eating well, training appropriately, and prioritizing mental health and physical well-being are likely beneficial and will help your running rather than hinder it. We all have different genetic body types; some build muscle easier than others, and that's okay! What's important is that you feel good and enjoy training as you take care of your brain and body. By embracing your own definition of strength and giving your body the fuel it needs, you'll be that much closer to running sustainably.

> Whatever body composition changes occur when you're eating well, training appropriately, and prioritizing mental health and physical well-being are likely beneficial and will help your running rather than hinder it.

Get Started With a Strength Training Plan

Getting started doesn't have to take a lot of time or energy. Simply dedicating a few minutes to an active warm-up before or after our run can make a big difference. "Over time, you can gradually build up your strength training volume and intensity, keeping in mind not to do so when you're also increasing running volume and intensity. Something simple like standing on one foot while holding your other knee up with your hands, then letting go and using your hip flexors to maintain the position, is great for improving the strength of your stance leg," says Drew Watts, a professional strength coach who has guided Tina for years. "This control will help every time your feet strike the ground. You may feel off-balance at first, but over time those muscles will get stronger, which will help you run more efficiently. Additionally, you can add some lunges, pogo hops, and even planks before your run to improve performance."

You'll likely be sore after diving into a new strength training plan, so dial back your training as needed to adjust. If you are too sore to run, that probably means you went too hard, too soon. Allow time to warm up and cool down before and after your strength sessions just as you would with running. Dynamic movements (jogging, leg swings, walking drills) are ideal for getting warm and for helping the body wake up and get ready to lift.

Our journey as a runner teaches us to be patient, to understand that improvements and breakthroughs take time. We know this applies to everything else too, but when beginning a strength training plan, we look for quick changes and get frustrated when they don't happen. Strength training is another part of a sustainable running plan that will take time to construct. The more consistent you are over weeks, months, and years, the better off your body will be. It is

Tina Muir

Strength training helped Tina stay healthy and avoid injury during her years as an elite marathoner.

better to start slow, picking just a few exercises to work the major muscles consistently week after week, than to jump into a one-hour program that you can't handle or maintain. "Split squats, glute bridges, push-ups, rows, and planks are great starter exercises. Completing two to three sets of five to eight reps (or 20-30 seconds per exercise) is a simple way to incorporate some strength training to your program," says Watts. Build up those exercises by adding weight, or load. If it starts to negatively affect running, back off a little. "If you are uncertain about how to properly perform these exercises, please find a fitness professional in your area to help you. Doing them incorrectly may not injure you, but it probably won't help you either. We don't want to develop bad movement habits when our goal is to become better movers (runners)."

It is always best to start with lower weights (or bodyweight to really nail the movements) and short training sessions, 20 to 30 minutes, to help ease your body into a routine. It might be tempting to dive right in, brand-new strength program in hand, and go hard right out of the gate. Resist this temptation! Any new habit requires deliberation and finesse, especially something like strength training. An important rule is to never lift more than your technique can support.

Integrate a Strength Training Routine

Journal articles that demonstrate the utility of strength training are all well and good, but what do we do when we are short on time and energy and don't exist in the perfectly controlled confines of a scientific study? Just as we are each wonderful, beautiful, totally individual people, our strength routine should be individual as well. There is no one "best routine" (no matter how many clickbait articles claim there is). It's important to consider our background, goals, and available resources when thinking about how we want to integrate strength into our running routine.

Compound movements that integrate multiple muscle groups (e.g., lunge with a shoulder press) are more functional and have been shown in research to more effectively increase running performance (Kraemer and Ratamess 2005). For instance, many athletes, swayed by the six-packs splashed across the cover of *Sports Illustrated,* might wear themselves out doing crunches and other abdominal exercises. Instead, athletes should focus on building a strong trunk that provides a stable foundation for the limbs to move. To quote Charles Poliquin, "You can't fire a cannon from a shaky canoe." Think about the types of exercises that will better allow our limbs to move like independent levers, as opposed to exercises that will give us six-pack abs. Crunches could result in tightening muscles and potential lower back discomfort; those should be a hard pass. We like to use crunches as a way to weed through potential strength training coaches: If a coach is all about crunches and sit-ups, keep on looking!

Bodyweight exercises are convenient, especially for runners who are frequently away from their gym or home setup. It's also a great way to build a strength-training habit and focus on technique while minimizing injury risk. One of the hidden benefits of strength training is that it slows us down, even if only for a little while. Since technique is such a critical part of effective strength training, we are given the opportunity to perform our movements in a controlled manner. Running involves repetitive movements but also fast actions that occur quicker than our brain can process and change our individual steps. Unless we are highly skilled and developed in understanding technique, we aren't able to decipher what our joints are doing every time our feet strike the ground. "If we focus on these things during our strength training sessions, it reinforces those finer points and carries over to our running. While getting our muscles stronger is good, if our joints can't direct the forces we're creating properly, we may not be improving our efficiency," says Watts. If we're rushing through strength exercises to "check a box," we could be missing out on the many benefits and increase our injury risk. If time is not on our side, it might be best to stick to something that we can commit to before each and every run, like a slightly longer dynamic warm-up consisting of running-related movements and priming exercises. However, if we are not setting time aside each week for strength training, be warned: Performance may not proceed as we hoped, and injury risk increases.

You should have a designated space for strength training. Research shows that it's easier to build a habit in a space that facilitates it, like writing at a desk, sleeping in a bed, or doing strength work in a designated exercise nook. Cordoning off that physical space can motivate and make the habit stickier, because the space acts as a visual cue, a reminder to fit your routine in each day. Zoë's workout nook is just outside her office, and each day when she logs off, she's forced to walk past her yoga mats and dumbbells, which act as a potent reminder to get her strength and mobility work done.

In training as in life, there's no free lunch. Stress is stress, and you need to be sure strength training works *for* your running and not against it. Most runners like to stack their biggest strength stresses on harder run days (like workouts) to avoid spreading it out throughout the week, which could create a chronic stress–training stimulus. More experienced runners may like to focus on controlled movements the day before or the day after their hard running workouts. Test it out to see what works; you are the one who knows your body best.

Chronic stress (e.g., trying to do an hour of strength five times a week) can negatively affect the endocrine system by increasing cortisol and causing unhelpful fluctuations in estrogen and testosterone. While this is more of a concern for heavier strength training (versus lighter, physical therapy-style mobility work), all training should be flexible and responsive.

The biggest key is consistency. The perfect strength routine won't make a lick of difference if you only do it a couple of times, so the best routine is one you can regularly complete. "If a runner is doing bodyweight strength training, I love to see a 10- to 20-minute session after every run. This acts as a cool-down, helps build strength, and reduces injury risk. If a runner is willing to lift weights at a gym, those workouts only need to be done twice per week since they're more challenging," says Fitzgerald.

Feeling sore week after week is a sign that your body is breaking down rather than adapting. Don't view perpetual soreness as a validation of training. Make sure that you feel motivated, energized, and healthy more days than not. While it's normal to occasionally feel soreness, especially if you're incorporating new moves or starting a gym habit, it shouldn't be persistent, and it shouldn't come at the detriment of your running training. Similar to your running training, some days might be tough and make you a bit sore, but if every day leaves you feeling exhausted and too sore to pull a sweater over your head, then it's not sustainable and it's time to ease up.

Strength training can seem intimidating if it is something you have never done. It can look like the elite runners have a personal strength coach standing by their side, perfecting their form with every move (and often they do!). We might believe we are not at the level to require that, but we are. A little strength work is better than nothing, even if a five-minute dynamic warm-up is all you can handle right now. If you truly want to reach your best, dedicated strength training time each week is a must. Find a coach to teach the correct technique, and then watch your running form smooth out as it becomes more efficient and reduces your injury risk.

ACTION STEPS

- Aim for consistency; it matters more than intensity.
- Consider a dynamic warm-up before a run to prime the muscles.
- Find a routine that fits your life and circumstances.
- Choose strength training exercises that support running and what you want out of it.
- Determine the volume of strength training that's ideal based on where you are at in your running journey and running season.
- Find a strength coach who can prescribe an individualized program, especially if you are new to strength training. Make sure they have a heavy focus on correct technique; if not, keep looking.

5 | Reduce Injury Risk

Imagine never getting sick, injured, or overtrained again. Think of a world where we could run every day without the fear of crossing the invisible but well-known line runners like to dance on. Picture life without that well-trodden line where we can do as much as we want with no repercussions. It would be the runner's ultimate dream.

Or would it? While we might daydream about guaranteed, hiccup-free training, what would we lose in the trade-off? If we knew there were no limit, no max to what our body could handle, would we love it as much? Would we even continue?

Part of the magic would be gone. It wouldn't be about finding our limits, because there wouldn't be any. It would no longer be about the enjoyment of running, because we would get even more wrapped up in the numbers of going further and faster. What else, or who else, would we sacrifice? When we have that much intensity for any one thing, it is often followed by the heartbreak of mental burnout, knowing we have lost the love for that part of us. In the same way that having a favorite food for breakfast, lunch, and dinner every day eventually makes it so we can't stand it anymore, we would likely feel the same about running, and move on to something new—anything to challenge ourselves in a new way.

> Being a sustainable runner means building a healthy relationship with our sport for life.

Being a sustainable runner means building a healthy relationship with our sport for life. Part of the excitement is knowing that we have this one body that is not indestructible. We each hit a limit for what our individual body can handle given the constraints of time and balance. For most runners, it's not about hitting pure physical limits; it is about approaching the limit created at the intersection of physical potential and recovery. We can manage some of those limitations, while others are relatively fixed and create an unavoidable gap to our pure physical limits. Our journey as a runner involves finding our limit and getting as close to it as we can.

Recognize Breakdowns

Sometimes the worst happens. We trip on an uneven sidewalk and require a visit to the emergency room. We feel burning on the ball of our foot at the start of a long run and end up with a blister and an overused muscle by the end. Those injuries truly suck and, unfortunately, they're a reality. But, for everything else, we must consider our role in their development. Setbacks, like injury, sickness, or overtraining, are in no way enjoyable, yet they serve an important purpose. "Someday, you will be glad this happened" is the last thing a runner wants to hear when working through a breakdown, but we need to hear it and accept it. Injury, sickness, and overtraining are indicators that we are overdrawing on our physical bank account, and it is time to put energy into recovery and rest. We find out how much running means to us—how much we care. They give us an extra level of motivation on race day, and these breakdowns remind us to live with gratitude for what our body has achieved in the past.

Breakdowns are a reminder that we have to love and respect our body every time we go out for a run. Despite our inner critic's best efforts to convince us otherwise, the world is not conspiring against us, wanting us to be miserable or fail. When our body breaks down, it is providing us with clear feedback that we are missing something important that can be easily addressed. Our body is trying to tell us we have a weakness to work on . . . even if our greatest weakness is ignoring our body! When the world places the same lesson in front of us time and time again, it means we are not getting the hint. Until we realize that working harder isn't the answer, and that we must pay attention to why we need to change, that lesson will keep showing up. Rather than being mad at our body for not being perfect, we could reframe our thinking to view it as an unexpected lesson that could help us be more resilient runners. While the timing may not feel ideal in the moment, things will work out. New goals will appear, and the experience can rekindle appreciation for what a gift it is to run at all. By picking up this book, we are reinforcing what we want for ourselves; these moments are a big part of the change we wish to make.

> Despite our inner critic's best efforts to convince us otherwise, the world is not conspiring against us, wanting us to be miserable or fail. When our body breaks down, it is providing us with clear feedback that we are missing something important that can be easily addressed.

When we ignore the red flags that warn us we are pushing our body beyond its limits, we end up in one of five situations: overtrained, injured, perpetually sick, burned out, or in a slump. While it is possible to experience more than one of these at the same time, because of our genetics, running form, and livelihood, we commonly experience the same breakdown over and over, especially if we haven't learned from previous experiences.

Small injuries that disrupt our training for a few weeks are a warning sign that we are coming up against a limit. If we have previously ended up in an overtrained state, there is a good chance it will happen again if we use the same approach. Or if we come down with a cold every time our toddler gets sick and it takes weeks to return to normal even when we have been diligent about our nutrition, it shows that our immune system is struggling (as Tina knows all too well!).

Let's dig into the five types of breakdowns to see what causes them, and then go further to find out what we really want to know: What can we do to stop it from happening in the future?

Overtraining

Overtraining is an imbalance between training and recovery, exercise and exercise capacity, stress and stress tolerance (Lehmann et al. 1993). Increasing training volume to an unsustainable level is often what causes overtraining in runners. If a state of overtraining is reached, accumulation of exercise and nonexercise fatigue, stagnation, reduction in maximum performance capacity, mood state disturbances, muscle soreness, and long-term competitive incompetence can be expected (Lehmann et al. 1993).

What this looks like is exhaustion. When we push our body too far, day after day, we become overtrained. Suddenly, every run becomes energy sapping, no matter how easy the pace. Workouts become near impossible. Every run gets slower no matter how hard we try. We are unable to get anywhere close to the distance, time, or pace we were able to run just a few weeks ago.

This is different than having a bad day or a bad week. Those are inevitable. Overtraining means bad days every day, every week, with no letup. Sometimes while training, we might have four bad days in a row, followed by one really good workout, and then another three runs in which we struggle. In that case, it's probably not overtraining. Overtraining means our body is incapable of having any version of a good run. It is totally depleted.

A 2015 article in *American College of Sports Medicine's Health & Fitness Journal* described two limiting performance states as overreaching and overtraining (Brad 2015). An athlete who struggles with their exercise routine and may feel stale or drained is overreaching, which also features persistently heavy muscles that are stiff and sore. While soreness is expected 24 to 48 hours after a hard workout, if it lingers for more than 72 hours, or we wake up sore after an easy run, it suggests we are struggling to recover between workouts. When a runner has been overreaching, workouts are no longer enjoyable or productive and running is a struggle. However, a few weeks of easy running or rest and plenty of nourishing food is usually enough to bounce back. Overtraining, on the other hand, is a severe case of overreaching that requires a much longer recovery period of rest or very light activity. In addition to extreme fatigue and soreness, there are other lesser-known side effects that can affect life quality. Sleep disturbances, decreased mental concentration and restlessness, increased irritability, and mild to severe depression are all signs of overtraining. Once overtraining sets in, the fastest way to recover is the one thing runners don't want to do: Rest. Total rest, or running very easy for multiple weeks, along with lots of nourishing foods, sends a signal to the body that it is safe. It can take six weeks or longer to feel normal again. Our bodies have to regain trust that we are out of danger.

Overtraining is a diagnosis no runner wants to receive, but one review found that many of the negative symptoms of overtraining or overreaching may, in fact, be caused by underrecovery through not consuming enough calories for the energy expenditure, also known as relative energy deficiency in sport, or REDs (Stellingwerff et al. 2021). In this review, 86 percent of the studies showed either an energy availability discrepancy between the individual's needed and actual consumption, or a decrease in their carbohydrate availability during the time they were thought to be overtrained. The symptoms of REDs and overtraining syndrome are similar and could lead to misdiagnosis of overtraining syndrome, requiring rest, when in fact the runner could have continued training had they increased their caloric intake and carbohydrate consumption. Later in the chapter we'll look closer at REDs and learn why it is so detrimental to runners, and then discover how one simple change can get us back on track within a few weeks.

The most important lesson when we are in recovery from overtraining, or are experiencing any of the breakdowns, is to learn from errors and make prevention the key to avoiding it in the future. This means truly running easy on recovery day. No, not the random pace we have deemed acceptable for recovery on that day, but covering up the watch, or at least turning off the pace-per-mile beeps so our body can tell us what easy feels like. On days we are especially tired, that might mean running one to two minutes slower per mile than our recovery pace on a more rested day. We also want to make a habit of fueling well throughout the week, especially after workouts and longer runs, incorporating adequate protein and carbohydrates, particularly if we are plant-based. We must make sure we have enough time between peak races and our next training cycle, and finally, taking time away to rest and heal after a race or hard training block can make the difference between experiencing a breakdown or not.

Injuries

It's normal for minor aches and pains to pop up when we're training hard. Stiff muscles in the morning, the odd case of shin splints, or an achy arch of the foot are almost rites of passage as a runner. If we are getting enough sleep and fuel, those small injuries will pass quickly, and we will get back to training full strength.

When pain increases in intensity during a run, or hurts for the rest of the day after a run (including the next day), we recommend taking an immediate three days off running before reassessing. It is better to take a few days off to recover than to add thousands more running steps for the sake of not wanting to miss a day. That is a surefire way to turn a little niggle into a major injury. During that time, try to do light activities like mobility work, self-massage, and gentle movement to determine what type of professional to visit if the rest days do not do the trick. We all know the struggle. We don't want to miss a day; we want to get back to running as soon as possible, but we also need to respect our body enough to let it heal.

Need a little motivation to take that step? We can journal about our feelings. All of them. The fear of missing race day. The anxiety of losing fitness. The paranoia about body changes. The race flashing before our eyes. By working through the emotions in a journal or private document and keeping it handy for the future, we can read it on a future race day if need be. Our raw, emotion-filled words will be a reminder that we made the right choice by stepping back even though it was hard and will provide extra strength when the going gets tough. We will know that the reason we are racing right now instead of sitting on the couch in regret is because of that choice.

If journaling holds no appeal, an alternative is recording a video talking about how bad it feels and keeping it for the future. Yes, it can be uncomfortable (we all feel awkward on camera), but remember this is just for one's self; we can keep it in a hidden folder on the phone it was recorded on. Or we can talk through our feelings with a running friend. They will know the situation all too well and will be happy to support us, likely reminding us of the same words we would say to them if they were injured and panicking.

If we notice small injuries occurring often, it's an indicator that something is going on. Our body is informing us that it is close to its absolute limit and that we are not addressing the cause of these issues. It is letting us know that our body is about make a drastic change to protect itself. It is about to shut down, and not just for a few days, but for weeks or months. A big injury is imminent if we do not back off. As runners, we try to write off our injuries as a fluke, but if they keep happening, it is time to accept the hard truth that we are making errors.

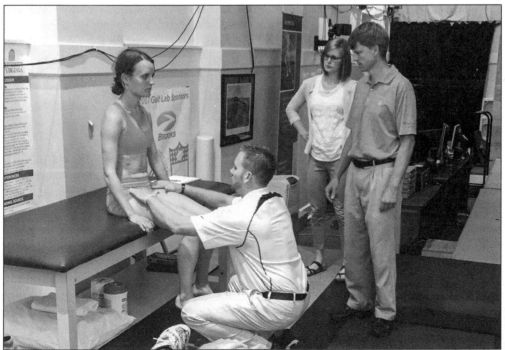

Tina getting a body mechanics assessment with Dr. Todd Nieder at the UVA Speed Clinic. When regular breakdowns are occurring, it is time to step back and consider all the factors that could be contributing.

Dr. Margo Mountjoy, MD, PhD, lead author for the 2018 International Olympic Committee (IOC) consensus statement on relative energy deficiency in sport (REDs), highlights the importance of looking beyond the symptoms to figure out what is happening in our body as a whole. "There are many reasons an athlete becomes injured or unwell. Sometimes it is due to training errors; sometimes it is related to under-recovery or under-fueling," she says. "The important thing to evaluate with a medical professional is the *reason* for your injury or illness, not just the identification and treatment of the problem. In this way, you can help to prevent it from recurring in the future."

In hard training, we want to push the edge. That is how we reach our potential. However, if multiple injuries arise within a short period, a conversation with a knowledgeable medical provider is needed to determine the source of the breakdown in body mechanics. This is also a good time to consider working with a coach. Having a coach is not just for elite athletes, marathoners, or ultra trail runners. The primary reason that runners need a coach is to be objective about how much is too much when we undoubtedly try to push beyond what our body can handle. When we look at our own training, we always think we could do more. A good coach will be able to determine the minimum effort needed to reach our goals, while also considering the impact of general life stress on our training.

> The primary reason that runners need a coach is to be objective about how much is too much when we undoubtedly try to push beyond what our body can handle.

With or without a coach, we need to be real with ourselves. We have to be honest about whether we are pushing too hard for where life is right now. Backing off to make a tough run an easy one, or cutting a long run short, is not going to make as big a difference to our fitness as we might think. If it means we get to the start line healthy and remain injury-free, it is well worth it. It is always better to go into a race slightly less fit than not at all.

Sickness

Getting sick is a part of the human experience. We all get colds in the winter. We all require rest days for the occasional flu, and sometimes we just feel off. This is not to say that anytime we get sick it indicates we need a life change. Sickness happens, no matter how well we take care of ourselves, but frequent bouts of not feeling well indicate that we are overdoing it in our training and in life.

While stress-induced cortisol in the short term can be beneficial, long-term exposure to cortisol leads to chronic inflammation (Hannibal and Bishop 2014). It also decreases the body's lymphocytes, the white blood cells that fight infection in our body. The fewer lymphocytes we have, the weaker our immune system is and the more we are at risk for viruses.

While stress has a bad reputation, our human response to stress was actually developed as a survival mechanism to prepare us to fight, flee, or freeze. However, our brains have not yet evolved to understand that sending the wrong text to a friend or trying to speak Spanish in *la panadería* in Seville is not, in fact, a risk to our life. Our brain can't tell the difference. Stress is stress to our body and mind.

When we get busy, we cut corners in the self-care department. We are not talking about massages or relaxing in a hammock (although those are always good ideas when stressed!) but rather the simple necessities. We stay up late to finish a work project and get up early to prepare kids' lunches. We forget to eat for a few hours after a run while we're completing errands, or we grab our fifth packaged bar of the day instead of sitting down for a meal, leading to a serious lack of nutrients (and hunger!). And we rarely drink enough water, leading to dehydration and frequent headaches.

Daily gastrointestinal (GI) distress may be a symptom of chronic inflammation. On race morning, runners go to the bathroom a lot. Our body recognizes that something big is happening. It is emptying our body of waste, so it is prepped for fight or flight (it interprets our nervousness and excitement as danger) and trying to prepare to be our best. But if daily life is causing stress, our body will act like it is race morning every morning. Of course, we need to empty our bowels daily, but when we find ourselves in a panic on every run (changing our route to make sure we have plenty of bathroom stop options), stress is affecting our body's ability to digest. Even if we are eating plenty of nourishing food, our body is not able to absorb and utilize it when food is quickly pushed through our digestive tracts due to stress. If we are in a constant state of stress, we do not utilize critical nutrients that we need to function, even though we are consuming them.

For runners who have kids at home, colds and sickness are going to be a part of life. But cold after cold, when others in the family are not getting sick, indicates an overrun and struggling immune system. One study found that poor sleep efficiency and shorter sleep time (something we sacrifice in busy times) resulted in a substantial increase in the risk of developing a cold (Cohen et al. 2009). Sleep efficiency is defined as the ratio of total sleep time to time in bed, and less than seven hours in bed per night was considered short sleep time. While sleep may be hard to come by when we have a lot on our plate or are in the stage of parenting in which young children need assistance at night, it is possible to catch up on sleep by other means. Letting go of guilt and feelings of laziness associated with daytime napping is one way. Even 20-minute naps can be what our body needs to handle the rest of the day. Longer naps can be even more beneficial during this time. It is also important to consider the duration of colds as a sign of a body struggling to cope. Most colds should last under a week, but if they last for weeks on end, it indicates that our body is not able to fight back or return to health.

Burnout

Burnout has become a bit of a buzzword since the pandemic, with many folks weary of video conferences, the unending and boundaryless hours of working from home, and the doldrums of training with few races in between. While this word is bandied about a lot in the press, it's not something that affects only office and health care workers. Athletes can also suffer the consequences of sustained, inappropriate training loads and stress.

Even if we never reach the point of physical injury, the body has hard limits on what it can do. Without incorporating harder and easier periods of running through periodization, and getting enough recovery and downtime in micro- and macrocycles (such as rest days in a week and down weeks in a year), cumulative fatigue builds up. And it's not just physical. Stress is stress; emotionally trying times in life can increase the chances of burnout in running too.

While runners are typically poor at recognizing how much is too much, there are clues to indicate that we are overdoing it and must relieve some of our stressors. When we have no time to socialize or unwind because we have too much to do, we are barreling toward burnout.

Burnout is defined as "exhaustion of physical or emotional strength or motivation usually as a result of prolonged stress or frustration" (Merriam-Webster n.d.). It is difficult to motivate ourselves to do anything once we reach this point, so we want to avoid it. We can go through short periods of jumping from one task to the next, falling into bed exhausted to wake up the next morning to do it all over again. However, if we find we go to bed exhausted but lie awake for hours because our mind is still on overdrive, we are putting our physical and mental health at risk.

> Just as we want to become sustainable runners for life, we also want to be sustainable human beings for life—people who have a zest for life and can fill others' cups, because they make sure to fill their own first.

Just as we want to become sustainable runners for life, we also want to be sustainable human beings for life—people who have a zest for life and can fill others' cups, because they make sure to fill their own first. Running is a great way to prevent burnout from the buildup of stressors in our daily lives, but it can only do so much. We have to take care of ourselves in other ways too.

Being busy is rewarded in society today; many feel it demonstrates the importance or value of our work. It's tempting to use busyness as a proxy for worth in a culture that values productivity, output, and performance above all. But once we become so busy that taking a little time to read or watch a favorite sitcom becomes hard to squeeze in, we are well on our way to burnout. Once we start skipping social events with friends or family because we cannot find the time or energy to go, the time is coming. We need connection to others. We need periods in which we are not working or processing—time spent doing what we love to do, filling up our cup with joy.

Burnout should not be confused with overtraining or overreaching, as we discussed earlier in this chapter. With burnout, an athlete's training load might be appropriate, but the recovery or stress management side of the equation might be out of whack. Poor nutrition, lack of sleep, or life stress, such as family responsibilities and work requirements, all add to the likelihood of burnout. Sometimes runners note that it is not the physical feeling of exhaustion that is holding them back but the emotional and mental lack of desire to push themselves at all. Not all stressors are necessarily bad, but their toll needs to be acknowledged and factored in.

While life circumstances are most commonly the major contributors to burnout, that doesn't mean running can't play a role in getting there. A lack of autonomy in training can be associated with burnout. Feelings of autonomy and efficacy are crucial in maintaining motivation and commitment to training long term. Maybe we feel like we're not getting the return on investment that we used to in training. Maybe life stress has kept us from building the same race schedule that usually motivates us, or family responsibilities are creeping into the time that we usually save for running. Feeling like we have no control over our lives can lead to burnout and takes a big toll on mental energy.

Common burnout symptoms are mental exhaustion (it can also present as physical exhaustion), decreased performance, lower motivation, and, at its worst, some folks may want to quit running altogether. Some runners might feel mentally and emotionally stable but struggle with overwhelming physical fatigue from poor nutritional habits and critically low levels of sleep. Others might be physically fine while their hearts and minds are a million miles away from training. In our experience, athletes are more reluctant to take time off for their minds than for their bodies, though mental burnout is just as real as physical burnout. Continuing to push through compulsively will only prolong the burnout.

When we have an ambitious goal on the schedule, it's tempting to focus on weekly mileage and vert goals or workouts and strength training volume, but the most important thing to focus on is an *input* that makes that volume sustainable long term. When choosing goals, and designing training on our own or with a coach, the most important thing to consider is available resources like time and mental and emotional energy. The best training plan in the world won't do a lot if it's incompatible with our current input levels.

If running makes you feel like you're missing out on the opportunity for social connections, try to rearrange training to include more social time. Join a running club. Invite a regular group of friends to the park for a morning meetup. Find an accountability buddy or join a virtual challenge.

When holes open in our lives—a relationship ends or a schedule changes—it may be tempting to cram ever-increasing amounts of training into the void. The wrong reason to increase our training volume is because we have more time, or because we want to drown out the thoughts that are going around and around in our mind. If we're not able to increase the rest of our inputs and double down on self-care, increased training volume will soon outpace our ability to care for ourselves. When we continue to strain the demand on our body and mind without replenishing resources, we can set ourselves on a path toward destruction. We have been there, and it's not fun. We may feel tempted to tell ourselves that it won't happen, we will be fine, but the reality is, we are not the exception (no matter how much we want to believe that). It is just not worth it.

The best prevention methods are also the simplest: minimizing inputs and focusing on good sleep, nutrition, and other things that fill our bucket, like a mindfulness or gratitude practice, time with friends and family, or whatever returns us to training fully rested and ready to go. Chris McClung, CEO and head coach of Rogue Running, encourages runners to also check in with their *why*, "revisiting your reasons for running and making sure your training and goal setting is in line with that purpose, along with making sure you have plenty of space for variety and novelty to keep things fresh."

The "Burned Out" Checklist

If your training exhibits any of these signs, it might be a good idea to take a step back and make adjustments to your training and goals. Though your noggin may be tempted to persevere, resist the temptation to white-knuckle through. Stepping back rather than gutting it out is the best way to ensure healthy, sustainable, long-term progress and growth.

Poor Recovery

If you can't recover from intervals during a workout that has previously been a breeze, you might want to cool your jets. Add in more easy days or bonus rest days to the training plan. Likewise, if you aren't able to recover between runs, and are tired before you even tie your shoes, try the 10-minute rule discussed in chapter 3.

Lack of Motivation

If you're typically highly motivated to run and complete workouts, but lately just haven't been feeling it—your body is trying to tell you something important. Listen to it; it could be you're headed toward burnout.

Weird Appetite

An irregular appetite (beyond normal increases associated with training volume) can indicate that your hormones are being affected by cortisol, a stress hormone. If you find yourself frequently overeating, even on light training days, or skipping meals because your stomach feels off, your training likely needs an adjustment.

Abnormal Fatigue

It's normal to feel a bit tired after a long run or workout. What you want to avoid is feeling abnormally tired, to the point that it interferes with daily life. If you're regularly having trouble focusing at work, or normal activities like walking the dog or getting groceries feels overwhelming, it's time to take a break.

It can be tempting, but don't ignore the signs of burnout. Burnout doesn't mean we did something wrong, that we're stupid for messing up, or we're weak. We're human beings trying to do a lot, which means treading a fine line between doing enough and doing way, way too much. By paying attention to and acknowledging what our body and brain are telling us, we'll train stronger and longer than we ever thought possible. We can be a sustainable runner, even if our history makes that hard to believe. Everyone needs reminders when we are doing too much. We have all been there. Yes, we have made mistakes in the past, but they don't have to define our future.

Zoë's Thoughts

Many folks may struggle to recognize that they're on a collision course with burnout before it's too late. People just like me. In 2018, I had just wrapped up a graduate degree in environmental journalism and moved out to Aspen, Colorado, to start my dream job at a public radio station in the Rocky Mountains at 8,000 feet. I was elated. I was also completely exhausted.

As the radio station's morning host, I started work at 4:30 every morning. Anxious to prove myself, I went to bed each night with my stomach tied in knots. My worst fear was sleeping through my alarm and arriving late to the station with thousands of listeners tuned in. So, I barely slept.

Though I had only moved up a couple thousand feet in altitude, I was winded going up and down the stairs. I lived a couple of blocks from the grocery store, but the thought of walking there and lugging food back home and up the stairs to my apartment overwhelmed me. I had to psych myself up just to get off the couch and check the mail.

I had previously completed several ultras and had been training regularly but could now hardly complete a four-mile jog around town without walking. Instead of stepping back, reducing intensity, or taking a rest day, I doubled down. My flawed logic was that I must be out of shape. Surely if I just *worked harder* I would be able to shake this!

Nope nope nope.

The harder I ran, the worse I felt. Because my runs were so low quality, I felt guilty for taking even a day off (the mother of all exercise red flags). I dug a deeper and deeper fatigue hole, unwilling to do the single thing that my body was begging for: Rest. I was trying to cash checks that my body did not have the funds to back up.

It became a struggle to do the 20-minute walk to work. And when I finally got to work, I had trouble focusing, the fatigue was so heavy. *I must not be cut out for this job*, I thought. *I guess I wasn't as smart as I thought I was.* I did the same thing in training. Reluctant to back off, I doubled down. Again. I tried to get to work even earlier, to take shorter lunch breaks, to force my fried brain to focus. When I felt the quality of my work slipping, I tried to produce more, work longer hours, and come in on weekends.

Spoiler alert: None of that worked. I was good and burnt out.

Finally, a stomach bug and ankle injury forced me to take time off work and running. If we don't make time and space to step away, our body forces our hand. I learned this the hard way, and it was a long road to recovery and health. Looking back, I can see that every time I put my head down and worked harder, I pushed myself further into a hole. But it can be hard to realize when you are in that moment, especially when we are runners who are acutely aware of our fitness levels, and burnout symptoms can feel strangely similar to a return to running after taking time off.

Slumps

While some folks are familiar with the full-body "meh" that is burnout, a slump is different. With burnout, solid rest and an emphasis on recovery should be sufficient to turn things around. But what if we rest and still don't feel as springy as we'd like? We might be in a slump. How can we really tell if we're burned out or just in a slump?

Since there are myriad benefits to rest and no benefit to charging our way through burnout (despite what we might tell ourselves), it's best to respond first with rest. Take a week to sleep extra, eat extra, take easy walks outside, and disconnect from social media and devices that monitor activity. If we still feel awful after a week, it could be worth dipping our toe gently back in the waters of movement.

Sometimes slumps can be related to our mental health or inner state. Depression can make us feel unreasonably tired and make it tempting to stay on the couch or in bed all day. While it's not a panacea, movement is one of the best ways to work through the fatigue that accompanies depression (along with adequate support from a mental health professional—but a walk or jog won't hurt either). However, if the fatigue doesn't seem to have a physiological underpinning such as work stress or lack of sleep, then the best way to reverse it might be to get active rather than acquiescing and watching more *Succession.*

Sometimes, for reasons unrelated to mental or physical health, the prospect of running might not sound that enticing. And that's okay! Training is not always going to be a carousel of pleasure. Slumps can occur when we feel a mismatch between effort and outcome. Our previous effort may not be yielding the same results, and maintaining that effort might become increasingly taxing and less fun. While we can't always control our level of exertion, because time and energy are limited resources, we can control our focus on outcomes.

To get out of a slump, we need to shift our training focus away from outcomes.

After taking a few days off, the stoked feeling should return. If it doesn't, we need to keep resting or find other activities that do get us excited. Tina once took three months off running before the desire to hit the roads returned. We could consider an activity we have always wanted to do but never did because we had to save ourselves for running. When the enthusiasm to run does return, especially if it has involved an extended period away, we shouldn't dive right back into rigid or intense training but instead should take off the watch, log off Strava (or at least dive into the community side of it), and jog it out. It's important to take stock of anything that gives unhelpful feedback, like apps, social media, data, or a watch. Often, overreliance on numbers and outcomes can diminish the fun in running, something we desperately need more of in times of slump or burnout.

If we are overemphasizing results at a certain distance and feel the pressure mounting race after race, doing something new and exciting can shift the focus away from getting a PR and more toward simply enjoying the experience. If trying to beat a previous marathon time starts to feel more like a burden than a joyful journey, signing up for a trail race might be just the ticket. The challenge of new terrain takes the pressure off getting a PR and can still spur long-term growth and progress.

Zoë's Thoughts

When I was in graduate school, a busy schedule of work, class, and freelancing gigs dominated my calendar. Without races on the schedule, it was hard to feel motivated to put in the miles when there was so much else to do. So I made up my own event: The Boulder Taco-thon. Why didn't it catch on worldwide? I don't understand either.

The event would take me to every taqueria in Boulder on a route just over 26 miles. The goal was motivating because it struck a sweet spot between just serious enough to be appealing and just silly enough to avoid negative pressure.

So, what's your Taco-thon? Can you connect all the sub shops in your hometown? Create a silly scavenger hunt with friends or on your own? What's interesting enough to get you out the door but goofy enough to feel lighthearted? It might feel silly to run to every donut shop in town, but if you think about it, how much crazier is it than running exactly 26.2 arbitrary miles? You might as well get a tasty pastry out of the deal.

If the pressure of racing at all feels like an onerous goal, then it's time to get even sillier!

Slumps are often caused by too much attention on one factor or doing the same thing over and over. The best way to break out of a slump is to find a new focus for our attention. It doesn't have to be a big idea or a grand objective, just something. According to Chris McClung, "Slumps can also happen when training isn't polarized enough. Your easy runs aren't easy enough and your hard workouts don't have enough variety. Or, you are stuck training for the same distance over and over again without variety. Marathoners need to train for 5Ks and half marathons occasionally versus going through the same marathon cycle over and over."

Take Time Off

Runners love to run; we know that. But more than that, we hate to take time off. It is hard to ignore the little voice of insecurity telling us we are losing the hard work we have spent months putting in. While we logically know that is not true, it is not always easy to follow through and step back.

We can benefit immensely from and thoroughly enjoy easy running for a few weeks or months. While we may lose some of our sharpness, it is surprising how much fitness we retain. It is an opportunity to simply maintain, especially during crazy periods of life in which our mental energy is diverted elsewhere. Once hard workouts are sprinkled back in, speed will return after a few rust-busting (and potentially humbling) efforts. It often comes back surprisingly quick, and we will feel rejuvenated and ready to challenge ourselves again. During this rebuilding time, it will feel like we are starting over, but training is not about one season or one particular moment of fitness. What builds our fitness are months and years of training, which compound even if we take time off. A few weeks or months of easy running is still building fitness, potentially making us more efficient, and therefore, more sustainable runners in general.

Taking a break after big races and experiencing regular downtime is imperative to our sustainability as runners. Even if we have been injured and don't feel like we deserve to take time off, it is critical to rest and rejuvenate, and it's important for runners to proactively plan recovery phases. It is more beneficial to our bodies to train seven days per week for a month straight, followed by three to four days totally off, than to take off individual days and never allow a block of time for recuperation. Our bodies need downtime sprinkled throughout the year to be able to give our best when it is most important.

If we don't take time off when we are healthy, we will be forced to take time off via one of the major breakdowns mentioned earlier in the chapter. It is important, especially as highly motivated runners, to take days off before we need them. We want our brains to feel mentally ready to return. We want to be craving runs and be excited to get started again, because if we do not occasionally have time to miss it, burnout and losing our love for the sport are the alternative down the road.

We need to take time off even if a goal race did not go to plan and we feel like we didn't give our all, even if we had to drop out at mile 75 of a 100-mile ultra, and even if we ran easy every day for the last six months. Taking time off is as much a mental break as it is a physical one. While our brains may eagerly search for a reason to resume running too soon, our muscles and bones are still repairing from the physical carnage of an ultra, a marathon, a season of 5Ks, or just months of running. It is not about a race itself, but the months of training. Just as the old saying goes, absence makes the heart grow fonder; we want to give ourselves time to miss running— time to understand how much it means to us.

While the amount of time off depends wildly on the intensity, distance, terrain, and our individual traits as human beings, we recommend taking at least one day off for every 10 miles raced

Courtesy of T.J. David.

Zoë enjoying a run in Marble, Colorado. Regular bouts of downtime combined with finding ways to feel joy in your run leads to a lifelong connection to running.

for trail running and a minimum of five to seven days off for a road racing season. This is very individual, so there is going to be a different answer for each of us. We need to be honest as to when we are ready to get back to running or whether something else is internally driving us to come back too soon.

When it comes to alternative activities during time off, it is okay to go out for a hike or an easy 45-minute swim in the morning, but it is important to ask ourselves why. Are we doing it because we enjoy that activity and don't usually get to do it? Because we are better humans when we are outside in nature each day? Or is it because of calorie control or an obsession with training? (If you felt your stomach drop as you read that last statement, you are not alone; we have both been there too.) It doesn't mean it has to always be the case. Cross-training, or other forms of exercise during time off from running, should be primarily for health or enjoyment reasons. If it is for anything else, it is likely a psychological attachment that should be addressed with a mental health professional. It took Tina years to untangle this relationship, but it can be done, and it feels empowering to get that freedom back.

We need to be honest about why we struggle to take time off. If we fear weight gain or are unable to sit still and rest, this is a good opportunity to seek out a therapist who can help us work through this mentally and emotionally.

If we find breakdowns happening time after time, we need to redefine how we measure ourselves as runners. Without doing so, we will never make the changes necessary to avoid them. According to Chris McClung, "Most of us measure ourselves on the wrong things" (how fast we can run a long run, for example, instead of how easy we can run our recovery runs). So we push in all the wrong ways, leading to the issues discussed in this chapter. Instead, we should measure ourselves by the following factors that make running sustainable.

- Long-term consistency and the ability to deliver consecutive months of work, not perfectly, but by putting in 90 to 95 percent of the prescribed work and adjusting the body as needed.
- Our ability to recover by making easy runs easy enough, as well as getting proper sleep and nutrition to feed the work.
- How we feel doing the work.
- Race results over time—no single race result should be the end all and be all, but we should rather consider the trend and overall trajectory of our results over 12 to 18 months.
- The quality of what we learn in each cycle. We win or we learn, so we can always declare victory if we learn after a tough workout or race.
- Are we enjoying the journey? This is only worth it if we enjoy the process and the work, surrounded by people who inspire us.

The world is not out to get us, even though it can feel like we are being thrown one curveball after the next and that all the bad luck comes at the worst time. These things often happen because we ignored the warning signs and a more insistent message was needed for us to listen. This is a reminder to be honest with ourselves. If our body tells us something is wrong, we need to listen. Right away. Or it will find a more aggressive way to get our attention, and none of us want that.

ACTION STEPS

- If you are frequently injured, overtrained, or sick, it is time to remove stressors and take time to rest and recover. If more sleep is not an option, how can you limit additional calories spent on other activities?

- Recovery runs should be completed at a pace comfortable enough to talk to others. Do not select a specific pace beforehand, but run what feels right at the time, even if it means slowing down and running solo.

- Get in the habit of getting blood work done a few times a year. Blood work is a much more accurate indicator of how your body is doing than weight or BMI. Keep an eye on iron, Vitamin D, cortisol, DHEAS for women and testosterone for men.

- Work with a training coach if your body breaks down frequently. Or, at a minimum, talk through your training plan with another runner to hear their perspective. (We often feel we are not doing enough, but an outsider can see when we are doing too much.) Remember, coaches are not just for elite runners; every runner can benefit.

- Create a silly goal. What is your Taco-thon?

- Forgive yourself for being human. Sometimes you will overdo it and your body will break down. That is part of life and part of your journey. It is okay to be mad, but then forgive yourself and move on.

6 | Explore Your Surroundings

Running offers a multitude of benefits to our physical and mental health, and yet, some of us don't spend much time considering how our day-to-day runs could enrich our lives. The days that easily blur in the passing of time could become the best part of our training. Our easy or recovery runs could transform from training into childlike play with a simple shift in perspective. In this chapter we will talk about boredom in running and how to break out of it, even if we run the same loop every day for years on end. But first, let's address the tiresome conversation we all have had when someone discovers we are a runner. The "running is boring" conversation.

It usually goes something like this. We are getting to know a nonrunner, or someone who is not yet a runner, when running comes up in the conversation, to which they respond, *But don't you get bored? What do you think about out there?* Here we go again. As they wait for our response, they stare, head tilted, with a look of genuine confusion on their face. *How can running be anything but boring? How do you do it? Why do you do it?* For them, running brings back memories of miserable PE classes and discomfort. *No, thank you.*

As proud runners, we promptly launch into defense mode, as if someone has insulted us personally. How could anyone say that our sport is boring? Even though, yes, sometimes we do get bored. But we can't let them know that; we have to defend our sport. We give our best description of what running brings to our lives, then change the subject. To each their own. We enjoy it, and that is all that matters.

The reality is, running can definitely be boring at times. We all know it. There are days when the sidewalk stretches ahead of us, like a tortuous, never-ending slog. Even runners with a profound understanding of the sport, who are able to enrich their runs through a deep appreciation of the earth, get bored occasionally. Even the runners who recognize that

Even runners with a profound understanding of the sport, who are able to enrich their runs through a deep appreciation of the earth, get bored occasionally.

each and every run is a gift may occasionally find a run tough or, yes, monotonous. We have run 17 laps around a supermarket parking lot on an out-of-town work trip or run on the same cleared path for weeks on end during bitterly cold, snow-filled stretches of winter. And, of course, treadmill runs also leave much to be desired.

Most of us, at one time or another, have found ourselves in a rut where running could easily be considered boring. Sometimes we look for a different avenue of exercise and try something new, but most of the time, we continue to run day after day, almost out of compulsion. If we are honest with ourselves about why, it could be to maintain weight or health, to have something to talk about with friends, or simply because we don't know what life looks like without running. At times, we lose zest and enthusiasm, yet we are as consistent and committed as ever, finding a way to get out there, even if we're emotionally and mentally checked out. It can show up as zoning out during runs, constantly keeping our eyes on the ground, and rarely looking up to appreciate what is around us. It might mean we spend our runs thinking about everything except running. In some ways, this is a necessary phase as a runner, and we have to work through it to rediscover our love for the sport. It doesn't have to last, though. Even when options are limited, we can still find excitement, joy, and appreciation. Each run can be something special, if we look deeper to discover what that means. By reigniting our love for the sport, we stay on a path toward becoming sustainable runners who can find joy on even the most routine and mundane runs.

The problem is, most runners have to train around life. Running is second, third, or even further down our priority list, and that means squeezing it in between other things. While elite athletes may be able to travel to a beautiful new park, cool trail, or exciting location to keep things fresh, the majority of runners may only have that luxury on occasion. For many of us, that means home is the primary start and end point of our runs. Whether we are 20- or 100-mile-a-week runners, options get pretty limited. It is easy to feel bored before we even begin. We have seen everything hundreds of times before, and therefore there is nothing new to see or explore. It can feel like we have done every loop in every direction possible to be excited at all.

It doesn't have to be this way. It is possible to get out of the mundane, even if every run looks the same from the outside. As runners who have decades of running between us, we have had plenty of practice with repetition of miles, loops, and training plans. Let's dive into some of the ways to change up our runs when things get stale.

Vary Workouts

An important element of becoming a sustainable runner is keeping our training stimulating enough to remain physically and mentally engaged. That does not mean continuing to push the pace in workouts, looking for constant improvements

Tina's Thoughts

During the writing of this book, my husband, Steve, was deep into his cross-country season as a Division II collegiate coach and was working more hours than he had in many years. With Steve leaving at 5:45 a.m. most days, having two young kids and a business to run, most of my runs, regardless of the distance, started and ended from our doorstep. I began to rely on podcasts and music to get me through my runs, but I wasn't even enjoying them anymore; I was just using them to pass the time. It reminded me of overnight flights home to England in my 20s in which I would watch movies for the sake of passing time. I would barely pay attention to the storyline, but I'd know that when it was finished, I was two hours closer to being home. I was doing the same thing with my runs. By the time I made it through *The Greatest Showman* soundtrack, I would only have 10 minutes left. Or once I listened to an episode of Brené Brown's podcast, my run would be over. Box checked. I was seeing my run as a means to an end and was losing appreciation for my favorite listening experiences. I love *The Greatest Showman*, and I wasn't even enjoying it!

While recording an episode of my *Running for Real* podcast with a friend and fellow runner, Mishka Shubaly, I had the opportunity to face reality and make a change. Mishka asked me why I listened to music and podcasts every day. I couldn't give him a good answer. He challenged me further (oh, how I love friends who are not afraid to do this!), reminding me of what running without distraction could be giving me instead. I suddenly realized music and podcasts were actually sucking the fun out of my run. Of course they were. Listening to them removed all connection to my body and surroundings. I thought about how I usually use music and podcasts to motivate me: during chores like washing the dishes or cleaning. When did running fall into that category? I was robbing myself of the gift of running by never being in the moment. I removed my headphones. For a few months, I enjoyed my runs again, or at least appreciated them. But soon, I was back into the "have to run" mindset, my runs were passing slowly, and I was counting the minutes until it was over. I knew something had to change.

This became the major impetus for the body scan and senses check-in that I use in Together Runs. During the pandemic of 2020, I decided to take a microphone with me on a run once a week to feel more connected to my community. Together Runs provide an opportunity to experience running alongside a friend without actually being next to them in person.

Runners could join me for a run, even if we were thousands of miles apart. Together Runs breathed life into my runs and reminded me to reconnect my body with my surroundings. Even though at the time, each Together Run involved running the same few quiet roads near my home, I felt connected and engaged. I was able to take in new details and experiences, and see each run as unique and special. It made me realize there were better ways to change up my runs than tuning out. I needed connection, not disconnection.

at the same distance year after year. It means changing things up. Occasionally we need to do the workouts, distances, and paces we feel are our greatest weakness. Yep, the workouts we dread the most. Variation in training can reduce the risks of injury and overtraining, which we discussed in the previous chapter.

We might believe that improvement comes by deepening our commitment to a discipline. Often, what we really need is to step back, decrease distance, time, or miles, and change things up. In chapter 7, we discuss how stress + rest = adaptation, and if we know we are getting adequate rest but adaptation is not happening, we need to adjust the stress on our bodies. Modifying stress does not necessarily mean adding more stress but involving a different type than what we have been including over the past few weeks, months, or years. Some of us respond better to higher volume or intensity, and others do not. We need to avoid thinking that more is always better; sometimes different is what we need.

Ways to Change Up Workouts

Hills are a great way to let go of expectations and do something that cannot really be compared to other workouts. It does not matter how fit, fast, or strong we are, hills will always humble us. Here are some hill workouts to try after a proper warm-up:

- Run a long, continuous uphill tempo pace of one to five miles.
- Run a one- to five-mile loop with rolling hills as fast as possible.
- Run hill ladders of varying times or distances over a one- to five-mile loop, running hard on the uphills and very easy on the downhills.
- Run speed hills of 100 to 300 meters, running as hard as possible on the up, with a walk down.
- Run descending hill ladders, such as eight-minute, six-minute, four-minute, or two-minute hills with as much rest as needed.

Shorter or faster workouts after extended periods of long workouts can be a great way to challenge ourselves (and it can feel good to complete our run in less time!). While they may be a shock to the system and feel uncomfortable when our legs physically can't move any faster, the improvements will come fast, and it is very rewarding to see progress. Here are some speed workouts to try:

- 10×1 minute hard with 1-minute recovery
- 6×2 minutes hard with 1-minute recovery
- 1 minute, 2 minutes, 3, minutes, 4 minutes, 5 minutes, 4 minutes, 3 minutes, 2 minutes, 1 minute with 30- to 60-second recovery
- 1.5 mile hard, 1 mile hard, 4×800m with 90-second recovery
- 8×400m on the track with 2-minute recovery

When we run from home or squeeze in runs around a busy schedule, it is easy to default to road running for the majority of training. Getting on trails, dirt, or grass can provide major benefits by strengthening different muscles and allowing our body to try something new. Many road runners (Tina included, for many

Courtesy of T.J. David.

Zoë enjoying a run in Zion National Park. She regularly runs on trails to prep for upcoming races, change up terrain, and take in the scenery.

years) have such a fear of rolling their ankles that they avoid trails at all costs. Yes, there is always some risk, but by running on uneven terrain regularly, especially on easy days, we strengthen our ankles and condition our body to handle more on and off the road. This has the added benefit of making us much more resilient as runners, reducing our risk of injuries. Soft terrains are more forgiving to our muscles, helping us recover from tough road workouts.

Change It Up

We suggested fun as a way to get out of a slump in chapter 5, but for those who squeeze runs in the early morning, a short lunch hour, or while kids are at soccer practice, the reality is that sometimes a run just has to get done. When our choices are limited, there are still ways to keep training light and fresh. Here are some ways to do just that.

Reconnect With Nature

In the Tina's Thoughts sidebar from earlier, she explains how doing a body scan and checking in with her senses invigorated runs that had become monotonous and disconnected. This experience is shared with podcast listeners through Tina's *Running for Real* episodes called Together Runs. Listeners begin each Together Run by connecting to nature through physical touch and then completing a body scan. By connecting with nature, and then to our body, we are awakened to the experience of running itself. Rather than thinking about other things that we have to do or how long we have left to run, we get in the practice of being in the moment—something we want and intend to do more of but struggle to put into practice. We find it hard to set aside 10 minutes a day to meditate or to appreciate the frantic nature of life with kids. Running naturally lends itself to being present in the moment once we put technology aside, making it the ideal place to practice grounding ourselves.

Taking Yourself Through a Body Scan

Picture a body scan as a wave of light slowly covering your body, beginning at the top of your head and working its way down to your toes. If it is safe to do so, close your eyes; if you are running, simply soften your gaze instead. Check in with as many body parts as possible, paying attention to how each individual part feels. Relax any tightness you feel in any areas, especially the eyes, mouth, and shoulders, where we tend to hold tension. If you do feel tight, pause for a moment to relax that area; feel that body part melt down as you relax it.

The entire scan should take at least a minute, if not a few minutes. If you are running, it is helpful to do another scan at the end to see how your body feels in the final few minutes of a run. Once you finish the scan, take a moment to reflect: How does your body feel as a whole? Can you feel your feet connected to the ground? Remind yourself that even if you stand on layers of concrete or man-made material, the earth is underneath it all; we can still ground ourselves in this moment.

After the body scan, the next step is a senses check-in. The five primary senses can be used to experience the run through our surroundings. Even if we have completed a running loop thousands of times, this encourages us to find something new and different. By paying attention to the sensations of the run, we may notice a sound that our brains usually filter out as unimportant or a smell that reminds us of a meaningful memory. When it comes to our overstimulated sense, vision, picking out a small detail can bring something novel and beautiful to the run.

Jay Shetty spoke of this concept in his book *Think Like a Monk*, in which he describes walking the same 30-minute loop every day for hundreds of days. "Every day the monk asked us to keep our eyes open for something different, something we'd never before seen on this walk that we had taken yesterday, and the day before, and the day before that. Spotting something new every day on our familiar walk was a reminder to keep our focus on that walk, to see the freshness in each 'routine,' to be aware." Jay used this practice to bring color to his walks, and runners can do the same by simply paying attention in a new and unfamiliar way in our overstimulated, overscheduled lives.

Jay goes on to say, "Truly noticing what's around us keeps our brains from shifting to autopilot." He then shares wisdom that can be easily applied if we run the same routes day after day: "Monks understand that routine frees your mind, but the biggest threat to freedom is monotony." When we run the same paths each day, if we are not consciously finding ways to stimulate our minds and hearts, we are apt to lose the freedom, the simple joy that comes from connecting our body and mind through running.

> When we run the same paths each day, if we are not consciously finding ways to stimulate our minds and hearts, we are apt to lose the freedom, the simple joy that comes from connecting our body and mind through running.

This is a practice that can be done anytime, anywhere, or multiple times throughout the run. The body scan and senses check-in can be done together or separately and can remind us of the gift of being able to run. These practices also help us to acknowledge areas of our body that are not feeling so great and can prompt us to do something about consistent pain before it becomes an injury.

Find New Perspectives

When we repeat the same loop regularly, it is easy to head toward monotony. We end up on autopilot, spending our runs thinking about our to-do lists, and what we will do upon our return.

Another simple shake-up is to reverse the direction of the loop you are completing. Runners are creatures of habit who tend to run a route the same way each time. Running it in reverse may feel awkward, but you will get a different perspective and notice new things along the way. Try turning down the street you often cross over, wondering where it leads (yes, even if there is a big hill that you have never felt like tackling). Commit to it one day and see where it goes.

A different take on this challenge could be to select five houses, buildings, trees, parks, or other monuments that you will take a mental photograph of during a run. Stop to read the worn sign that has stood in front of a statue for longer than you have been alive. Or slow down as you run past a tree that stands higher than the rest, recognizing its years of steady growth and how the world has changed in its lifetime. If you live in an area with dense housing, select five homes on each run and acknowledge the little touches residents have made to make them their own, or send love and empathy toward a home that needs some care. What might the people inside be needing during this time?

Pay attention to the small things in each route. Revel in the minute changes that shift with the seasons or in a simple change of scenery. After thousands of runs covering the same path, truly observing something can bring richness to our runs. Maybe it will even provide the opportunity to connect with others who also appreciate the beauty. One day when Tina was admiring a tree near her home, the person living there came outside, and they sparked a friendship centered around their appreciation of nature.

Set a Challenge

One popular method of keeping things interesting when our start and end point is always the same is to run every street in the area. In 2018, trail runner Rickey Gates set out to run every single street in San Francisco in an epic feat of endurance and urban discovery. After 1,300 miles and 46 days, Gates had covered every single street in the city, documenting what he saw and the people he met along the way. In an interview with *Runner's World*, Gates said, "It provides its own mountaintop to get to and come back down, and it's right there." Part of what made Gates' adventure so incredible was how he documented it, taking careful notes of the extraordinary—and ordinary—things he saw along the way. Paying close attention to the mundane allowed Gates to see the extraordinary in the everyday around him.

We often find ourselves running down the same streets, skipping dead-end roads or big hills we are too tired to tackle. By setting a challenge to cover every street in the area, we can discover new joys in our old running routes while we learn which roads connect to one another. After the run, we can jot down notes of what we have noticed. Honoring our attention by recording these observations will sharpen our ability to see more and cultivate a curiosity that squashes boredom. This is especially enjoyable during holiday seasons or times of celebration when houses may be decorated or themed. We might spend an evening run in December seeing how many Hanukkah candelabrums are glowing in the windows of houses or observe colored powder filling the streets from a Holi celebration in the spring. Changing up our runs in this way allows us to become an expert tour guide for visiting guests, and we can smoothly navigate our way around a traffic jam because we know the back roads.

Courtesy of T.J. David.

Zoë finding a way to keep the fun in her runs through her love of sugary foods.

We might challenge ourselves to learn the names of all the trees in the area throughout a season and then spend time observing or even counting how many of these trees we see on an average run. We can learn which ones are native to the area and which are invasive, potentially harming the local ecosystems. The same can be done for plants and flowers: What does native wildlife look like in our part of the world? Then when we travel, our eyes will be prepped to notice the environment in new places.

You can also tailor these challenges to your own personal interests and hobbies. If you are a dog lover, count the number of dogs you see, or pay attention to dog breeds you see the most. Look for houses that have a certain feature you like, and count how many are along your route. Or count Little Free Libraries on your route so you know where you can drop off books the next time you need space on your bookshelf. There are endless ways to count and find new sensory information on a run. Each challenge encourages us to look up, look around, and take in our surroundings, rather than mechanically operate on autopilot. The coming sections will provide further ways to develop this practice.

Create Random Shake-Ups

Ever notice that a run passes by more quickly when it is broken up into sections? We aren't talking about anything structured or intense, especially if we follow a training plan that is delicately balanced with ample recovery and intensity. Instead, we are referring to ways to break up the run—for example, running fast up a hill that we usually dread or adding in a few midrun strides to knock the rust off tired legs. It can mean picking up the pace to the next lamppost, followed by slowing down until the next one, or adding 20- to 30-second surges every five minutes.

Avoid sprinting, but aim for buttery smooth strides in a bonus speed-endurance stimulus for better running economy and a break for your brain. Play "red light, green light" on a street with lots of stops. Alternate by running at a tempo effort to one stoplight, then run at an aerobic effort to the next one.

Another way to have fun with routine runs is to select an object, person, or feature you see on occasion, and do something fun every time you see it. When a Ford Mustang passes, stop running and do some high-knee drills, or every time that you see a postal delivery person, thank them for the work they do. A green car could signal that it's time for a body scan or senses check-in, and falling leaves might mean you have to catch one before you continue your run.

Looking for loose change is another popular way to give some energy to regular loops. While you want to make sure you are looking up and around, you can create a runner's piggy bank that becomes a monthly challenge. How much change can you find? It is not unheard of to find bills or notes, which could be a way of fulfilling the dream of being a paid runner!

Finally, if training for a race is not currently on the agenda, try a "segment slay," as Zoë calls it. Are you able to run your fastest time on a Strava segment, or even go for a top spot? Run a regular route at an easy pace, except for the Strava segment of choice. Run that part as hard as possible and see just how fast you can do it. Tina did this upon returning to her college town last year, and she enjoyed chasing down segment records along courses she had run hundreds of times before Strava existed.

There are endless ways to sprinkle in fun bursts of effort without them becoming something that beats up our legs or affects our training.

Treadmill Tips

Want to slow down time? Just step on a treadmill for an easy run. Workouts on the treadmill might feel quicker to some athletes because they are typically broken down into smaller, discrete segments. End points and intermissions make the time go faster, and workouts often feel very purposeful and connected to our larger training goals. Easy treadmill runs, not so much. How can you make easy miles on the treadmill feel bearable?

Try starting an easy treadmill run with a short warm-up hike or uphill walk. Set the treadmill between 5- and 15-percent grade, and jog, hike, or walk slowly uphill. Keeping it easy, change the grade every couple of minutes to mix up movement patterns. Make sure to keep it a low enough grade that it doesn't become a strength workout. This warm-up jump-starts the aerobic system and can lower perceived effort for the rest of a flat, easy run.

Once warmed up, play with the grade ever so slightly. Start at zero for 8 to 10 minutes, then increase the gradient by one percent every two minutes. At six percent grade, start over with another eight-minute chunk at zero. Make sure to keep the effort easy and purely aerobic as the gradient changes.

For a bit of speed (but not too much), add in a dash of spice to a treadmill run. After a warm-up, do 30 seconds of smooth but fast running, alternating the grade between zero and four percent for each five-minute block, if you're feeling good. This is an easy fartlek that lets you get feisty with some speedwork without overdoing it. The 30 seconds give your brain something to latch onto and look forward to without overdoing it on intensity.

For the treadmill-reluctant trail runner, add in some mountain training. Every five minutes, alternate between a completely flat grade and then a five-percent grade. If you are training for a steep race like a mountain ultra, make every other hill a 10-percent (or 15-percent—advanced runners only!) hill. Treadmills offer the opportunity to get aggressive on a sustained hill year-round, no matter where you live. While it may not offer the same scenic vistas, there are ways to make treadmill training fun and effective.

Make Runs Fun

If you have a running friend in your neighborhood who you can never quite meet up with, consider a scavenger hunt as a fun way to share a run without physically doing so. With a little preparation and an agreed-upon day, one runner spends their run dropping hints or clues, and the other spends their run following the trail and bringing the findings back with them. Just be sure that any missed clues are promptly picked up and that you remain considerate of others in the area.

Brittany Charboneau, a 2:33 marathoner, makes sure to bring joy to her runs through weekly themes, even when she is in hard training. "Keep every day novel on your runs by thinking about it as your 'playtime'! Run places where you can collect every color, or make a color your theme; you'll run to different locations with that color's name. If your theme is 'animals,' look up street names ahead of time; you can run them in order to change up your route. You might run to Wolf Avenue or Dinosaur Ridge, and be amazed at all of the new things you see on that run."

In 2022, Brittany took her playtime runs to a new level by winning every race in Disney World's Dopey Challenge, consisting of four consecutive days of racing, each increasing in distance, concluding with a marathon (which she ran in 2:44!). Brittany brought fun to these races by dressing up as a Disney character each day and finding ways to race each event as her themed inspiration that day. She ran the 5K as Elsa from *Frozen* with her intention being to "show yourself that you can do it your way." Another day, she ran a half marathon as Joy from *Inside Out*, with her goal for the day being to "be the joy for everyone."

There are creative and perspective-shifting ways to bring fun to every run; we just have to think outside the box to find them. While we know that running enriches our lives, and we thrive on the postrun endorphin rush even at the busiest of times, we can still find new ways to appreciate our runs. Running keeps our bodies and minds healthy and strong, and they can also add elements of play into our week—something that we need now more than ever.

ACTION STEPS

- If you have lost the ability to be present on your runs, participate in a Together Run with Tina, available on her *Running for Real* podcast feed.
- Sprinkle in body scans and senses check-ins to your runs.
- Run your regular loops backward.
- Turn down that street you have always wondered about.
- Select five things to take a mental picture of during a run. It could be reading a sign you have run by hundreds of times or selecting houses to reexamine.
- Aim to run every street within your neighborhood.
- Find ways to play on regular treadmill runs.
- Add a random shake-up by picking up the pace to the next streetlight or doing a press-up every time you see purple flowers.
- Dress up as a favorite character or person, and race using them as inspiration.
- Create a scavenger hunt for a running friend.
- Chase down a Strava segment record or run your fastest time for that segment within a regular run.

7 | Replenish the Body

Our body lives, breathes, and endures for us; it is our vehicle for life. We accept that it is affected by our physical choices, but it is also affected by the psychological, emotional, and mental situations we experience. In this chapter we dig into utilizing our basic survival elements to not only run to our potential but also live our best sustainable lives. Becoming a sustainable runner means setting ourselves up for a lifetime of running (if we choose to run for life; again, it is okay if we do not want that!). No matter what level we compete at (or don't!), we need to give our body the best opportunity to thrive. That means focusing on sleep, fueling appropriately, and doing what is best for our individual body, regardless of what that looks like for others. This chapter will go into the daily factors that affect us, highlighting some of the dangerous negative behaviors we engage in, often without realizing. The aim is to untangle our emotions from societal pressures we face and provide tools to maintain the best version of ourselves, no matter what life throws at us.

Get Enough Sleep

During stressful periods—work or personal stress, injury or illness, or other challenging scenarios—sleep is often reduced, intentionally or not. Our sleep schedule may become erratic, or our bedtime constantly changes. We may use time we should be sleeping for additional errands or tasks we need to complete.

Mild sleep deprivation can be a risk factor for a body breakdown, but it can also leave us more susceptible to a mental breakdown. We don't think we are losing enough sleep to cause harm, but consistently missing a few hours a night quickly adds up. Interestingly, one study found athletes from individual sports (swimming, triathlon, cycling, racewalking, and mountain biking) went to bed earlier, woke up earlier, and obtained less sleep than athletes from team sports (Lastella et al. 2015). The study concluded that the individual sport athletes got far less than the recommended eight hours of sleep per night. If even elite athletes are not able to get enough sleep, adding in the life demands of many recreational runners, the reality is, most of us are sleeping less than we should.

Research has demonstrated the importance of sleep for athletes and therefore runners. Sleep allows us to repair the microtears in our muscles created through the load of training. These microtears are not bad; they help our muscles become stronger, but the human growth hormone (HGH) released during sleep repairs our muscles and strengthens our bones. When we have a sleep deficit, less HGH is released, and our ability to recover is impaired. Optimal sleep is critical to reaching peak athletic performance and yet another reason not to commit to big goals during stressful times.

It has also been found that early-morning swimming training sessions severely restricted the amount of sleep obtained by elite athletes (Sargent et al. 2014), and with many runners getting up very early to run, we are in the same sleep restriction. Runners who go out in the evening may struggle to fall asleep after their late-night jaunt as endorphins rush around their body. Cutting sleep not only limits running performance but also the ability to perform all other daily tasks.

Despite the evidence and clear correlation, prioritizing sleep can be hard to do. When we have had another busy day and feel like we need just a little time to wind down on the couch, one more episode of *Ted Lasso* sounds much more appealing than a nighttime flossing, brushing, and mouthwash routine. We all do it, and sometimes it is okay to do so. Those moments watching TV, reading, or even, yes, scrolling social media can be a part of our connection to others, and that matters too. Next time you feel that first wave of tiredness in the evening, go push through your nightly routine. Even if you do end up back on the couch, at least you are ready the next time tiredness hits, and maybe a little closer to actually going to bed.

On the note of sleep, one other important topic to address is insomnia. As Tina struggled with insomnia most of her adult life (ironically, until she had kids), reading about "utilizing sleep" or that sleeping less than eight hours a night would never allow someone to reach their potential was incredibly harmful. It made the insomnia worse and added a lot of stress through worrying about the lack of sleep. What is important to note, though, is that in most cases, sleep is actually not the problem. We will address some of the challenges that can lead to insomnia (and led to Tina's) in coming chapters. But for those working through insomnia right now, we see you, and it is miserable. Let go of what we shared above, and be patient for the advice to come.

> If we want to progress in our running, then we need to remember that stress + rest = adaptation.

If we want to progress in our running, then we need to remember that stress + rest = adaptation. If rest is adequate but we are under too much stress, we will not improve. The same outcome will occur if we reduce stress but get insufficient rest. We will not reach the adaptation and, therefore, our running potential.

Understand the Symptoms of REDs

We cannot talk about how the body recovers without bringing relative energy deficiency in sport (REDs) into the conversation. REDs is a multitude of symptoms that result from not getting enough fuel and is directly related to caloric intake that is significantly less than caloric expenditure. Runners rarely end up injured, sick, or overtrained from "overfueling." While habitual overeating is not ideal, it is preferable to underfueling. Underfueling is what can cut a runner's training short, so fueling that aligns with our bodies makes it better equipped to handle the strain of training.

While the most widely known REDs symptom is a disrupted or missing menstrual cycle, REDs can affect anyone. Decreased testosterone is a major indicator for male-identifying runners, and there are many more symptoms that can be debilitating if left unaddressed. A woman can maintain a regular period but experience many of the other factors and be diagnosed with REDs.

One major symptom of REDs is often celebrated as an achievement of fitness, but it can be a signal our body is in a depleted state: bradycardia. Jennifer L. Gaudiani, founder and medical director of the Gaudiani Clinic, explains how bradycardia can affect our long-term health:

> *Many athletes think proudly that their resting heart rate below 60 beats per minute, a condition called* bradycardia, *is a sign of fitness. It's true that a well-trained, well-rested, well-hydrated, and well-nourished athlete is likely to have a slow resting heart rate because the heart muscle is so efficient and strong that it can do its work pumping blood with fewer beats per minute. In fact, this athlete's heart rate will barely budge when they get up and walk across the room and back, because mere walking doesn't put much stress on skeletal and cardiac muscle.*
>
> *By contrast, if an athlete is undernourished or underweight (for their own body type, regardless of BMI), bradycardia may be present for a very different, and much less healthy, reason.*
>
> *Malnutrition (deliberate, as in the service of an eating disorder, or accidental, as can happen with REDs) causes the brain to change how the body manages fuel, slowing the metabolism so that fewer calories are burned in the context of inadequate intake. One of the ways the body spares calories is through a slowed resting heart rate, accomplished through elevated vagal tone (much like that of a hibernating bear).*
>
> *So how can an athlete tell if their resting bradycardia comes from a vigorous, strong heart or from a starving heart? Besides a realistic review of rest, fueling, and hydration practices, the answer is by walking across the room and back. The person who is underfueled will have muscles that are depleted, even if they are not pushing themselves athletically. This often causes the heart rate to increase by 75 percent or more from resting to slowly walking. While this measurement is not validated, years of expertise have shown that this indicator plus a thoughtful history of recent self-care can help highlight for athlete and provider that all is not well.*

Leaving it to the experts, Renee McGregor, a sports dietitian with a specialty in REDs and eating disorders, explains how digestive issues and recurrent injuries are two of the most common symptoms of REDs, but are often ignored or written off as something else. According to McGregor, "Individuals who are in low-energy availability frequently experience gastroparesis and dysbiosis, which often present as IBS-like symptoms but are associated with a lack of energy in the system to digest food efficiently. The problem is that if an individual suspects IBS then they often look to exclude further food groups, which just adds to the energy deficit. Another early warning sign is soft tissue, ligament, and tendon issues. Although we often associate REDs with bone stress, it can start to manifest much earlier."

When we have a lot going on, it is easy to forget to prepare or purchase the nourishing foods our body needs. I can wait a little longer, we tell ourselves, when in fact, we can't.

While these symptoms are easy to write off as a part of life as a runner, they drastically affect quality of life, and we need to accept what they are trying to tell us. Both Zoë and Tina have experienced REDs, and both denied its contribution to their performance decline and stagnation. It was only once they accepted that a caloric deficit was what was causing the issues that they were able to begin the recovery process.

The REDs symptoms let us know we are doing too much for what we are taking in. When we have a lot going on, it is easy to forget to prepare or purchase the nourishing foods our body needs. *I can wait a little longer*, we tell ourselves, when in fact, we can't. This element of self-care is critical not only to our health but to our self-respect as living beings. When we do not replenish calories burned, our body begins to believe we are living in a dangerous time when there is not enough food available and that we need to be ready to flee. We are not thriving; we are surviving.

Tina Muir

Tina at the London Marathon, and, yes, that is Prince Harry turned away in the background! While Tina ran fast in her road running career, she often wonders how much faster she could have run if she had been fueling correctly.

Say No to Diet Culture

In addition to working to reject the societal norm that tells us we need to be hustling all the time, there is

Tina's Thoughts

Nine years of missing my period was the most obvious way my body tried to tell me I was not eating enough, but there were many other warning signs I ignored. I always felt cold, and my fingers would turn white anytime I got even slightly chilled. I told myself I had Raynaud's disease, but in reality, my body was protecting my central organs and directed blood to areas that needed it most: the brain, heart, and lungs. And then there was my sugar addiction.

From the moment I got up to the moment I went to bed, I could not go more than two hours without sugar. I told myself I just had a sweet tooth—that it was a genetic trait. Not untrue; my grandma was notorious for having a scone, clotted cream, and jam for her lunch with a dessert after. Once again, I wrote this off, but I should have known something was up when I was unable to think of anything else if I did not have sweets or chocolate every few hours, or when I *had* to have dessert every night, without fail. I scoffed at anyone who would tell me their sweet treat at night was four squares of dark chocolate. That was my prebreakfast sweet. Dessert had to be a massive bowl of ice cream, or multiple big chocolate chip cookies. Sometimes, when others would serve me dessert at a gathering, I would look at the measly (note: normal-sized) portion, devour it, and spend the next 20 minutes hoping they would offer more. If they didn't, I would think about it for hours. Even if I had to walk a mile in negative temperatures to a gas station; even if I had to wake up early for my race the following morning, I needed my dessert before I could go to bed. Instead of taking that to be a neon warning sign from my body, I wrote it off.

The worst symptom, though, was anxiety, especially at night when I was trying to sleep. As soon as I lay my head down to rest after an exhausting day of training, work, and life, my brain jumped into action. I would roll around in bed, agitated and frustrated. Once I did fall asleep, I was restless until 4 a.m., when it felt like someone flicked a switch in my brain. I was wide awake and starving. I would toss for 30 minutes before eventually launching myself out of bed, too angry to lie there anymore. Five hours of sleep for over 90 miles per week was not enough. Worse still, everyone in my life had to suffer the consequences of my mood swings. I tried to convince myself I was "one of those people" who could get away with less sleep. (For the record, Matthew Walker, professor of neuroscience at UC Berkeley and author of *Why We Sleep*, has concluded that very few people are "that person" who can get away with less sleep.)

Now I think back to those symptoms and wonder how much faster I would have run, and how much happier I would have been, had I just given my body what it was begging for: more fuel.

---

another giant battle going on in our minds: the impact of diet culture and the beauty industry.

A 2021 report cited that the global weight loss and weight management diet market was valued at $192.2 billion in 2019 and is projected to reach $295.3 billion by 2027 (Allied Market Research 2021). Fortune Business Insights, a global market research report company, shared a report in 2021 that projects the global cosmetics market will grow from $287.94 billion in 2021 to $415.29 billion in 2028

(Fortune Business Insights 2021). The weight loss and cosmetics industries invest a lot of money into telling us we are not good enough and that we can't thrive as we are. It's an industry that tells us perfection exists but we can't get close to it without them. While we may understand intellectually that is not true, we still acutely feel our inadequacy while scrolling through social media feeds. Some of the world's best psychologists, marketers, and research companies convince us that the only way we will feel better about ourselves is by buying what they're selling. It doesn't matter that an estimated 95 percent of diets fail or that one-third to two-thirds of dieters regain more weight than they lost (Mann et al. 2007); the messaging hits us where we are most insecure.

As runners, we are surrounded by people whose bodies are defined and lean. We celebrate professional athletes and follow their careers as if they were our own family. Magazines, brands, and media primarily show thin bodies rather than the broad spectrum of runners that exists in our community and bombard us with images and messaging that tell us we are not where we need to be. We are left feeling it is our own fault if we don't look that way. We don't have the willpower, desire, or strength to make the right choices to do so. What social media doesn't show is the time and financial resources, as well as the baseline genetics, that are behind every social media six-pack.

When we fall for it and end up restricting our food, at some point, we "cave in" and binge the foods we have been avoiding. We become those people who "failed" their diet or can't control themselves, and believe the lie that we cannot follow through or stick with anything. Most diets fail because they rely on an extreme level of restriction that is not healthy or sustainable in the long term. But rather than blaming the diet, we blame ourselves. And those feelings of shame, coupled with unhealthy restriction, can cause more weight gain than was originally lost and catapult us toward the next diet. We did not "fail" our diet; it failed us, intentionally, because then we continue to spend money trying to reach the unattainable or unrealistic goal weight.

Nutritional labels have also become a confusing mess—a victim of a tug-of-war between weakened regulators and empowered industry. Some sectors (like diet and nutrition supplements) aren't regulated at all and aren't subject to regulations around labeling and advertising.

There is a wealth of confusing and, at times, conflicting advice. High-fat or low-carb? Intermittent fasting versus same-day energy deficits? Keto, plant-based, all-natural, and paleo dogma tell us that it's not just personal preference but a moral failing if our diets are insufficiently pure or don't live up to some arbitrary standard. And then the food and supplement industry is good at hiding what we don't want to see. The Food and Drug Administration states that "conventional food and dietary supplement manufacturers *should* declare small amounts of nutrients and dietary ingredients on nutrition labels," but then goes on to say, "The use of the word 'should' in FDA guidance means that something is suggested or recommended, but not required" (2016).

We're becoming wiser to the ways that industry leverages our insecurities against us, and we're tuning in to how renewed focus on food and nutrition can be a source of empowerment rather than insufficiency. Shopping at our local farmers markets for fresh, wholesome ingredients is one way to do just that. Testing our skills in the kitchen to incorporate unfamiliar fruits and vegetables from our local community supported agriculture (CSA) share can be fun. We can stimulate our community economy by choosing to support a local bakery rather than purchasing packaged cookies. And fruits and vegetables that have traveled a dozen miles taste better than store-bought apples that have traveled thousands of miles. When we inevitably head to the grocery store, we know we have local bakery cookies, fresh seasonal produce, and fun new vegetables to explore with when we get home, and all we need are a few basics.

Intuitive eating can seem incredibly intimidating, and it can be difficult to disregard the fear that once we let go and allow ourselves to eat what we want, there is no going back. We may genuinely believe that we will be unable to stop eating or consuming those foods we crave, and it may feel like we have lost our ability to know what hunger feels like. Articles from the early 2000s that gave us "tips" for how to eat less are still subconsciously imprinted on our brains today. We need to question the assumption that hunger is boredom and that we should go out and take a walk before eating or should down a glass of water before dinner so we don't eat as much.

As runners, we are used to ignoring unhelpful comments from those who do not "get" our sport, when they repeatedly remind us that we will have bad knees for life. Yet, while they may not understand, it is important to pay attention to loved ones who do not normally comment but show concern. That is an important time to listen.

Our bodies know what to do, but many of us stop listening. Intuitive eating requires a leap of faith to trust that we will recognize hunger cues and that if we let our bodies tell us what and when to eat, we will get better at understanding what we need. If we have spent years ignoring hunger cues or hushing our bodies' cries for food, it will take time to learn those indicators again. Once we accept that there are no bad or off-limits foods, and we allow ourselves to have what we want, we will make good choices because we won't obsess over the food we have always denied ourselves. We will be free. Free to untangle the relationship between our body and our running. Free to untangle our running from our self-esteem. Free to enjoy a lifetime of sustainable running, knowing we are doing it because we love it, not as a punishment for eating too much.

Consuming nourishing, nutrient-dense foods alongside those we daydream about eventually changes our taste buds so we start to crave the wholesome, nutrient abundant options, and we won't always obsess over the "forbidden" ones. Once we allow the foods we love to come into our lives without condition, the temptation won't be as strong. We can do all the right things to build a loving relationship with food, but we need to address our relationship to our bodies first, so let's dive into it.

The journey to loving our bodies can be a difficult one, especially if we hear from a young age that thin is beautiful

> Once we accept that there are no bad or off-limits foods, and we allow ourselves to have what we want, we will make good choices because we won't obsess over the food we have always denied ourselves.

Tina's Thoughts

Toward the end of my elite running career, I represented Great Britain and Northern Ireland in a World Championship. The race happened to be in Wales, which was a nice excuse to see family and friends. I returned home to the United Kingdom intending to stay the five weeks between the championships and the London Marathon. I was the lightest I had ever been, and I knew it. I had weighed myself obsessively for years—always naked, because I wanted to track my "true" weight. While I knew deep down documenting my weight was damaging to my physical and mental health, I wrote it off as something I needed to do to be the best runner I could be. I loved seeing that number drop year after year.

When I arrived home, my dad gave me a hug and winced, saying, "Tina, I can feel the bones in your back." At first I felt excited; I was getting to a place where I was as lean as "everyone else," but then I thought it through later that day. My dad does not interfere in other people's lives. He does not make comments like that and certainly not about the way someone looks. His tone was filled with so much disappointment, so much worry. I felt my chest tighten and tears well up. It was the first time I started to accept that my relationship with my body was not good. While it took another year before I truly began my recovery journey, his comment stuck with me because he wasn't someone who would usually say something like that.

I spent so much unnecessary energy obsessing about the way I looked. Even though it had no real impact on my racing at that point, it began as performance-focused. I wanted to eat well to have steady energy for my workouts and consume a variety of foods to power my training, but it soon morphed into a situation in which the way I looked was more important. I started to eat packaged bars that tasted like birthday cake, spouting how "amazing" they tasted, when I was actually telling my body to hold out a few more hours until the next meal. Why eat something that tastes like birthday cake over the real thing? What stopped me from having some cake midafternoon if that's what I wanted? Why lie to my body and mind time after time? I would feel irritation when my stomach would rumble; how could I possibly be hungry already? It was time for an apple or a few carrots to keep me going until I deemed it acceptable to eat again.

On race day, I would stand on the start line, look at my fellow elite competitors, and genuinely believe I was "the big one," when there was an imperceptible difference between myself and the rest. I would make comments to friends about not being "that skinny," when I was. My self-confidence was destroyed and led to an obsession with trying to lean down all the time. It also took away so much joy from the sport because I struggled to celebrate the accomplishments of my fellow competitors even though I knew how hard they had worked to get there. Now, having grown and delivered two children, I look at my body in a different way, with gratitude and love. I wish I had known back then how powerful self-love and appreciation could be.

and fat is not and that value and respect are awarded to those whose physical bodies look like what we see in the media. The Health at Every Size (HAES) movement has taken the conversation a long way, and minds are changing, but we still have a long way to go.

Randomized controlled clinical trials have indicated that the HAES approach is associated with improvements in physiological measures, health behaviors, and psychosocial outcomes and that the HAES approach was more successful than weight loss treatment in promoting those outcomes (Bacon and Aphramor 2011). According to the Association for Size Diversity and Health, the HAES principles and framework are a "continuously evolving alternative to the weight-centered approach to treating clients and patients of all sizes. The HAES® Principles promote health equity, support ending weight discrimination, and improve access to quality healthcare regardless of size."

Love your body. It sounds so simple, but we know it's not. It should be something we do automatically. Deep down, we know how much our body does for us, yet appreciation for our body is something we just don't often consider. A Dove Global Beauty and Confidence Report from 2010 included feedback from 10,500 women and girls from 13 countries around the world. The research highlighted a universal issue: As girls and women grow older, beauty-related pressure increases while body confidence decreases, which means we are not able to see our true beauty on the inside or outside. Only 20 percent of women and girls in the United Kingdom like the way that they look, and only 4 percent of women around the world consider themselves beautiful. More than three-fifths of women (69%) and girls (65%) globally say that increasing pressure from advertising and media to reach an unrealistic standard of beauty is the key force in driving their appearance anxiety. The study also found that 80 percent of women agree that every woman has something about her that is beautiful, but they do not see their own beauty. This is another example of treating ourselves with less compassion, empathy, and forgiveness than we give to others.

Most of the studies have been focused on women; however, those who identify as male are not exempt either. While female-identifying runners are given one ideal, male runners face opposing and conflicting ideals that can be even more challenging. Men are told by society to look muscular and have a triangle-shaped body, and male runners are informed that lighter and smaller equals faster. In many ways, it is more difficult for people who identify as male because they are suffering alone. Conversations on male body image just do not happen for most. The women's body image movement has gained powerful momentum, but anxiety-provoking conversations around male body image are kept under the surface. One study found a significant correlation between body dissatisfaction and anxiety and depression in men (Barnes et al. 2020). The connection between anxiety and depression and body image is further exemplified in additional underrepresented identities, such as women of color, people with disabilities, and trans athletes. Those pressures to reach an unattainable perfection can feel even greater.

We spend a lot of time thinking about the parts of our body we dislike and very little time appreciating what we value. Being body confident is not about loving every single part of ourselves. The problem is, we hone in on the areas we struggle with most and allow them to affect the way we view ourselves as a whole. We convince ourselves that everyone is staring at our imperfections and sees just how "ugly" we are.

We aren't encouraged when we see celebrities on the red carpet flaunting their six-week postpartum bodies as we look down at our own recovering stomach. Despite what we see, media figures often struggle with their body image even more because they know they are being watched and judged by millions of other people. Taylor Swift, in her Netflix documentary, *Miss Americana*, talked about how the pressure occasionally caused her to skip meals because she felt she was constantly being judged. When we look at a magazine cover of Taylor Swift, we see perfection. All Taylor saw was flaws.

Then there are the physically perfect specimens: athletes. We are astonished at their bodies and what they can accomplish. We also respect bodies that overcome incredible obstacles and show inner strength: friends who fit back into prepregnancy clothes in a few weeks; runner friends who defeated stage-four cancer, using running to deal with the adversity; those in bigger bodies who confidently share themselves with the world. We value everyone's bodies except our own.

Why do we do this to ourselves? Because our body seems so ordinary, flawed, and unlike those bodies we admire, even if we know their bodies have broken down too. We don't see the internal struggles they have, and it can feel like their struggles are in the past while ours are constant. Talking about our bodies in a negative way has become almost a pseudo-bonding experience; while it can make us feel like we're connecting to others, it also perpetuates the negativity we feel toward ourselves. McGregor, the sports dietitian who specializes in REDs and eating disorders, reminds us to keep the following in mind: "Athletes in general tend to be a certain type of personality—motivated, highly critical, focused, obsessive, and often with a perfectionist mindset. While these are traits that help athletes achieve, they also need to be understood and managed well. If this group of personality traits is put into a competitive environment, it is like walking a tightrope. If we push too far, these same traits become dysfunctional. Athletes need to learn how to manage their own expectations but also need to learn to accept feedback so that it is not always seen as criticism. Perfectionism is not about drive; it is just an addiction to a set of beliefs that give you a false sense of security about your worth. Athletes need to learn to embrace failure as this is also the place where most growth occurs."

> Talking about our bodies in a negative way has become a pseudo-bonding experience; while it can make us feel like we're connecting to others, it also perpetuates the negativity we feel toward ourselves.

While we may assume McGregor is referring to elite athletes, the word *athlete* does not apply to only those at the top. Many of us runners, including you, dear reader, possess a number of these traits and need to challenge our perfectionistic mindsets. We need to free people, particularly the women and girls of tomorrow, from these suffocating traits that suck the joy from our lives and running.

Build Body Confidence

Becoming a sustainable runner means learning to love our body from the inside out, respecting and valuing it, just as it is. If we constantly criticize our body, we will continue to suffer consequences from those actions. These activities may help you view your body differently and let go of the belief that the way you look is who you are.

Send an Email to Loved Ones

We are generally very good at showing love and affection to those who matter to us. We are kind and warmhearted toward family and friends, admiring the things they are good at. We know no one is perfect, and they may have things that frustrate us, but we appreciate the good they bring to this world.

Your loved ones feel the same way about you. Maybe they tell you; maybe they have a strange way of showing it, but they think it. This task is going to seem daunting and scary, and it may be tempting to skip ahead and move on to the next. But there is a magic to this activity that may change the way you view your body, mind, and heart. It will help you get one step closer to seeing what others love about you.

For this exercise, download the email template available at becomingasustainable-runner.com/body and send it to three loved ones. The email message will be written from Tina and Zoë and will look as though we are emailing them. It will ask them to respond to Tina and Zoë (but actually you) with what they believe are your three greatest superpowers. The message will remind them that most of us struggle with seeing our strengths, and sometimes we need a friend to remind us. As one of the most treasured people in your life, their opinion is valuable. If you are not comfortable using the template, you can create your own or tweak the template as needed.

Unfollow or Mute Those Who Make Us Feel Bad

If you have a friend who makes you feel bad about yourself, who puts you down, and who talks about how amazing they are but tells you (either literally or figuratively) that you're not good enough, would you remain their friend?

Even those of us who are people pleasers would not keep such a person close, ask their advice, or see them often, because that person makes us feel bad about ourselves. Yet we do it on social media. We stay connected because we don't want the awkwardness of unfollowing or unfriending them. We can, however, mute or hide people who do not serve us. If we want to feel good about ourselves, the people we surround ourselves with matter. And that includes online. Muting or hiding someone is not public information, and it can be a temporary change while we work through something painful.

We need to be honest with ourselves. Is someone else's "success" (or what we perceive to be success) harming us or poking at one of our greatest fears? Are we intentionally choosing not to celebrate them because of envy (we have all been there), and because we have been sold the message that one person "winning" means we lose? Sometimes it means forcing ourselves to support them, even if at first it feels fake. We all know true authenticity when we see it—when we know deep down they are doing good work and doing their part to make the

If we want to feel good about ourselves, the people we surround ourselves with matter. And that includes online.

world a better place, but they provoke feelings of insecurity in us that make us want to resist. The more we push our way through to be supportive, the more we move away from being a casual observer (or, let's face it, lurker). The more we acknowledge the work others are doing, the more we see that we too are doing important work, we too have something to offer, and the success pie isn't a finite number of slices. The more we live that belief, the bigger the pie gets. Good things come our way too.

Regardless of the reason, if we want to be better at self-love, giving love freely to others who see the goodness in this world and detoxing from people who don't help us is key. It may not seem like much, but it can make a big difference.

The same goes for brands. While you are never going to avoid ads, you can tell the algorithm you are not interested in posts that are diet culture–related. There is a block or "I don't like this" button for ads on social media. Let them know that this type of ad is offensive or unappealing. Do this for any ads using triggering words that make you look critically at your own body or life.

This applies to magazine subscriptions too. If you are subscribed to a magazine or online publication that is constantly talking about weight loss and getting a flat belly (or how others did it), either email them to say you are not comfortable with that content or cancel the subscription. If a brand or organization is still promoting weight loss and perfectionism, they are probably not the kind of brand you want to align with or support financially. Your purchasing decisions matter, especially when accompanied by feedback to explain your actions.

Remove Ourselves From Conversations About Someone's Body

This one can be tough and can make some interactions awkward, but it will have an impact on us and may also inspire others to rethink their effect on conversations. When we contribute to or stay in conversations that are based on judgments of other people or judgments of ourselves, we are reinforcing that behavior. We will continue to judge others, knowing those we talk to in this way could also scrutinize us in that way too. We then begin to feel like the world is full of people watching us, waiting for us to screw up. Living a sustainable life means sharing that we are no longer comfortable participating in these conversations. If we ask others to join in a gossip detox and they laugh, it doesn't necessarily indicate failure or that we should abandon the idea. We have planted a seed in their mind; give it time to grow.

If they react negatively, it may be worth reassessing whether that person should continue to be in our life. How can we stop criticizing ourselves if we continue to look for flaws in everyone else? We all know the old saying "When you point one finger, three are pointed back at you." We are most critical of behaviors that poke at our greatest fears.

The more we practice, the more our inner self-talk is kinder. We are all judgmental. Human beings will always look for differences and similarities between ourselves and people we meet. We all have those thoughts, and we don't need to judge ourselves for being judgmental (talk about a confusing no-win battle there!), but we can change how we react to those thoughts. Instead, we can acknowledge the thought, then try to determine that person's motivations or what their side of the story might be for that action. Finding a way to empathize with them might help us understand their behavior or situation (or even better, ask with curiosity about their choice). It will change the way we view the world, and build our self-love muscles.

Thank Our Bodies

On an intellectual level we know that the human body is incredibly intricate, complex, and smarter than we will ever comprehend. But on a day-to-day basis, we forget those attributes and feel frustrated for what it can't do in the moment. Sometimes we need to be reminded of its accomplishments and everything it does for us without being asked.

Writing a letter to your body to thank it for all it has done can be a powerful exercise. Think about all the times it has carried groceries, lifted a child, powered you up a hill—all the things it has accomplished for you beyond general living. You have come so far as a runner or within your fitness journey. Once you wouldn't have been able to believe what your body is now capable of at this moment.

Courtesy of T.J. David.

Zoë casually running along a crest. By trusting her body, she is able to do things fear could easily prevent her from trying.

Start the letter with "Dear body," and then let the feelings flow. Don't think; just write. No one has to read this. The first few lines may be a little clunky, but it doesn't matter; what matters is you are doing what feels right for yourself.

Keep a Gratitude Journal

Take a few minutes each day to write down some things that you feel genuine appreciation for. Maybe it's appreciation for your feet carrying you through a tough run or a little yellow flower growing between slabs of concrete making you smile. It could be for a friend who lifted your spirits and made you laugh or someone who held open the door for you this morning. Once it becomes a regular practice, you will start to appreciate little things everywhere that give life more meaning. Writing down gratitude, even as a simple bullet list each morning or evening, helps you live with more awe, appreciation, and thankfulness for the world and for yourself.

Accept All Parts of Ourselves

This one can be tough to wrap our brain around. We all have things about ourselves that we like less, and that is normal. This is not about loving every single part of ourselves all the time. As humans, we are always going to find flaws. Finding self-acceptance and love is not about forcing it. Instead, if we can see the functionality, and how it serves us, it changes our perspective from judgmental to thankful, and that can be a big shift.

Not a fan of your stomach because of pregnancy stretch marks? Mama, you are a warrior who physically created a child, and those scars are like a tattoo representing that beautiful life. People get tattoos with their kids' names on them; you have your own natural tattoo that should remind you every day of the incredible feat your body accomplished. Your torso also contains your actual stomach and many other organs that help to digest food, clean out waste, and survive! Feel insecure about your nose? That nose alerts you to smoke that could save your life, allows you to smell delicious baked cookies fresh out of the oven, or reminds you of your grandma when you open a keepsake box of her belongings.

We each have our own area of insecurity, likely stemming from a distant childhood memory that is still affecting us. We may not be able to free ourselves from the hold it has on our life, but we can reframe it to limit its power over us.

Engage in Positive Self-Talk

How we talk to ourselves matters. We need to speak to ourselves the way we would to a loved one or a friend. How would we treat them if they made a mistake, or they didn't run as fast as they thought they would? We would tell them it is okay, that they did their best, and that everyone makes mistakes.

We must give ourselves that same compassion. This will not stop negative thoughts coming in; that would be impossible. We can, however, change our response. Rather than letting the thought go round and round in our heads, we can think about what we would tell a loved one in the same situation.

It is easy to say "give compassion" but a lot harder to do in practice. As Tina was asked by a sports psychologist years ago, how we would talk to our 17-year-old daughter can be an easy reframe. If a 17-year-old were talking to herself the way we were, what would our response be? Imagine the insecure, fearful 17-year-old is still in us (because they are!) and sometimes needs a reminder that things are going to be okay—that we are okay. Love and kindness are the best and quickest way out of a spiral of negativity.

Surround Ourselves With Positive People

If we spend time with people who are negative toward others and degrading toward themselves, we reinforce that approach with ourselves, no matter how hard we try to avoid it. When it comes to family, we accept who they are and that they will always be that way. But we can consider our friends; we should get in the habit of reflecting whether they make us feel rejuvenated, filled up, or refreshed after we leave them or if we leave feeling sad, down, or self-conscious.

If it is a longtime friend, it can be painful to recognize that the relationship has come to its natural end point, but that does not erase all the special memories. We can still live with gratitude toward that person for the times spent together while recognizing that a close friendship is coming to an end. We must gradually pull away and remind ourselves that we could always reunite in the future.

We can spend time surrounding ourselves with positive, inspiring people in other ways: listening to audiobooks, enjoying podcasts, or reading books by uplifting authors who make us believe we are unique in a beautiful way or that we can continue to improve. There are plenty of people who make us feel good if we soak up everything we can from them.

Why spend so many pages on how to feel good about our bodies? Because feeling confident in our skin—in who we are—is critical to becoming sustainable runners. Once we detach our self-worth from the way we look and view running as more than a weight loss tool, we can unlock the magic in the sport that takes each experience to the next level. It means we can make smarter decisions about our running based on how our body feels rather than what we think we need to do to maintain or improve our figure. Once we hop off the hamster wheel of striving for the ideal body, we can get back to enjoying our sport. It requires work to reach this point, but the rewards will be reaped throughout the many years of our running journey. This builds a foundation of trust in ourselves and enjoyment in life. Committing to changing the relationship between our body and food changes everything.

When in doubt, always return to the body. We need to stop listening to the noise and connect to what our body is telling us. Treating ourselves with empathy and compassion is the best way to run for life. Running can be the loyal, reliable friend who is there to listen during difficult times or when we are emotionally struggling, but it is not a therapist that can fix

> Treating ourselves with empathy and compassion is the best way to run for life.

everything that is wrong in our lives. Our mental health is part of our total body health, and until we learn to prioritize it, we will never find the peace we are so desperately looking for.

Keep Things in Perspective

One damaging contributor to a lack of self-confidence is comparison to elite athletes. Elite runners have access to professionals and recovery tools that help them handle high training volume and intensity. Comparing our commitment to theirs is only hurting us. They have a chiropractor who can get them in with 30 minutes' notice, and they have the freedom to take naps when sleep was elusive the night before. Elite runners consider the time required to create nourishing meals as part of their training and have a network of support people who are heavily invested in their goals and will do whatever they can to help them perform their best. They may have assistance taking care of family, delegate a lot of life errands, and be giving up a 40-hour workweek to be able to handle 110 miles a week.

Not all elite runners have this privilege. Many inspire us by making time to do it all and still run fast, but we have to be careful not to hold ourselves to that standard or think we are a failure if we are not able to do it all. Even those with less support than most elites will still have more than the average recreational athlete.

What our individual bodies can handle is unique to each runner. We may have a similar finish time as other runners, but we do not arrive at that result in the same way. Comparing is a natural human behavior, and in this world of social media, numbers, stats, and performances are posted for the world to see. Just because we train less or differently than someone else, that doesn't make our training worse or better. The best training for us as distinct human beings is our own individual training. Even if we could handle someone else's volume, it wouldn't necessarily be productive or add to what we already do.

> Comparing is a natural human behavior, and in this world of social media, numbers, stats, and performances are posted for the world to see. Just because we train less or differently than someone else, that doesn't make our training worse or better.

It's one thing to say all that but another thing to trust in it. We can trust a coach while still fearing letting them down or disappointing those who have invested in us. In that way, we can be thankful for not having the elite lifestyle, considering the pressure and stress elites feel knowing how many people they may let down with their performance!

Our bodies are doing the best they can in every moment of the day. They meet the ridiculously high expectations we set for ourselves, but most of the time we still yearn for change while we push harder and harder for goals. We can help our body to do its best by loving it for where it's at and what it can do.

When our life is surrounded by a lot of runners (as training partners, as friends, in our social media feeds), our perspective is skewed. We forget that human beings come in every shape and size, speed, ability, and resilience. While runners are good at pushing through pain, and our bodies can be more physically defined than nonrunners, we also forget that running even a mile is an impressive feat for the average human being. To many people, runners are seen as incredibly strong and tough. The idea of being able to talk while running is something hard to even imagine. We forget that perspective and spend our energy focusing on what a small percentage of the human population is able to do.

Tina's Thoughts

I used to struggle with looking at other elites who were regularly running 100+ miles a week—many of them running closer to 120—yet my highest ever was 99.7. (Yes, you read that correctly, 0.3 short of 100, and yes, it bothers me to this day.) I felt inadequate, behind, fragile. I would look at the workouts elite runners shared on their social media and think that there was no way I was ever going to be able to handle workouts like that. In my head, they continued to improve week after week, month after month, year after year. I would be that runner who everyone thought had already reached their ceiling: time to give it up already. Of course, we think other runners are all improving rapidly, constantly bouncing back after time off and launching back into the next race, whereas for us, we are moving slow, having lots of setbacks, and never getting to our destination fast enough.

I was wasting precious energy thinking that way, and I wish I realized that they were sharing the workouts and paces that made *them* feel confident about their upcoming races. I couldn't see it at the time, but they too struggled with confidence. Just as I didn't want to announce my paces on my bad days, they kept theirs to themselves too.

However, in the moment, we forget that and compare our worst workouts to their best days. Had I been looking at my strengths, I would have been in a more confident place. I would have appreciated that I could finish my long runs at a mind-boggling pace or that I was strong, resilient, and had very few injuries. I would have been a better friend to other runners I considered friends. I would have genuinely celebrated their successes, accomplishments, and confidence-building runs rather than seeing it as a reproach for how "slow" I was. I can't change my past, but I can change the way I view my future. You can too.

Trent Stellingwerff, director of performance solutions and applied sport research at the Canadian Sport Institute, has worked with dozens of Olympians and believes it is important to consider the way we compare ourselves to running heroes who are performing on the largest stage in the world. When we see Olympians or other world-class performers running their best races, they are at their absolute peak. It is easy to fall into the trap of thinking they look like that year-round. When we see them compete, they have controlled everything possible to be in absolute prime shape. Professional athletes have been training their entire lives.

While it is good to be energized and motivated by others, we can also do more than we thought we were capable of if we stop holding our bodies to the standards of others. We want to be the best we can be, not a counterfeit version of someone else. It is inspiring to see someone being fully themselves and loving who they are. We will only be able to run our very best when we do what is best for us, not what's best for everyone else.

We can have all the apps in the world, pore over every stat, and track every element of our lives, but our bodies always know best. We have simply lost our ability to listen. We have filled our lives with so much stimuli that the simple, small differences in the way we feel are almost imperceptible. The advice given in this chapter alerts us to the ways our body tries to warn us, but we have to be ready to accept the message, and that requires slowing down long enough to hear it.

The next time we compare ourselves to someone and get a sinking feeling in our stomach or a tightness in our chest as envy rises up, we must catch ourselves. How is it helping to compare ourselves to that person? If we look up to someone who is at a much higher level (in running or in anything), we can remind ourselves that this is their strength and they are giving their all. Their achievement does not take anything away from our accomplishments and who we are. That said, we recognize it can be difficult to pull ourselves out when we are deep in, and sometimes it can even feel a little good to wallow in self-pity for a bit. Think about that 17-year-old in us: What would we tell her? See if she has the answer we have been looking for.

ACTION STEPS

- If any behaviors from the REDs section of the chapter resonated, especially a missing menstrual cycle, digestive issues, or recurring injuries, or if you suspect (be honest!) you are not consuming enough calories (yes, even if your weight is not where you want it to be), consider working with a registered dietitian for fueling needs.

- If there is a psychological component to eating, and you struggle with disordered eating behaviors, consider working with a mental health professional to break free from those debilitating thoughts.

- Ensure you are getting a minimum of seven to eight hours of sleep every night. Life happens, and a full night of sleep won't always be possible, but you need to prioritize sleep over "one more thing" to do at bedtime.

- Remember that there are a lot of factors at play to make you feel dissatisfied with the way you look (including the billions of dollars spent on ads that play on our insecurities), and it is not your fault. But you can choose intuitive eating, even if it scares you to try.

- No foods are bad foods; the more you restrict foods, the more you crave them. Once you give yourself the freedom to follow your body, the cravings will subside (or will be replaced with cravings for nutrient-dense options instead).

- Avoid pseudo-bonding experiences that consist of talking negatively about your body to others and stop participating in conversations about other people (especially judgments on another's body).

- Unfollow or mute toxic personalities who harm your mental health.

- Be supportive of others doing good work, even if it feels forced at first.

PART II | SUSTAIN YOUR RUNNING COMMUNITY

8 | Find Your Place

We do early-morning workouts in total darkness, squeeze in a lunch-hour run between meetings, zip through the streets in the evening, untangling the day's stress from our bodies and minds. It can feel like we are alone out there. Even if there are other runners around, our paths cross for only a few seconds before we are back in our own world. We have an agenda, a plan for what we want to get done that day. Running can feel individual, or yes, even lonely.

Running becomes a reliable friend who encourages us to keep our bodies and minds healthy. But, even during our busiest phases, we can still be part of the running community. If we cannot make group runs work for our schedule, and the mental energy required to coordinate meeting a friend is more than we can spare, we are still not alone. Community can always be part of our lives, providing small hits of connection in the daily hustle of life.

Enrich Your Running Through Connection

When our training is isolated, like it was for most of us in 2020 during the COVID-19 pandemic, it is difficult to stay engaged. We often forget every other runner is out there with us. While we may not be together physically, we can be emotionally and mentally. We all struggle to push against the discomfort of running hard no matter how experienced or fit we are, and if we look around, thousands of other runners are fighting their way through too. We are out there reaching for the same finish line, but on our own journey to accomplishment and fulfillment. Thinking about other runners can give us comfort and strength. It is one of the reasons we feel empowered and strong at the finish line; the energy and collective effort fires us up for the rest of the day.

In 2020, there were no races to shift our perspective, and that shook many of us. We can get so wrapped up in our own lives that we forget there is a world beyond our own dreams and goals, a world that is welcoming, rewarding, and satisfying, and gives us an opportunity to enhance our running experience with just a little extra investment. It is effort that comes back to us tenfold.

If 2020 taught us anything, it is that we need other humans. We need connection and to communicate with those who understand our experience. Service to others is one of the quickest ways to discover our purpose and meaning in life, which we will talk about in more detail in chapter 9. Building relationships with other runners can help us realize how fortunate we are to be a part of this community.

Giving back to the running community is motivating and gets us out of our own heads. This is especially true when we are not hitting our goals. If we are feeling demoralized that running has broken our heart again, but we can't figure out why it is not coming together, it is time for a change. Achieving goals and setting new personal bests feels good, but sometimes that love fades, and connection is what we crave. That said, getting involved in the community doesn't have to mess up our training or goals; it can enrich our entire running experience by giving us purpose and meaning.

When we hear about the adventures and stories of others, it increases our own running passion and exposes us to new ways of looking at the sport that we thought we knew everything about. There are a few ways to get involved depending on available time, stage of life, and location.

Run With Others

For someone whose experiences of running are a miserable high school PE class, or running through the airport with bags awkwardly bouncing from side to side as they try to catch a flight, the idea that running can be enjoyable seems laughable. The idea of running with others, absolutely mind-boggling.

You can run . . . with others? And you can talk while you run? And *like it?*

How is that even possible?

New runners often wonder this. As their lungs burn and legs shake from effort, it is disheartening to see a group of runners gliding by, laughing and chatting as if they could run forever. *Those "real" runners make the sport look so easy, when it is definitely not.* It is hard for new runners to even imagine being at a point where they could do that.

Except it could be; it should be. Hear us out as we explain why.

Running with others brings a shared accountability and honesty that cannot be put into words or quantitatively studied. It allows us to speak openly and freely in a way we are generally unable to do. As we travel side by side, the intimidation of eye contact removed, we can let our guard down and be vulnerable, building a deep connection. It can help relieve anxiety or energize us for the day ahead. It is astounding how quickly an intimidating run passes by when we complete it with someone else.

Tina's Thoughts

Running as a professional sounds like a dream, and in many ways it was. I loved all the extra perks I was fortunate enough to be given. I loved the special treatment and the opportunity to maximize my potential on every occasion. For many years I thrived, cutting my marathon time by four minutes (which is a lot in the elite world) for four consecutive races. In 2016, fourteen years after initially setting my lifetime running goal of being in a world championship, I was finally close. It motivated me to push just a little harder.

Once I achieved that goal, my motivation began to tumble. I was envious of other runners who ran faster times. I started to look over my shoulder in races to make sure no one was catching me, and I couldn't bring myself to support my closest running friends in their endeavors. Every race became about how good it was going to feel at the finish line. I pushed harder because surely that was the answer. My running joy became inexorably tied to my result at the finish line; I just had to get through training to get to that point. When I began to dream in January of the finish line for a July race, I knew something was wrong. I trudged my way through my runs, despised my training, and started to hear a little voice saying, "I'm done."

I did end up quitting the sport, not sure I would ever train for a race or even run again. Maybe it was time to close that chapter and find a new sport. All I knew was that quitting took a lot more courage than continuing. I was going against everything I knew. Tough people don't quit. Except on this occasion, I learned they do, and it was one of the best decisions I ever made.

Coincidentally, around that time, I was starting my business Running for Real, and while I feared no one would ever want to hear from me, a quitter, I took a deep breath and went for it anyway. I launched the brand and my own podcast a month after I stopped running. It turned out that giving back to the running community gave me new energy, new life. I loved seeing other runners reach their goals; I loved having conversations with runners on my podcast, talking about their running and how it connected to every other area of their life. I loved the idea of running with others without being concerned about them slowing me down. I understood the power of giving back. It felt better than receiving accolades, because it was rewarding and fulfilling every single day, rather than only on the days that everything lined up. It was daily gratitude, rather than being appreciative a few days a year.

I did begin to run again, and with others as often as I could, which was wonderful. Now my running is about much more than finish lines. In fact, the races I enjoy the most are those in service of others. I find ways to give back to and connect with the community every day, and it leaves me inspired, appreciative, and loved for who I am, not what I do.

Experiencing the joy of running with someone can start off as a happy accident: An out-of-town friend and lifelong runner cajoles us into it or a spontaneous cousin suggests lacing up together during a visit. The first few minutes of the run feel strange. *We can hear one another breathing. We are too close. What pace are we going to run at?* Then, suddenly, it clicks, even if only for a few minutes.

We get into a rhythm, our breathing calms, and we become *those* runners, ones who enjoy running side-by-side.

For some, group running is all they have ever known, and was what made running a part of their life. Group running can be a powerful connector. There is something beautiful about running with others, syncing movement with another human being. The effect becomes even more robust with a large group in motion together. It is not only the endorphin rush flooding our body, but the feeling of connection, a shared experience that makes us connect to our animal roots—a pack of runners covering ground as one unit.

It is not only about the mental and emotional side either; there are biological reasons that we thrive on running in groups. We came across this concept reading Brad Stulberg's *The Practice of Groundedness*. Brad discussed Kelly McGonigal's work on the collective joy that our species is hardwired to feel when we move in synchrony with others. We know that running is energizing, but there is also the release of oxytocin, a bonding neurochemical that connects us to our running partners on a euphoric wavelength. There is also the concept of identity fusion, defined as a "visceral sense of 'oneness' with a group and its individual members that motivates personally costly, pro-group behaviors" (Swann and Buhrmester 2015). People who experienced identity fusion within their groups felt strong self-agency, meaning they took action toward what they wanted in life. Runners who experience identity fusion form a family-like bond with group members and feel strength as a unit.

> We know that running is energizing, but there is also the release of oxytocin, a bonding neurochemical that connects us to our running partners on a euphoric wavelength.

For those who have been committed to a solo path, following their own running dreams for many years, it can be hard to surrender some of the control to a group. When we are used to deciding every aspect of our training by ourselves, allowing a group to dictate pace, route, and to a certain extent, duration, can be a big step. In these moments, it is fear of the unknown trying to protect us, but we can be safe trying new experiences as a runner. Just because we are used to running hard when we want and easy when we don't, doesn't mean we won't benefit from another's company or pacing. Letting go is something that many runners struggle with (including both of us), but the more we settle into the group, and go with it, the more we can enjoy the process. This does not mean we do every run with a group or running friend, or even most runs, but finding time for it regularly can be beneficial.

As first discussed in chapter 6, if group running is not possible in your area, try a Together Run. After a few meditative activities to bring runners' bodies and minds into the present moment, Tina begins a conversation that is as close as you can get to running alongside a friend without actually being next to them in person. Together Runs were immediately a big hit when introduced in 2020, and a great way for the community to experience the joy of running with someone else, at a time when it was not physically possible.

We have all seen or experienced the joy of celebrating others' successes as part of a team. There is a special friendship created by caring for others with similar or even identical goals. It takes a level of trust and maturity to want what is best for the group, as well as for the individuals in it, a maturity we may need to work toward before we can truly actualize the feelings. Running regularly as part of a group is one way to work on that personal growth. The bonds made during runs will be strong. It is only through this process that we begin to understand that someone else's success does not diminish our own accomplishments, even if they are better than us. We can celebrate those moments together, and strengthen our sport and other people. As long as we did our best, that is all we can ask for.

Joshua and Aaron Potts, founders of the Running Report YouTube channel and hosts of the *2 Black Runners* podcast, believe in the power of group running to enrich our own running journeys. Aaron reminds us, "The bond formed when you grind through miles together is like nothing else. You'll create lifelong relationships with people you never thought you would have, and you'll push each other through your hardest day. As the saying goes, 'iron sharpens iron.'"

And Joshua recognizes the impact community has had on his running journey: "Some of my best memories have been made in the sport from club, elementary, middle school, high school, college, and outside of competitive running. Also, those are some of my favorite memories with my best and closest friends. There is nothing like a bond created through hard workouts, disappointing races, and the joy that comes with conquering a running goal you never thought you could achieve."

The Power of Running for Social Change

Chris Mosier, an athlete and activist, defines community as "a group of people connected by a common interest, identity, or location." He adds, "While living in a particular area provides an immediate community, it is not as powerful for me as my communities from my interests, like the running community, and my identity, like the LGBTQ+ community. Community affiliation should, in its best iterations, uplift, support, embrace, and advocate for its members. It's a place where we have a common ground or foundational starting point of likeness that can help us bridge our differences."

The running community has the potential to bring each of us something special. You likely would not be reading this book without believing in the power of community and shared passions, both within our sport and outside of it, that bring us together. The running community has come together to evolve into a more inclusive and diverse place to be, literally and metaphorically, supporting those who have traditionally felt unseen, unheard, and unwelcome. While we awkwardly work our way through some long overdue cultural changes, in our own weird and wonderful way, runners are making a difference. Running is one way we can make changes in the community at large; it can be a vehicle for social change. It helps us to be more optimistic, empathic, adaptable humans who are capable of understanding how minds can change and grow, just as our muscles adapt to the small microtears that occur each time we head out for a run. Our bodies get stronger as the training compounds year after year, and so does our compassion and understanding through hearing other runners' perspectives.

While our sport may have only changed the lives of a small percentage of the global population, the potential impact can be especially powerful. We know the rush we get from converting a lukewarm runner into a lifelong committed one, but always wonder how much better the world would be if everyone had a running practice, or at least a getting-outside-into-nature-to-move practice, in their daily routine. While we wish running had the opportunity to change more lives for the better, we understand that it is something others have to want to try. It cannot be forced.

While the COVID-19 pandemic brought a lot of suffering, it offered more people the opportunity to experience the true magic running brings. Runkeeper reported a 252 percent increase in its app registrations, and a 44 percent increase in monthly active users in 2020 compared to 2019. It also reported a 62 percent spike in people around the world heading out for a run. Similarly, MapMyRun noted a 65 percent increase in runs logged in 2020, and Garmin noted 27 percent more new users in 2020 (Smith 2020).

New runners bring in fresh perspectives, challenge us to find new ways to be inclusive, and help us understand the experiences of others. We want to convert new runners into sustainable, lifelong runners. One of the best joys a runner can experience is seeing someone transition from a suffering, default pandemic runner to someone who gets pure joy and life satisfaction from the sport we love.

Improve Individually Through Group Experiences

With that, we have to stop apologizing for our own running story or ability. We have all done it. Running with someone who is faster than us, or when we are feeling tired from a challenging workout the day before, our inner critic begins to pipe up. We fear we are holding people back so we apologize for being "slow." Even the best runners have off days, or days when it's beneficial to slow down. We owe our bodies the respect of listening, and taking it as easy as needed, even if that means our usual running buddies go ahead and leave us to run at a slower pace, one that keeps us running healthy and strong.

In these situations, when we know that we will feel tired or understand we are slower than our running partner, it is good practice to set boundaries. Get in the habit of having a conversation about expectations before a group run begins. We can tell our training partners that we "expect to go about *this* effort level for *this* many miles." Getting expectations out in the open, making sure everyone is on the same page, will make the group feel more comfortable. We are collaborating on a run together, so having a conversation about what we all want out of it is only going to make it better. It also means confronting vulnerabilities we might have about our athletic ability instead of allowing them to fester deep down inside. It's always better to get it out in the open and talk frankly, rather than push it down and explode at a friend when we can't hold it in anymore. In the situation where we are the faster runner, validate our friends' feelings and remind them that we chose to run with them. Make it clear we have committed to running with them regardless of pace, and encourage them to say something if the run feels too fast.

We can get into trouble in group runs if we don't bring up the objectives for the day. When no one discusses pace or effort level prerun, through competitiveness, the emotional nature of the conversation, or just excitement, the pace can wind its way up. Before long, everyone is hammering, and each person in the group feels as though they are the only one struggling, wishing someone would say something. We end up running in silence. No one enjoys the run because we are frustrated by the situation. Be that brave person; say something. Chances are most, if not all, of the runners in the group will thank you. It may also inspire them to speak up next time. They will be able to see that saying something does not hold back the group or sabotage the run, but helps everyone, especially on easy days that are critical for staying healthy. The tension in the group will disperse, and a laugh may even arise out of the awkward situation.

If you find yourself feeling really good in a group run and want to go ahead, share your thoughts with the group and invite others to join you if they like. That way, they have the choice, rather than being unwillingly thrown into a faster run than they intended. Some of the group will likely hang back and run at a pace that feels comfortable to them. Again, dialogue is key.

It is important to ask ourselves what we want to get out of our runs and workouts in that moment and be strategic about running with others. One study found that women who exercised alone reported feeling calmer and more relaxed in comparison to individuals who exercised with a partner (Ginis et al. 2006). If we are looking for some quiet time on a busy day, or an easy run to recover from a tough workout the day before, it might be better to skip the running partners and head out for a solo run. Alternatively, if we want to rev up some motivation or have had a tough day and need to talk to someone who knows the situation, running with others could be just what we need. Another study noted that if we want an intense, hard-hitting workout, pairing up with someone who is fitter (or faster) can level up our workout (Plante et al. 2010). It all comes down to listening to that intuitive feeling of what is best for our body at that moment.

We view those who run faster than us through rose-colored glasses, but every one of us has insecurities we face, struggles to work through, and unplanned days we need to take it easy. It is not something to be ashamed of, but something to be celebrated; we are all humans with limits. If someone chooses to run with us, it's exactly that: They choose to run with us.

Women are especially guilty of putting ourselves down. We simply don't need to do it; society does it for us each and every day. Those of us who identify as women are socially conditioned to apologize for totally normal things. It is like we try to beat the world to the punch by preemptively degrading ourselves. Doing so is not helping anyone; it is encouraging other women (and young girls who look up to us) to do the same. It is wasted energy, energy that could be spent performing our best or enjoying the experience. Break that habit, and call others out for doing the same. We are all perfectly imperfect just as we are. Apologizing constantly is destroying our self-esteem.

Tina's Thoughts

After many years of connecting with recreational runners at every level, hundreds of runners have come up to me at events over the years. Within the first 30 seconds, they usually put themselves down, comparing themselves to my former elite status. They tell me they run, but they weren't a "real" runner like I am, or that they are slow or only run a few miles a week. As they share this, they look down at the ground as if they are protecting themselves from my disappointed glare, or that I will be repulsed by how "slow" they are. It hurts my heart to see runners degrade themselves like that, taking away their hard work and commitment because they believe only through running a 16-minute 5K is someone a real runner. I tell them it doesn't matter. I don't care about their pace, nor should they. A runner is someone who runs, that's all. When I run with others, I remind them prerun that I do not care what pace we run, so we can run what feels right for them. I will be by their side, regardless. They agree, but often start off too fast, not wanting to "hold me back," and reach a point midrun where they tell me I can go ahead if I want. To me, all I feel is empathy and love for them. They are spending precious energy worried about it, meaning they miss the best part of our time together. All I want to do is get to know them as a human being, regardless of speed.

But then I think back to a race in 2016 where Molly Huddle was racing. She was almost superhuman for what she was able to do at that time. I felt nervous to even be around her. I ran my cooldown with Molly and a mutual friend. I remember being worried that she would be thinking about how "slow" I was running and that she would be feeling irritated with me for holding her back. I apologized, to which, of course, they didn't agree. It was a cooldown, after all! I share this to bring home that point about running being relative and that we *have* to stop apologizing for being who we are, and where we are. While my speed at the elite level was mind-boggling for many runners, I viewed myself as slow compared to Olympians. If we continue this cycle to the next generation of runners, we will never be happy within our sport.

When we see ourselves as part of a community with ideas and experiences to contribute, we take back our narrative. Whether we're a newer runner or an experienced runner trying something new, we never know who we will impact. Conversely, we never know whose advice could be beneficial to us. Maybe we have a lot of experience in a particular area, but another runner has a different insight, a different perspective that could add value to our own running. We should always be listening.

Find Running Buddies

Making friends through school and extracurricular activities when we are younger is relatively easy, or at least the discomfort dissipates fast. But unless we live in the town we grew up in, making new friends is more difficult than it would seem. Why didn't anyone tell us it was this awkward to make friends as an adult?

Sure, we can do a quick search to find running clubs in our area and check them out on social media to see if we are a fit. The real compatibility assessment begins when we bravely show up, hoping there will be another equally awkward person who made the same choice, and we can gravitate together. But doing so requires confidence to even get there, let alone talk to someone when there is little time before and after. Just like anything else in life, the best way to meet people who have similar interests is to go where they are, and show up consistently. The group may seem like they are deeply bonded, but within a few visits (if not right away!), people will recognize the commitment you are making and welcome you into the fold.

Getting to know new people is unfortunately like dating. We might see someone who we think has the potential to be a friend and we engage in small talk to see if we have common interests. Taking a running friendship to the next step may require gathering courage to ask to meet up outside the run to determine if there is potential for a long-term friendship. That is when the "dating" begins. With new friends, as with new potential partners, we have to see if our personalities match, if both people feel excited about the relationship, and if it is worth the effort required for a friendship to grow. Sometimes we might feel that is the case, but they do not, and other times, we might be the one pulling back. Don't be afraid to make that first connection! Many times, would-be relationships languish because folks are reluctant to be seen as too forward.

Either way, the most important thing to keep in mind is to be ourselves. If we are not compatible, it is better to find out early over excuses that prolong the hurt. As the dating advice goes: Mixed signals usually mean no. The same goes for us: If that person doesn't make us feel good about who we are, or make us laugh and appreciate the time together, then maybe we need to reconsider. It takes some thought and some time, but once we figure out who we are aligned with in values and morals, it will be worth the effort.

Zoë's Thoughts

My friendship with Tina started as many relationships do in the 21st century: online. We were mutual admirers of each other's work, occasionally tweeting compliments and liking posts. As a newer podcaster and writer, I admired Tina's entrepreneurial spirit and commitment to sharing stories that touched on topics she was interested in covering. The Venn diagram of mutual interests would have been a perfect circle. But, I hesitated in reaching out to Tina, nervous that it might seem weird or awkward to cold-email someone who I had been following as a fan for years. Although I wanted to make a connection, particularly in the male-dominated space of running media that often pits women against each other, I just . . . didn't.

It turned out that Tina felt similarly. But after I posted a picture of my compost setup, Tina felt there were enough commonalities to work up the courage required to take things to the next friendship level and take them off-line and into the real world.

Tina slid into my DMs, and the rest is history. If there's someone whose work you admire, or has common interests, or is working to solve a shared problem (like climate change!), take that first step and reach out; you won't regret it.

Tina Muir

Friendships can be created in the most unique ways. For Zoë and Tina, a shared love of composting led to the creation of this book and a lifelong friendship.

Running with people in your area and finding space within your local community is more intimidating. We cannot hide behind our computer, but there is also the genuineness of having another flawed human in front of us to keep it authentic. When we move online, there is a pressure to get it right, to be the best version of ourselves or we fear becoming the next victim of cancel culture. That said, online communities are not only a wealth of information, a place where we can learn from the mistakes of others and be inspired to be our best selves, but also a place to connect with people all around the world who share our passions. It can foster lifelong relationships in our local communities and beyond that we otherwise would have never known. Let's explore that more.

Create Your Own Running Group

What if you attended group events in the past and either didn't feel welcomed, or it didn't feel like the right fit? This can be particularly relevant to those who hold marginalized identities and historically haven't been privileged in spaces like running. BIPOC or LGBTQ+ runners might encounter struggles specifically related to the pressures and expectations that white, cisgender-heteronormative society and running culture places on runners of diverse backgrounds. While finding a community or group that immediately makes us feel like we belong is ideal, that doesn't always happen. When we have a negative experience with a group that left us behind on a run in a new city, or made us feel isolated as we stood alone, it can be difficult to put ourselves in that vulnerable situation again.

Maria Solis Belizaire wanted to join a running group, but had not come across any for Latinx runners, so she decided to start her own inclusive groups, Latinos Run and Latinas Run. Even when the primary reason is to create a safe space for typically underserved runners within the running community, it doesn't mean fun can't be a priority. As Belizaire explains, "For many of us, running is a social adventure. It's an opportunity to connect with a group of people with shared interests." Belizaire has advice for runners creating that place for those with shared interests: "When starting a new club, the best advice I always try to give is to first, 'start with a vision.' Write it down and create a framework to what you want. For instance, what type of club are you looking to create, and what is the location, demographics, and practice dates and times. Once you have your vision set, start setting expectations. Whether it's a regular 5K run, group training for races, or running on a particular surface, let runners know what to expect when they attend your events." Belizaire cites the importance of consistency, especially when it comes to communication, dialogue, posts, and meetups.

If you are determined to create a group that provides all the features and values that you wish had been there for you, go ahead and build that community. However, there are a few things to consider before taking that step. First, take a deep dive into what is already available, and attend other groups' runs and events to see if there is an opportunity to make that group even better. Often, we try to re-create the wheel when there are ways to work with established groups that are not able to see their own blind spots. How can you fill in the gaps of what the group is missing? If we were left behind on runs in the past, could we volunteer to lead a slower pace group on a run, or take a vow to always run with the person at the back? Could we strategize with local communities on how to create welcoming group run opportunities for those in Black and Brown neighborhoods, and make sure voices of color are centered in those conversations? Could we reach out to new runners in the group and be the first person to welcome them?

Most running group leaders welcome suggestions to improve attendance and retention. If they do not, others within the group may already be thinking about a change in leadership. Our questions may prompt a movement within the group to push for more inclusivity. If there is not an existing group willing to work alongside you and the energy is there, go for it. Make the club you wish had been there for you.

Some remote locations may not have running groups at all and creating a running group may fall squarely on our shoulders. If so, spend time researching successful running groups in other similar cities or towns to determine what they do that makes people want to come.

Parkrun and November Project are fantastic examples of successful, free, worldwide community events that were developed with inclusivity in mind. Parkrun organizes free, weekly community events all over the world. November

Project is a free fitness collaboration in multiple cities around the world that uses physical activity to motivate and encourage people of all ages, shapes, sizes, and fitness levels to get out of their beds and get moving. Both are made possible by the generous support of their volunteers and partners, and it has taken years to build them to their current level. If we are willing to put in work, embrace the setbacks, and invest the money required to create a community event that we feel is missing, there are resources that can be cultivated for support.

When setting up a group, it is critical to have a healthy sense of perspective and realistic expectations about how fast it will grow. While we want to have a grand vision of our future running group flourishing with new and experienced runners, growing every week from dozens to hundreds, the reality is that most groups take time to pick up steam. It may mean six months (or more) of a few loyal friends turning up because they don't want you to be alone. It may mean hours of effort invested, and sometimes feeling like it will never go anywhere. It may even mean that you never get to see the full effect and growth of what you have created. As quoted in *Think Like a Monk* by Jay Shetty, monk Gauranga Das told his students, "We should plant trees under whose shade we don't plan to sit." Starting a running group means taking an oath or writing ourselves a contract to commit for a year before reevaluating—even if it is just one friend who shows up week after week out of pure love for us. While we may think our idea is just what the running community needs, as we know, life can be busy, and often people who promise they will turn up, don't. Keep showing up. The lessons learned each week will help you grow as a human and a leader, lessons that can be applied to everything else in life.

Maria Solis Belizaire has been extremely successful in building her groups, and credits part of that success to utilizing social media and finding strong leaders: "As we live in the digital age, connecting through social platforms often gives you a larger audience to connect with. Build an online audience and presence. Most runners today use social media to find out about events." Belizaire recognizes that an indicator of a group's success is to "create a team of great leaders. Having great leaders can help your reach and can increase the quality of service you provide."

Finally, be prepared to shift the group slightly if some time has passed and it does not fit the community. As Belizaire noted, keep the vision, but adjust as needed.

Find Online Communities

While in-person activities are preferred by many runners, meaningful connections are possible online. When the COVID-19 pandemic reframed the way we approached relationships, we found creative and effective ways to keep in touch without being together in person. While they do not provide the physical connection, online communities can be a wonderful place to connect with others, or to work up the courage to speak without the rejection we fear when opening ourselves up to another person. One of the benefits of online communication is that it's not restricted by location, potentially making a truly global community.

Through their Running Report YouTube channel and *2 Black Runners* podcast, Aaron and Joshua Potts have created a community for runners who are fans of

Connecting With Runners Through Social Media

A 2016 study examined detailed, daily exercise behaviors and social network ties of approximately 1.1 million runners over the course of five years and concluded that exercise is socially contagious (Aral and Nicolaides 2016). This meant, on average, one friend running an additional kilometer influences the other to run an additional three-tenths of a kilometer on that same day. The runners also influenced one another to run faster on that same day. While it is not always beneficial to run further or faster, this study shows the power of the running community's influence.

In a 2015 study of runners, researchers assessed over 3,400 runners to examine the correlation between their running behaviors and social networking sites, finding two interesting connections (Mahan et al. 2015). First, the use of running-related social networking generally corresponds with the amount of running involvement. A highly involved runner may use social networking sites to extend their participation beyond running. They may make new friends through the network, taking their love of running beyond the miles logged. Second, social networking use also influenced runners to run more miles per week, and made them more satisfied with their social life. Runners who used running-related social networking sites became more engaged in running, which promoted their physical and mental well-being.

Social media and training apps can be a negative presence in our lives when we allow them to take over, but seeing others getting out there can help us to feel good or stay motivated in our own training. When we are going through a difficult time, it is easy to feel isolated or alone, and when we are busy, it can be easy to skip a run or cut it short. That small, quick reminder of the connectedness of the running community can be enough to keep us on a path that makes us feel good.

Sharing our training through apps like Strava, or on social media platforms, can provide that connection, and allow us to give back to the community with a few taps of our thumb. By giving friends kudos, likes, or comments about their own training, we are supporting them while also being inspired by them, whether we realize it or not. We get to choose who we surround ourselves with in person and through the media we consume. That means we also get to choose whether we are inspired or demoralized. Connecting with motivating runners who support our journey can help us tap into an energy source we didn't know existed. As Strava tests more community features beyond the competitive and training elements, there is a bright future for runners looking to engage with others online through Strava running clubs and beyond.

track and field but are also interested in discussing social issues that have been ignored in the past. It can feel as if we are alone in our passion for a particular topic, and not all of us have a sibling to geek out with over our shared interests, but Aaron encourages us to find that space for ourselves, even if it originally feels like we will be a micro group . He recognizes how a community, even one created online, can become a lifeline and energizer for others with the same passion.

"The community means so much to me because the community raised me. I've made some of my closest friends, mentors, and gained tons of opportunities through the running community. One thing I've learned about the running community is that there is a place for everyone. So whatever you like about running, I promise you there is someone out there just like you."

It does not have to fit the traditional community definition—being a group of people in the same location coming together—because we can find others with shared passions, even without a leader's presence. As Aaron explains, "Nowadays there are so many different ways to be involved in the community, and some don't even require running. Obviously, you can easily join a running club in the area, but you can also just listen to podcasts that interest you or subscribe to a newsletter that speaks to you. There is so much media in the running world that is relatable and inspiring. As you start to follow a podcast, an influencer, or newsletter you will start to feel a part of the community and you'll be inspired to put on your shoes and go for a run."

As with in-person group running, the first step should be to explore what is already available and ask other runners for recommendations. One of the difficult parts of the modern approach to living is that with so many places to find information, it can be tough to know what we are looking for. But by seeking out experienced people who know the best places to look, we can remove some of the overwhelm. Once again, it is better to contribute and help grow a previously existing community rather than building something new, unless after deep research, we have found that there is nothing available for the group we envision. In that case, go ahead and make the group you wish could have been there for you.

Tina hosting a group run in Venice, California, with Allbirds. Regardless of whether a group is created online or in person, building the group you wished you had earlier in your life is key to maintaining consistency in your commitment.

Defining a "Real" Runner

As runners, we all have different definitions of what a "real" runner is. To some people it means committing to a certain level of competitiveness. For others, it's a speed thing. You are a real runner when you can hit a certain pace. Still others see anyone who puts on a pair of shoes and heads out the door as a runner. For the record, this last definition is what we believe a real runner is. We believe we cross over into the runner category as soon as we lace up our shoes and take our first steps, but it can be hard for many to view themselves as "real" runners when they compare themselves to others who fly by on the trails. *Now **they** are real runners; I'm just out here jogging.*

Here's the thing, though: We are all runners. Running is relative. A 10-minute-per-mile pace is fast for some, and slow for others. The same can be said about almost every pace (unless you are Eliud Kipchoge of course!). One of the most interesting aspects of our sport is that we can all cover the same course, but we each have our unique journey. We can be together, both literally and figuratively, but also be on our own adventure. We all start each training block and each season as slightly different people than when we finish a goal race or transition into the next season. We learn a little more about who we are. With each race, we feel more confident identifying ourselves as runners. We all consider skipping a run to stay in a warm bed on a cold winter morning. We all traverse the same paths, some covering those paths in less time than others, but there are runners of every speed out there every day. We are part of a community, a group of people that welcomes new members with open arms. We know that everyone is different and has their own experiences that made them into the person they are today, yet we all share one thing in common; we are runners.

Mirna Valerio has long advocated for runners of every speed to see themselves as runners. "Slow is relative. Your slow may be someone else's fast and vice versa. You never, ever have to apologize for being slow. Just like they say to 'hike your own hike,' you can run your own run. As long as you are moving your body in a way that (eventually) feels good to you, move it as slowly or as quickly as you want or as it will go. If your friends, family, or running group has something to say about your pace, find new people to run with! I love that running forces us to see, feel, and use our bodies in challenging ways. I learn a lot from simply moving my body and traversing all different types of terrain on my own two feet. It makes me feel uniquely human and very close to the earth."

Every single runner covering a race course has their own unique path to that moment. While it may feel at times that the running community only cares about what the top runners have to share, in actuality, all of us have something special to offer. We all have advice and lessons that could assist another runner, help them through a difficult time, or make them feel more connected to the sport, to themselves, and to our home, Mother Earth. And, despite what some running magazines and social media accounts may show, running is not just about races or the finish line. Living for fantastic finishes will leave a runner fed up and unfulfilled. Running is about what we learn about ourselves and who we become along the way, even if we don't know where that is yet.

Find Where You Belong

Verna Volker, founder of Native Women Running, has grown a huge community on Instagram by sharing experiences from runners who previously did not have a place to feel valued. "As someone who never saw herself as a runner, I now know that each of our journeys is unique. I struggled with it for a long time, but as time went on, I ran more races and realized what my body can do. Though I never saw my body as a runner's body, I realized that I could do things that some runners couldn't do, so I learned to adjust my thinking to stop comparing and embrace my own journey."

Volker also learned the value of speaking out regardless of how many people may be listening. By doing so, she has become an important voice in the running community by providing a space for others to speak about what their running journey has meant to them. "It's easy to become silent in our voices. We often think what we say is not powerful, but it truly is. I think each of us carry a call to do good and desire change in the world. Our voice is a simple, powerful tool. Yes, it's scary, but you soon find out that others will come along and encourage you. Many will support and believe what you believe in. Don't be intimidated. You have a powerful voice."

Mosier reinforces this point by reminding us, "None of us are born believing we do not matter—we learn this over time. Systems are in place that treat people differently depending on any number of factors, and those systems are challenging to overcome. But every negative thought that we have—about our value, our ability, our story, or anything else—was put in our minds by another person. We all bring a unique perspective from our own experiences and interpretations of them to this world, and every story matters. Sharing our stories can be empowering to ourselves and inspiring to others. Visibility and representation matter so much, particularly to members of communities who have been told they don't matter. For anyone who believes their voice or story do not matter, there are people out there whose entire lives could be changed by seeing you and hearing your story. Never underestimate your ability to impact others simply by being yourself."

Then there are those who might not consider themselves real runners or serious runners, but they inspire us with their consistent commitment to their running practice. Maybe running has been a part of their daily routine from a young age, prior to conversations defining a "real" runner. Or maybe they see "real" runners as those people who train for the Olympics, but their personal running has always been a part of their physical and mental health. There are many runners who do not need the label of "real," and do not care what others think about their running journey. For them, running is a way to promote longevity, is the antithesis of their job, and is valued for the simple act of it. We could benefit from learning what these runners have to say.

If we want to be a real runner, we are. No minimum mileage, speed, or background required, a simple definition for a simple sport. According to Mosier, "In many ways, we've been trained to value a certain type of athlete or certain achievements. But the truth is, not every runner will qualify for Boston, and even fewer will run the Prefontaine Classic. Not everyone wants to run a marathon or worries about the podium. The beautiful thing about running is that there are infinite ways to run and express yourself through running. We all share the commitment to move our bodies and to challenge ourselves. If you participate in the sport of running, you are a runner, and you deserve to claim that title and be celebrated as much as anyone else."

Not only does a broad and varied conversation within a diverse group stimulate more ideas, thoughts, and growth, but it helps to build a bond, and helps us all to feel a part of something special. These are our people. We understand the weird things runners do. Why not make the most of the opportunity to be around those people?

Volker reiterates this with what she has learned. "When we see ourselves in community, we become a part of something larger. For example, Native Women Running has become a virtual community where many runners see themselves and a place of belonging. When you find a community, you find support, representation, and space that is specifically for you. It's a safe place. I believe everyone should find that community to feel support."

Community means coming together because of a shared interest, but then moving beyond that initial mutual connection to form a deeper bond based on trust, on knowing that we can be ourselves, confiding in each other, and not being judged. It's a place where we belong.

Cultivate Community

We got together with activist Chris Mosier to think about ways to cultivate the community atmosphere we crave and how we can learn to value our own strengths. So grab a journal, sit somewhere quiet, and work through these questions.

What does the word *community* mean to you?

Who shows up for you when you need support?

Who do you show up for?

What can you bring to the running community that you wished you had at a previous point in your running journey (and if your journey is just beginning, what do you wish there was)?

How can you help develop the running community to reflect what matters to you?

What topics, identities, or interests do you bond with others about? Would you consider those your communities?

How much diversity and diverse representation do you find within your communities? How could you expand the diversity within your communities?

What ideas do you have for how to make sure new runners do not feel isolation or abandonment?

How can you be part of the change?

You belong, and so does every runner who laces up their shoes and heads out the door. The more runners that feel like they have a place they belong, the more our community can continue to grow and support one another.

Community means something different to all of us, but one thing has become clear: We all need some version of it in our lives. We live in an increasingly disconnected world, despite always being connected. Nothing can replace the physical and social connections of in-person interactions. Our busy lives make social interaction an easy sacrifice to make, but that has a harmful effect on our mental health and our purpose. Loneliness engulfs us if we become too detached from people and nature. Running, inherently a solo endeavor, has the potential to elicit meaning and joy through belonging. Finding community that welcomes us with open arms can be the key to unlocking a sustainable future for our running and beyond.

ACTION STEPS

- Make a pledge not to apologize for being slow. Tell your running friends about the pledge, and have them hold you accountable.
- Join Tina on a Together Run (find them on the *Running for Real* podcast feed).
- Try to increase the number of group runs you participate in, especially if you have been feeling stuck or lonely.
- If you are part of a running group in your area, how can you take a more active role in making the changes you would like to see?
- If you are determined to set up a new group and have researched what is already available, be consistent in your communication, dialogue, posts, and meetups. Commit to an entire year of showing up before reassessing.
- Get into the habit of setting boundaries in running groups or with running friends. Establish prerun agreements on the effort or pace. Make sure everyone has shared any considerations they may have for wanting to run slower.
- Use social media or training apps to connect with other runners and build your support muscles.
- Consider an online community. What interests or identities do you have that are important to you and could provide community and connection?
- Answer the questions in the sidebar "Cultivate Community." How can you implement the changes you wish to see in the running community?
- If you keep a training log or diary, look back through the earliest days of your running journey. How have you changed or improved since then?

9 | Give Back

While chasing goals and getting the most out of our own running potential can be rewarding, giving back to the community always creates the most meaningful and satisfying experiences. Acts of service can be life changing and signify something different to each of us. When our community has gifted us with many special moments, experiences, and confidence boosts, we want to make others feel loved and appreciated too. In addition to improving our mental and physical health, and helping us to fulfill our highest need as a human, giving back brings other like-minded people into our lives who encourage us to achieve new levels of growth and purpose. When we surround ourselves with people who believe in the power of service, we bring optimism, love, and energy into our own lives.

The means of giving back does not matter as much as the consistency to which we follow through. We each have a unique combination of passions that can contribute in a way that feels right to us. This chapter provides a few potential ways to share our gifts and experiences with the running community through supporting others. It allows us to reflect on the kindness others have shown toward us in realizing our own dreams. Knowing we can pass some of that on can give us purpose as we move into the next phase of our running journey . . . even if we are still focused on our own goals and aspirations.

Mentor Others

New runners have a lot to learn. Overhearing conversations between experienced runners can feel like listening to people talking in a different language. Someone who just discovered they need to purchase shoes specifically for running can feel embarrassed about their lack of knowledge. Tempos and paces, PRs and segment records, fartleks and thresholds . . . what does it all mean? While new runners catch on and

> By recognizing how to be the role model you wished for when you first started running, you can help other runners coming into the space.

quickly learn the lingo, we all know how intimidating it can be when everyone seems to know more than you do. We struggle with that feeling in daily life; why would we want it in our hobby too? That is not even considering the added stressor of running itself. If running a half-mile without walking is an accomplishment, excitement can quickly dissipate when others are talking about "only" running 16 miles the week before their marathon.

It can be challenging to see where you fit within the running community, but by recognizing how to be the role model you wished for when you first started running, you can help other runners coming into the space—many of whom started in pandemic desperation—to become a part of our community for life. While the media and running industry have traditionally lacked in showing the rich and diverse culture of our sport, you can be the change for the future. It might be intimidating to speak out about making change happen in your community, but once you take that step to advocate for yourself and other runners, you will be glad you did.

Share Your Story to Encourage Others

Runners listen to what other runners have to say. Whether you are new to running or have been doing it for decades, your experiences and perspective could be helpful for other runners to hear. Your message may resonate in a way that no one else's could, regardless of whether it is given virtually or in person. Your words could be the difference between others completing a race or giving up when it gets tough. Your words could mean they go seek treatment for an injury instead of running through pain day after day until a stress fracture forces them to take months off. If a newbie's only experience of running is Pinterest images telling them, "No pain, no gain," or endless photos of runners grimacing in a race, they may have inaccurate expectations of what it is to be a runner and conclude that they just don't have it in them.

By speaking up to a small group of people about the tough times and the moments you pushed through, you could change the path of a runner in your community. A "let's give this a try" runner may believe they are the only one experiencing their struggle, especially if they have been told they are not athletic and shouldn't bother trying to exercise. While elite athletes' stories may be inspiring to read, they don't resonate with most, and the new runner may feel like no other runner has been through this. New runners may also fear asking questions about fueling, hydration, timing, and other topics that experienced runners assume everyone knows. By sharing your experiences, they may feel comfortable asking questions they had originally been too nervous to ask. Maybe your story will help them feel welcomed, and make them feel like the real runner they are.

Helping a keen new runner dive into the sport is one of the most fulfilling ways to give back. Not only to translate those weird runner terms, but to help the new runner avoid some of the pitfalls that beginners tend to make. And let's be real, they are mistakes experienced runners make on occasion too! Be the friend who answers their questions and does not judge their inexperience, but instead embraces and celebrates the opportunity to create a lifelong runner who may go on to inspire countless other new runners. If you are an experienced runner or run leader, set aside time to run alongside newer runners. Get to know them, be a friend to them, encourage them.

While the word *mentorship* can sound stuffy, reserved for business executives grooming future CEOs, mentorship within running can simply mean being there for a new runner. The running world is welcoming, but to a new runner joining the community, it can feel like everyone knows the inside jokes except you. Recognizing the courage and commitment it took for a new runner to show up to a group run in which everyone knows one another is a great place to start. Welcoming them, giving insight into the logistics of the group, and introducing them to other runners can help solidify a future in which they belong. This simple gesture could make all the difference between a one-off, and them showing up every Wednesday for the next two years. These efforts help new runners transition from viewing running as a mechanical motion to recognizing its beauty and potential in the community for friendship and personal growth.

Mentoring does not have to be in a physical group setting, either. It could be as simple as messaging a new runner within a Facebook group, letting them

Tina at a Tracksmith shakeout before the New York City Marathon. Taking the time to get to know new runners in your community is a fun way to keep learning more about yourself and your sport.

know that no question is a dumb question and that you would be happy to help them, or noticing that your neighbor has started running and offering support if they need it.

While running mentorship may seem like something reserved for former professional runners, a running mentor can be any one of us. As a group leader or connector, there are simple ways to foster relationships within your own community, regardless of whether you are the mentor or not. After a group run, extend an open invitation for coffee. This is a great opportunity for all runners, regardless of speed, to get to know one another. This social time allows runners of every experience level to talk, and it's where unofficial mentorship can begin. Even if you have only been running a few years, your experience is valuable and important.

Joe McConaughy, a coach and runner, has seen the importance of mentors for his athletes: "We run for many different reasons—community, physical and mental health, adventure, self-improvement. The list goes on. In the same fashion, mentorship comes from just as many places. A mentor in the running community is someone who supports others in their goals, promotes community, shares their own experience for the benefit of others, and continues to dream."

Sometimes being a mentor means acknowledging what you don't know, and connecting folks with someone who has more information than you, demonstrating that it's okay to not have all the answers. Chances are you will learn from your mentee, too, and grow as a runner and a person, as you stretch those empathy muscles. It is not about the level of knowledge provided, but the camaraderie and encouragement to keep going.

If you have never considered that you could help other runners, Joe McConaughy has some advice: "If you want to be a mentor to other runners, get involved. You don't go out one day and 'become a mentor.' Join a running club. Organize a local run. Be empathetic. Ask people their goals and follow up with them. Identify a need in your group, community, or city and take action."

Sign Up to Volunteer

When we are unable to race because we did not qualify or we have an injury, our heart hurts and all we want to do is pretend the race isn't happening. Maybe we try to distract ourselves with something else because it's too painful to sit in our sadness. While it may seem counterintuitive, volunteering can be a great way to channel our grief into something positive and see how much work goes into putting on an event. We can regain control of our situation and develop perspective on what really matters.

Volunteering can help us work through the grief of missing out on an event, while also feeling good that we are giving back to the community.

Yassine Diboun is known for the fun he brings to volunteering. "Most of the volunteering that I do is in the form of providing aid stations at local trail races here in the Pacific Northwest. I always tell the folks that volunteer with us that 'we are not just filling water bottles, we are providing an experience!' We dress up in costume and aim to bring some levity to the often-grueling ultramarathons. For many people this is a lifetime achievement, and making an impression or an imprint in their memory of the experience is very rewarding and very inspiring for me! I also see how different runners strategically take care of themselves, and how they carry themselves with their attitude. I've always said that the best thing you can give someone is your time. Hanging out in beautiful areas with like-minded people is a fulfilling way to spend the weekend in my opinion!"

And he is right. We know the important role volunteers and spectators play within our own races. Staying hydrated and fueled can keep us on track toward achieving our goal, and a few supportive people lining the course can make all the difference between having a good day and mentally spiraling out of control. Runners can have a flawless buildup, but race day is where we really get to see it all come together . . . or fall apart.

Volunteering can happen on or off the race course, too. You can help with early race planning, prerace organization publicity, or prerace packet pickup. After the event, there are plenty of volunteers behind the scenes helping to tear down the race course and clean up the start and finish line areas. There are opportunities for you to connect your passion with supporting a race; you just have to think about where you want to contribute and what is available. Unsurprisingly, Tina has worked at a few of the Abbott World Marathon Majors and with their sustainability teams. Contacting a local race director, searching on the website of big races, or using the contact form on race websites is a great place to start.

Volunteering can change our entire outlook on the sport. We are immersed in community and culture, and can feel pride in the resiliency of runners. Race directors are often short on assistance, especially local race organizers, who are competing against the big budgets of giant race event companies. Volunteers can help make their events smooth and enjoyable for those participating, further growing the community.

Matthew Huff, author of *Marathoner*, believes in the power of volunteering to celebrate the running community: "There are two main reasons why I love to volunteer at races. First, it feels like such an easy (but so crucial) way to give back to the running community. When you're running a race, you *know* how critical those aid stations are. You need fuel and hydration, but you are focused on running, so to have people watching out for you and giving you what you need is life-saving. I love to be able to do that for others just as race volunteers have done it for me. Second, it's a whole heck of a lot of fun! You get to meet new people and cheer for runners. It's an exciting way to enjoy the race and feel like you're a part of it without having to run."

Giving back to the running community can remind us why we do it, what our purpose is. As Huff has experienced firsthand, "Sometimes when you're running a race (especially a marathon), you are overwhelmed by the amount of people working hard (sometimes for months!) so that you get to run. The organizers, the aid station volunteers, the

> Volunteering can change our entire outlook on the sport. We are immersed in community and culture, and can feel pride in the resiliency of runners.

medics, the expo workers. It's often thousands of people. I am so, so grateful as a runner to have those people making races possible, and so I really love to volunteer and give that experience to other runners. It feels good knowing that you are helping to provide those triumphant, once-in-a-lifetime, I-never-thought-I-could-do-this-but-I-proved-myself-wrong moments to others. Running a marathon, you're often focused on yourself so you don't get to see all the emotion the race brings to other people. Volunteering, you get to see how powerful a race can be for so many people, and you're making that happen for them!"

Appreciating the other side of racing means that when we race in the future, we can give a smile and a "thank you" to the volunteers who are holding out a cup for us. It means we treat the finish line volunteers with kindness and respect, even if we are disappointed at our race time. It means we recognize the sacrifice that they made on a freezing winter morning to stand outside for hours on end.

Volunteering doesn't even have to be around race day. Maria Solis Belizaire, founder of Latinos Run, has seen how the generosity of volunteers allows her groups to continue growing. Belizaire believes that "volunteers and partners are the backbone to how many clubs function. They both provide visibility to brands because they have a much wider audience. They also provide experience, help promote your events, and give credibility to the work you do."

Volunteering is a direct way to shift our running perspective toward gratitude and love for our community—a reminder we all need sometimes.

Become a Guide

Similarly, becoming a guide or support person for a blind, visually impaired (VI), or adaptive athlete can be another powerful way to connect with the community and find meaning beyond results. Whether you sign up to train once a week with a blind or VI runner in your area or run races as a support person as your schedule allows, it can be a powerful life motivator. If you have the time to dedicate a run each week to running alongside a new friend, it can be the difference between that runner getting outside to maximize their running experience, and yet another run on the treadmill. Deep connections and strong friendships can be built while running as we support one another through challenges in our lives. Becoming a guide is a way to connect with another human on a deeper level, with the recognition that the time commitment on both sides strengthens the relationship. Signing up at unitedinstride.com and achillesinternational.org means that local athletes or runners traveling through the area can find you and reach out.

> Becoming a guide is a way to connect with another human on a deeper level, with the recognition that the time commitment on both sides strengthens the relationship.

Kyle Robidoux, a motivational speaker and sponsored runner, has a beautiful way of thinking about the relationship between guide and VI runner: "Being a running guide combines your passion of running with volunteering. If you are already running three to five times per week, why not use one run to support someone else? It makes running a team sport and creates lasting relationships."

It is also a great way to connect with runners in the VI community, leading to opportunities to guide runners in a race we might otherwise never have had the opportunity to do. While the idea of someone's race plan resting on our shoulders can be daunting, any runner can be a guide. In the days prior to the race, the runner lets their guide know what is most helpful to them and how to best support them during the run. There will usually be an opportunity to go for a short practice run the day before, and you quickly get into a natural rhythm.

As someone who has benefitted from having guides alongside him for many years, Kyle has a message to ease your fears: "As long as you know your left and right, you can be an effective guide. Everyone starts on more runnable (safe) terrain such as a track or smooth running path, then progresses from there."

Tina's Thoughts

The first fourteen years of my running career were all about what I could achieve, what I could do, and how fast I could go. While I was proud of what I accomplished, when I began the next stage of my running journey in 2017, I vowed that things would be different. It would no longer be about taking from family, friends, or the community; it would be about giving back. I heard ultrarunner Mike Wardian talk about how much he enjoyed being a guide, and I knew that was one way I could follow through with my promise. I signed up at United in Stride and in 2019 was given the opportunity to be a guide for an athlete at the United States Association of Blind Athletes Marathon National Championships. Although I

Michael Anderson

was 13-weeks pregnant with my second child and unable to go the whole way, I ran through the halfway point with a first-time marathon runner from the Running for Real community, Joe Retherford. I was nervous going into it. What if I screwed up his pace and he couldn't finish? What if he fell because I missed something?

I was scared, but Joe made me feel at ease quickly. Despite not having run much more than eight miles in the recent months due to my pregnancy, the thirteen miles flew by and I kept going to fifteen, even tempted to continue. It was one of the most enjoyable experiences of my running life—much more meaningful than jumping in the race myself—and I met some wonderful people who have become dear friends. Since then, I have run three marathons as a guide and now I actually prefer running marathons as a guide over running for myself.

Tina running as a guide for Kyle Robidoux in the Boston Marathon. Giving back to the community can level up your connection to the sport.

Pace for a Race

Pacers are easy to spot on a race course: a flock of runners surrounding an individual who appears to effortlessly carry a sign in their hands or a backpack on their shoulders for an entire race. Many runners rely on pacers to keep them in the right zone without having to obsess over their watches (which are notorious for not working in big cities). Pacers have led to many personal bests and saved numerous runners from going out too fast. And yes, if we are being honest, many of us have started out with a too-fast pacer, and paid the price. While it requires extra effort to hold the sign or wear the backpack, the rewards of giving back, connecting with the community, and knowing you are a part of so many runners' special day is a gift in itself.

Stephanie Ormond, a marathoner and regular pacer, gets nervous each time she is about to pace a race, but as with racing itself, the experience is worth it every time. "It's not the same stress I feel before my own races, that fear of grinding and the wall. It's more about the responsibility. Knowing how it feels to race and that you can't do it for them. With that said, you only pace a group that would feel comfortable (but not too easy) for you, so you don't hit the wall and still have lung capacity to chitchat and communicate about the race strategy and check in with everyone. Through that 13.1 or 26.2, you really get to know a person. Through conversation, but also how they manage stress. I become so invested in their race, and getting them to that goal is such a rewarding process and keeps me coming back . . . and also making lifelong friends and running buddies!"

When we go off-road, the pacing experience is different, but just as rewarding. We hear elite ultra and trail runners talk about how essential their crew and pacers are to their successes. We know how much we, as runners, appreciate the fact that a running friend gave up a precious night's sleep to light up the way and keep our exhausted body upright and moving forward. Now that ultra and trail races are becoming more mainstream, the gift of crewing or pacing others is one that runners of every level can provide for their friends.

Either way, pacing is a commitment. We have to be fit enough to handle the duties without the recognition at the end. That said, it feels good knowing that we are helping other runners to realize their dreams. These give-back collaborations are something we see others do and admire from afar, believing we could never do it, or maybe never wanted to. Being a pacer requires sacrifice, running a race for others while risking our own bodies, and knowing that another runner's successful completion of the event rests on our shoulders. It can be a lot, and when we are already putting a lot of pressure on our own running journey, the idea of adding someone else's expectations can be too much.

However, in most cases, it will actually take the pressure off. Running for others can make us realize that even though the race means a lot to our friends, the outcome does not change the way we feel about them. If their race plan crumbles and they do not reach their goal, it does not make them any less of a friend. In fact, we may admire them more for the challenges they worked through or being smart enough to stop. That realization can translate into recognizing that we, too, do not have to achieve to be loved. Being a pacer, or crewing for someone, can help us see the love, energy, and compassion that running offers beyond our own accomplishments.

As a regular pacer for marathons, Ormond has some solid advice for those of us considering pacing, but afraid we might mess it up: "Every day you slip on your running shoes is a giant question mark. We've all had those runs that feel gross for no reason and also runs that feel great despite bad choices the day/night before. As with any run, you just do the best you can and be honest with yourself."

Professional ultrarunner Lucy Bartholomew owes a big part of her accomplishments (like finishing third at Western States) to volunteers, crew, and pacers, but has also experienced being there for others, and the satisfaction that brings. As Lucy attests, "I think that's just my philosophy. If you're injured or if you're not in it, still going to an event and volunteering or cheering or crewing fills you up just as much."

While confronting the pain of missing out requires courage, it helps us to process and work through our grief. Lucy recommends reframing the experience from one of missing out, to an opportunity we are given. "It's something that with the right mindset, you can be that person that's out there in the middle of the night, in the middle of the mountains, saying, 'Great job, John!' John will remember that."

If you are healthy and faster than other running friends, consider running alongside them in their race, pacing them if you feel comfortable, or simply being there for support. It is important to register for the race ourselves to make sure that it is legal and fair, but it can mean the world to a friend. Running with them means you can pay attention to pace to prevent them from going out too fast, and be the positive voice to counter the negative one in their head so they can finish. In races it is easy to get fired up by adrenaline and latch on to other people's paces early in a race, but having someone there to gently remind us to stick to the plan can make all the difference. Just make sure you talk through the race plan and find out what they need before race day. Some runners like to be left alone with their thoughts when it gets tough, others like compassion and support, and still others may want to hear motivating words or phrases to help them dig deep. Before the race, discuss a loose plan of what will help them most in their moments of struggle.

Advocate for Others

Another way to give back is getting directly involved at the city level with policy change. That could mean ensuring there are safe places in your area for all runners to get out there. It could mean advocating for members of frontline communities, who are bearing the brunt of crises, and whose running has been put on hold until they work through some bigger life challenges. We will go over some policy-related and big-scale changes that can be made within our local communities in the next chapter. It also could mean showing support for international groups and organizations that use running as a means to promote change, like Free to Run in Afghanistan, Runners for Public Lands, or Shoe4Africa. While donations are always appreciated, many groups could use extra hands or voices to get their mission out to as many people as possible.

Giving back to the community adds energy to our running journey, making us all more sustainable runners. It removes pressure and expectations by allowing us to see that even though our upcoming race feels important, it is actually pretty minor when we look at the big picture. A study about happiness found that those who were involved in socially engaged pursuits became more satisfied over the course of one year compared to those engaged in nonsocial pursuits (Rohrer et al. 2018).

While all but a few race-day memories fade away, the sentiments we feel when giving back to the sport stay with us a long time. Knowing that we contributed to someone else's life in a meaningful way can create a memory that will last a lifetime.

We have provided an extensive list of ways to give back to the running community. The busyness of life is unlikely to allow us to do all of these things, but we can select some that work with our current situation. While these are all potentially beneficial, check in to see which actions we align with most.

ACTION STEPS

- Offer support to a new runner and be there for them if they have any questions. Not only will they be grateful for a friend in the sport, but it also gives them the permission to become a mentor when they come across a new runner in the future.
- Sign up at unitedinstride.com to become a guide for a visually impaired or blind runner. This can mean running weekly or a few times a year as a running partner or race guide.
- Become a pacer for a race in your area. Be sure to pick a pace group that is very comfortable for you and nowhere near your race pace.
- Run alongside a friend in their goal race (be sure to enter it as a participant). Ideally this should be at a pace that is comfortable for you to run the entire race, but if you are unable to hold their pace the whole time, drop out at an agreed spot.
- Sign up to crew or pace a friend participating in an ultra race.
- Donate money or time to a nonprofit organization that is using running to promote change.

10 | Consider Activism

What comes to mind when you think of a climate activist? Do you have visions of angry protestors? Someone from Extinction Rebellion splashing paint on famous art? A hippie vegan in a Save the Whales T-shirt? Or perhaps Greta Thunberg putting politicians in their place with her infamous "How Dare You?" speech in 2019 at the UN Climate Action Summit. Our culture has not been kind to activists. Many movies, TV shows, and other corners of pop culture paint them as unreasonably emotional and ultimately politically impotent people who "care too much" about silly issues.

Despite what we might see as aggressive, in-your-face acts of forcing change, activism is inherently vulnerable and requires courage. It's stepping up to make a change and critiquing something you care about. Care too much about? Maybe, but it feels better than not caring at all. There is no social media post or public-facing article that attracts more unwanted attacks or criticism than those initiating systemic or societal changes, especially if they challenge our current way of living. Activism is tough and frequently misunderstood, but also a potent and powerful tool for change.

Now, picture someone you admire—someone you think of as brave and courageous. Chances are, they stood for something, even when it wasn't cool or fun or easy. They chose to speak up when no one else would, even if it meant they lost people along the way. Being prepared to accept the consequences of speaking up in a polarized world is not easy. We have all been in the situation in which we disagree with an issue, but we know there will be negative backlash from loved ones, friends, or yes, even social media followers, so we keep quiet and feel silent shame for doing so. It doesn't have to be that way. We have the option to choose bravery every single day in one million small ways—whether it's speaking up for the first time at a city council meeting, volunteering on a political campaign, or having a difficult discussion with a family member.

That said, this does not mean we should use Facebook to rant about what is wrong with our world. Lecturing people, especially by complaining about others, never changes anyone's mind, and it is likely to make people dig in their heels even more. No one, from a 4-year-old to a 100-year-old, likes to be told what to do or what to think. Speaking up is important, but it must begin with curiosity and truly listening to someone else's feelings. Responding to their thoughts in an empathetic and considerate way is a critical piece of finding common ground.

It also means we don't have to speak up about everything. We should select issues that are most important to us—ones that evoke a visceral response in us. If a topic produces a racing heart, a tightness in the chest, or a lump in the throat, then that is the one to get involved in. If nothing else, runners are people of action. We know how to get stuff done, even when it is incremental, one small step at a time.

Acknowledge Challenges

Diving into these issues can leave us feeling vulnerable and exposed, like our running pastime is totally mucked up with historical baggage and a dark future. But approaching these topics with honesty, vulnerability, humility, and a willingness to look inward can ensure everyone has more equitable access to the sport we love. We can all be advocates for environmental justice and action.

"Runners are used to all conditions. Snow, sideways rain, blazing heat—we typically push ourselves to be uncomfortable. And advocating for any type of change can be uncomfortable, especially when there are political or cultural barriers," says Clare Gallagher, a professional runner and environmental advocate. "For me, advocating for voting for politicians who prioritize climate policy can be uncomfortable. I get eye rolls, discouragement, and even experience folks peddling disinformation about climate facts. But the strength I get from running gives me the confidence to be that advocate, even when people scoff at me or say I'm wasting my time. Running has helped make me tough."

When faced with tough feelings like climate doom and grief, taking action is a powerful tool to push back. There are many things we can do to make a difference and alleviate our anxiety. As Katharine Hayhoe, a respected atmospheric scientist and professor, says, *we know what is happening, we know it's bad, we know it's our fault, and we know how to fix it.* "What's important is to develop a campaign that invites people in and respects your opponents," says Dakota Jones, a professional trail runner and founder of Footprints running camp, which supports trail runners pursuing climate action projects in their communities. "We've all seen how heartbreakingly effective it can be to be endlessly cynical and obstructive, but we have to believe there are better ways to communicate and accomplish these big tasks. We have to see the world through our opponents' eyes. The solution is not to demonize them but to show compassion and offer them a better way forward. It's hard and messy and never straightforward. We have to be humble and creative and as optimistic as possible. We have to maintain focus on the end goal and do our best to ignore the pain and frustration of the current battle."

Learn to Speak Up

To quote Katharine Hayhoe's eloquently simple line on climate change: "It's real. It's us. It's serious. But there's hope." There's no real scientific debate around these findings. An overwhelming 97 percent of scientists agree that climate change is caused by human greenhouse gas emissions (Cook et al. 2016). The oil company Exxon knew about climate change's impact as early as the 1970s and led an industry-wide attack on the truth, funding a false debate that prevented public action (Hasemyer and Cushman 2015).

It's important to listen to scientific consensus as well as to indigenous traditional and local knowledge. Around the world, community leaders are sharing observations of how ecosystems are changing. Synthesizing the collective knowledge of frontline communities and scientists tells us one thing: Climate change is real, and it is impacting our world right now. We are seeing the effects everywhere, but the most destructive changes are primarily affecting the global south. While we may not belong to the same country or live in the continent hit the hardest, we are all part of one humanity, one world, where each life deserves a chance to survive (and thrive), regardless of nationality.

If you made it this far in the book, you are probably already environmentally conscious, understand climate change, and believe that it is detrimental to our planet and population. However, not everyone is informed about the issues, and a few folks doubt that climate change is occurring or that it is a bad thing.

People are more likely to listen to a message when it comes from someone they trust or admire. The good news is, for many people, that's *you*. Trail runners are ideal climate communicators not only due to our experience but also because of our social leverage and interest in protecting the environment and people. "Start talking to people you look up to, ask them questions like, 'How do you give back?' It's hard to figure out your path of giving back alone. Take a deep breath and push yourself to engage locally. Talking to people in person is more effective and meaningful to me than connecting digitally," says Gallagher.

Climate change is tied to increased pollution, biodiversity loss, habitat fragmentation, and species extinction. While its toll on the physical world will be acutely felt, humans are already suffering and will continue to do so. It will amplify hunger and poverty, increase resource scarcity that could exacerbate political instability, and even hasten refugee crises. Since 2008, an average of 24 million people have been displaced by catastrophic weather disasters each year, many linked to climate change (IDMC 2022).

Your connection to this issue matters, and it's likely that there's someone out there that only you can get to. Whether through direct conversation or social media, you will be able to tailor a message in a way that feels authentic to you and your story. Ryan Holiday, a New York Times bestselling author, reminds us, "One of the things that I think runners don't get enough credit for is being there. I have spent more time on the rural roads near my house, up close and personal—that is, not in a car—than anyone else in the neighborhood. And I think that includes people who have lived there for decades. You are there—on the streets, seeing the people in your community, seeing the problems, seeing the opportunities, seeing the changes. I think that matters."

According to the Yale Program on Climate Change Communication (YPCCC), 54 percent of Americans think global warming is happening, but only a third of people say they talk with friends and family about it (Ballew et al. 2019). This leads to what the YPCCC calls the "Spiral of Silence," where people concerned about the climate avoid voicing their worry because they don't hear others doing the same, which perpetuates the cycle.

Research indicates that very few people deny climate change is caused by humans at this point, but those who push that message are loud, so it gives the perception that it is everywhere. A 2019 survey by the YouGov-Cambridge Globalism Project looked at 25,325 people from 23 countries and found that 13 percent of Americans agreed climate change is happening but also believed "human activity is not responsible at all." Only five percent said the climate was not changing at all (Milman and Harvey 2019), a much lower percentage than it might seem, especially with all the media coverage of climate denial. Most people we interact with are nervous about the planet's future but are too afraid to bring up those fears. Talking about it is not only a chance to get those fears out of our heads, but also a chance to build a deeper connection with those around us.

> Most people we interact with are nervous about the planet's future but are too afraid to bring up those fears. Talking about it is not only a chance to get those fears out of our heads, but also a chance to build a deeper connection with those around us.

In a fantastic TED Talk (2018), Katharine Hayhoe says that the best thing we can do to disrupt the confusing rhetoric surrounding climate-change discussions is to do the "exact thing we're not doing: Talk about it." The more people learn and hear about it, the more socially acceptable and validated those conversations become.

According to the YPCCC, common reasons for not starting conversations are being worried they don't know enough, not wanting to cause an argument, or thinking that they can't make a difference. Fortunately, we don't need to memorize climate models or have a firm grasp on the finer points of the albedo effect (basically, how much light ice reflects) to be an effective climate-change communicator (Ballew et al. 2019).

Meet people where they are. This is a conversation, not a conquest. People don't like being told they're wrong or being forced into a corner where they hold on even more tightly to their beliefs. The goal is to establish a connection, not conversational domination. Conversations about climate change are sometimes misrepresented as being politically charged and divisive, which doesn't have to be the case. "Lead with curiosity and ask people how their relationship with nature or the environment has changed over the years, and how they think their local community's relationship with nature has changed," says Vic Thasiah, founder of Runners for Public Lands. Find out what they're interested in and what they care about. Maybe they love fishing, and you can ask them if they've seen any changes in their local fish habitats. Maybe they're a runner, like you, and you can connect on that level.

Most importantly, keep it positive. Humans are predisposed to avoid negative emotions, and denial or inaction can be a physiological buffer against existential threat. Instead of focusing on doom and gloom, keep the message positive and focus on the benefits of taking action. Both hope and worry can produce constructive engagement, but staying positive is more important in the context of a productive conversation. "Avoid crisis language," says Thasiah, which "does not put people in an emotional state conducive to discussing the kind of thoughtful, long-term political work climate issues call for."

Tina's Thoughts

For many years, I felt like I wasn't doing enough to draw attention to the climate crisis. Not only did I feel a lot of climate anxiety as I worked through the phases of grief associated, but I felt like I had to do it alone (until I met some friends who were equally passionate about this, like Zoë, of course!). For years, I listened to and learned from climate activists who seemed so extreme, who did things I didn't have the confidence or ability to do. I couldn't commit to never flying again; if I wanted to ever see my family again, I would have to fly across the Atlantic. I noticed that when I began to mention policy with friends, family, and followers, their eyes would glaze over, but they often asked with genuine interest about what steps I took to reduce my own carbon footprint. I didn't talk about those things publicly because climate activists and environmentalists made it clear that individual actions make absolutely no difference. The harsh truth is, they don't. My refusal to use plastic bags does essentially nothing.

In 2022 though, I realized something. While those small changes didn't make the tiniest change to global emissions, by sharing them, it made others begin to think about their choices. It made them start to care about being sustainable and think about what small adjustments they could make, even if it was only putting fewer plastic items into the landfill. Friends would tell me that they stared at a roll of paper towels in the store, eventually putting it back on the shelf to get a reusable version instead. They held a Ziploc bag over the trash can before deciding to reuse it instead of throwing it out. These are tiny changes overall, but big alterations to their mindset. From there, they listened more, read further, and were prepared to make bigger changes. Friends who were race directors made their events cup-free. Friends with corporate jobs spoke up about changes that should be made to company-wide events. People who had historically thrown their electronic waste into the trash now made an effort to take them to a recycling pickup event. Eventually they began to consider the effects of their local politicians and the importance of voting at local elections. It might not make global emissions drop, but they joined the army of people around the world who care about making change happen. For me, that was the best way I could use my strengths to do my part—and drastically reduce my climate anxiety in the process.

A 2015 study surveying 6,000 people across 24 countries found that emphasizing the shared benefits of climate action was the most effective way of motivating others to action (Bain et al. 2016). People are more likely to engage in climate

New York Road Runners

Tina hosting a plogging event in New York City. Plogging (picking up trash while jogging) can be a great way to combine exercise and activism.

action when they believe it will produce social, economic, and scientific benefits. Emphasize that small actions like reducing fossil-fuel use, meat consumption, and food waste can result in meaningful impacts and help make steps toward commonly held goals like job creation and health and safety. Books like *The Future We Choose* by Christiana Figueres and Tom Rivett-Carnac paint a picture of how bright, beautiful, and green our future could be if we make some positive changes now. Reading messages of hope (and passing those along) can be the difference between allowing climate doom to drain the joy out of life and still finding love in our world (while continuing to evoke change).

Share the small steps you're taking, such as how you alter your driving or dietary habits to enact positive change. Emphasize the importance of action, no matter how small. The point is, keep talking—even as part of casual conversation at a friend's cookout, explaining why you became a plant-based eater for environmental reasons, or asking the local coffee shop if you can use a mug instead of a disposable coffee cup. Finding small ways to talk about climate change builds your confidence and brings awareness to the people around you. Then you can watch the beautiful growth as they become mindful in their own lives and begin to take steps too.

> Share the small steps you're taking, such as how you alter your driving or dietary habits to enact positive change. Emphasize the importance of action, no matter how small.

Help Make Running Accessible

Running is often heralded as being very democratic, something that everyone has access to. Anyone with a pair of shoes can get outside and run, right? Well, no.

Racism and the Environment

Environmental racism is the conditions under which, whether by conscious design or institutional negligence, actions and decisions cause disproportionate exposure of communities of color to environmental hazards and health burdens. For example, low-income communities and communities of color are unequally exposed to polluting infrastructure like power plants, landfills, trash incinerators, shipping ports, uranium mines, and factories. Black Americans are 75 percent more likely to live near facilities that produce hazardous waste; the majority of people living within 1.8 miles of a polluting facility are people of color (POC); Black families making $50,000 to $60,000 a year are more likely to live in polluted areas than white people who make less than $10,000 a year, meaning income alone does not account for the discrepancy. Black Americans are exposed to 56 percent more pollution than they generate, Latino populations are exposed to 63 percent more, and white Americans are exposed to 17 percent less (Fleischman and Franklin 2017).

When we hear stats like that, it can be easy to disengage and presume we don't have the ability to make change, but we can. Even sharing those numbers at local planning meetings for recreational spending can shift perspectives enough to reconsider where to spend funds and who *really* needs their recreational facilities updated. What's more important, though, is bringing people together to share their experiences. One mistake often made is speaking on behalf of a community rather than going into the community to ask. Using community connections to connect with leaders in underrepresented and underappreciated parts of town, bringing them into the conversation about the future, doesn't just gather a diverse group of opinions but will also make changes better for everyone.

Even something as seemingly simple as trail, park, and sidewalk access is affected by race and income. There is an unequal distribution of nature and access to the outdoors in America. The stories of Christian Cooper, threatened with violence while bird-watching in Central Park, and of Ahmaud Arbery, murdered while jogging in Georgia, are among the many stories of Black, Brown, and Indigenous people who, while trying to recreate outdoors, have been threatened, killed, or made to feel unsafe or unwelcome.

While we as runners might imagine ourselves as a welcoming and accessible group, according to the most recent Outdoor Industry report, 74.8 percent of outdoor recreators identify as Caucasian (2021). This statistic is not an anomaly or an accident but a predictable outcome of our nation's racist systems and history.

Historically, the United States has systematically segregated and excluded people of color from public lands and other natural places where one might recreate or trail run. From the Civilian Conservation Corps to the National Park Service, the nation's public lands have been bastions of legalized and institutionalized racism. People of color have been excluded from the American conservation movement. For over a century, the movement to protect parks, public lands, and other natural places have been dominated by white people and white perspectives. Framing conservation through this exclusive lens has perpetuated the racial divide in access to nature as well as the right to a healthy environment. For those readers outside of the United States, do some digging into the colonial roots your own country may have been founded upon. While the United States decides whether to face its past head-on or continue with feigned ignorance, the rest of the world also has to acknowledge its own role in perpetual racism.

So, where do we go from here, and what does this have to do with running?

Many of us run to escape. We run to escape the pressures of daily life—work, family, the challenges of living through a pandemic. The political atmosphere can feel increasingly charged and disconnected from reality. So it's understandable that we might take to the roads and trails in an attempt to escape. Tina and Zoë both enjoy going out to the trails to ground themselves in nature and remind themselves of the beauty life has to offer. Inevitably, when we use our running platforms to speak out against racial injustice, police violence, climate inaction or outright denial, there is a uniform response: Leave politics out of running and get back to giving us training advice!

It's an understandable sentiment. The low hum of political divisiveness has become a relentless background drone and, in many ways, has made us afraid to say anything for fear that our entire history and character will be put on display and criticized. But the problem with leaving politics out of running is that running has always been political. Were it not for the political action and organization of athletes years ago, women wouldn't be allowed to run the marathon, Black athletes wouldn't be able to compete at the Olympics, and Title IX wouldn't have made it possible for generations of women to participate in the sports we love.

The phrase "all you need is a pair of shoes" is more common than plantar fasciitis among runners; however, it requires money to buy gear and travel to races. We need resources to pay for childcare so we have time to train. Access to safe sidewalks and outdoor trails is the product of political processes.

Black, Brown, and Indigenous runners still encounter racism and discrimination within the sport today. Any woman who runs can tell you about the background noise of cat-calling—being just a part of life as a woman. Eliza Fletcher was murdered while out running one morning in September of 2022, which rocked the running community. It also highlighted the discrepancy in media coverage of white women and people of color. Indigenous activists struggle to get any mainstream media coverage or attention about missing and murdered Indigenous women whose cases are often left unsolved. In February of 2020, Ahmaud Arbery was shot and killed while out on a run by his Georgia home. Many Black runners don't feel safe doing what many of us take for granted: running around our neighborhood.

> While we may wish to run away from politics, the truth is that many of us cannot. Disengaging is a privilege that runners cannot afford, whether the issue is access to basic safety or a desire for trails unaffected by wildfires and air quality issues. If we drink water and breathe air, we need to be engaged in politics.

While we may wish to run away from politics, the truth is that many of us cannot. Disengaging is a privilege that

Getting Involved in Environmental-Justice Initiatives

Runners are people of action, and we get things done. Experts and activists say there are concrete steps and policy recommendations that will help rectify past and present injustices. "One first step would be talking with Indigenous people in your area about acknowledging their historic and current stewardship of the lands you run," says Vic Thasiah, founder of Runners for Public Lands. A land acknowledgment can be a formal statement or an informal location tag that recognizes and honors the Indigenous peoples while drawing attention to the enduring relationship that exists between Indigenous people and their traditional territories. "Talk with runners in your community about working toward greater equity in accessing safe and clean outdoor spaces," adds Thasiah. Often, environmental-justice initiatives are small and localized and might not explicitly identify as an "environmental-justice" initiative. We can educate ourselves around the various issues that connect to environmental justice—like water quality, sanitation, and indoor health—and then join groups focused on those individual issues within our community.

BIPOC-led environmental organizations and climate-justice initiatives tend to be underfunded compared with bigger-ticket fundraisers like the Sierra Club or Greenpeace. A recent study found that of the roughly $1 billion in annual environmental and climate grantmaking made by 12 top funders, only 1.3 percent goes to BIPOC-led environmental-justice organizations (Baptista and Perovich 2020).

We need to push for policy that funds the creation of new parks and open spaces, like the Great American Outdoors Act or the CORE Act (Colorado Outdoor Recreation and Economy Act). While the conservation movement has traditionally focused on protecting remote wilderness areas, as runners and policymakers, it is important to turn our attention to increasing protections and access to natural areas near urban centers. This is especially true for those with ties to historically nature-deprived groups, communities of color, and low-income communities. We need to be better at urging land managers to redouble their efforts to engage with and attract a more diverse array of visitors through outreach programs, cultural programming, and safe and equal access to all facilities. Signs at parks and trailheads should be multilingual and culturally appropriate.

We can push for improved tribal consultation and expand comanagement opportunities, as well as supporting LANDBACK initiatives that return lands to their original stewards. Indigenous-led conservation has been shown to improve lands' biodiversity and carbon-capturing abilities. In the United States today, skin color and bank account size are a predictor of whether one has safe access to trails and sidewalks, along with all their benefits. When we act at the local and national levels to help correct the racial and economic factors that contribute to unequal recreation access, little changes add up to a big impact, and feelings of climate anxiety and guilt will be reduced.

runners cannot afford, whether the issue is access to basic safety or a desire for trails unaffected by wildfires and air quality issues. If we drink water and breathe air, we need to be engaged in politics. The good news is that "getting political" doesn't have to be a big, scary thing. It doesn't involve tweeting controversial hot takes and yelling at strangers on the Internet. Getting political means assessing the systems and conditions that led us to be able to recreate and run where we do, and the systems and conditions that could be changed and improved to allow more equitable access for others. It means making change on a local level, with others in our community who have similar views. Those small changes add up to bigger ones on the national and even global stage. We are inspired to hear about what one small school with little resources has been able to accomplish or how a determined teenager sitting outside parliament every Friday inspired millions to do the same.

Failure to address the root inequities of unequal trail access upholds racial division, something that trail runners should be interested in dismantling. Dialogue is a good first step in promoting true inclusion. Without acknowledging the disparities that exist in environmental protection and outdoor access, the issue can't be fixed. Maybe we've noticed that trail signs in our area don't include culturally appropriate language and omit prominent languages like Spanish. Maybe we've observed that trail systems are only accessible from sidewalks of more affluent neighborhoods. Maybe our city ignores critical infrastructure like sidewalks, parks, and bike racks in some parts of town. Once we notice it, find a way to bring it up—to someone who can make change, through writing an email or letter to your town hall or through attending a city council meeting about revamping an area that already has all the amenities it needs.

Politics doesn't have to be a dirty word. It doesn't have to include two angry people on a debate stage. Often, politics involves engaged and caring members of a community coming together to identify and solve problems. Zoë's favorite response when people tell her to stay in her lane is that "her lane" is the planet and everyone who runs on it. And that's a pretty wide lane indeed.

Take Action

Individual action is taken by a single person, based on personal decisions. Collective actions are those taken by a group of people based on a group decision. For instance, biking to the trailhead rather than driving is an individual action. Installing a trailhead bike rack and increasing bicycle access to trails are collective actions. Collective actions often function on larger scales.

Thinking collectively through systematic changes isn't how our brains are designed to work. It's easier to imagine that tangible actions like forgoing straws or diligent recycling have an impact, because they feel more relevant to day-to-day life. It's much harder to contextualize the impact of actions like voting or urging fossil-fuel divestment. The consequences of these system-oriented actions are less immediate and visible.

When it comes to climate change, it's not an either-or situation. Individual action and systemic change are both required to move the needle on climate change.

Bestselling author Ryan Holiday puts it to us another way: "You can start very small. There's a great line in Milan Kundera's *The Unbearable Lightness of Being*. He says something like, it's better to rescue a half-dead crow from the road than to send petitions to the government. How many runners pass by the trash on the side of the road? How many of us contribute to it ourselves with plastic water bottles . . . or driving across town for a slightly better trail? The Stoics say you focus on what you control. Of course, collective action at scale matters . . . but so do the little things you're ignoring right now."

"I encourage runners to give back physically, in person. Trail stewardship and maintenance are always needed. I personally find in-person volunteering much more fulfilling, meaningful, and effective than online advocacy," says Clare Gallagher. We can start by assessing our daily practices and becoming more conscious of how our lifestyle and choices affect others. We should all ask ourselves, "What and who am I investing in with my lifestyle?" or "What buying habits, waste habits, and conservation actions are part of my daily life?" These questions can be a starting point for us to assess our current environmental practice and to think more deeply about how our actions have immediate impacts on our environment and communities.

For example, if you have made big steps to minimize the carbon footprint of your eating habits but haven't thought deeply about ways that your financial habits—like where you bank or invest your money—are fueling climate change, that can be an area for improvement. Maybe you ride your bike around town instead of driving, but haven't started a compost bin. Now is a great time. According to Project Drawdown, a multidisciplinary coalition of experts on climate-change solutions, these are the biggest actions an individual can take:

- Eat a plant-based diet
- Live car-free
- Avoid air travel
- Have fewer children

Having one fewer child is the lifestyle choice with the greatest potential to reduce annual personal emissions, saving an average of 58 tons of CO_2 each year. But discussions around that action can have, to put it mildly, racist overtones. And such a goal disproportionately burdens populations without access to health care resources. A better way to frame this might be to provide equal economic, educational, and social opportunities for women everywhere, which is correlated with lower birth rates.

Living car-free saves about 2.5 tons of CO_2 a year per person, while a plant-based diet saves around 0.80 tons. The EPA reports that aircraft contribute 12 percent of U.S. transportation emissions and account for 3 percent of the nation's total greenhouse gas production.

These four lifestyle actions may seem extreme. Even Tina and Zoë, who care deeply about climate change, do not live car-free or refuse to fly. While these are the biggest ways to make change on an individual level, it does not mean we have to go to extremes.

Talking about these things and making reductions and changes wherever possible are the most important steps we can take. We can choose to walk or bike rather than drive, or we can eat plant-based foods on most days. But the reality is, without alternative options or solutions for many of our choices (such as reliable and affordable alternatives to air travel), we are at the mercy of those power players in the space. Even if every person who reads this book fully committed to all four of these actions, it would have the tiniest fraction of a percentage impact on climate change. Once again, it comes back to systemic changes and the major contributing companies who have the power and resources to actually move the needle.

Outside of the realm of individual action, what's next? Succinctly put by Bill McKibben, an environmentalist and one of the 100 most important global thinkers in 2009 according to *Foreign Policy*: "The most important thing you can do is join with your neighbors and organize. The second most important thing you can do is join with your neighbors and organize."

Thasiah says, "Runners can make a positive impact in their respective communities and landscapes by talking with their running friends about how they can better promote the values of environmental protection and sustainable development in their city and region through their running group in collaboration with local environmental organizations and agencies." He adds that "finding that overlap between what needs to be done and what you are good at and/or love doing is ideal."

The most effective actions we can take as individuals are ones that can effect systemic change. If riding a bike to the trailhead inspires others to do the same, then that becomes a more meaningful action. Whatever climate actions we're taking, whether it's plant-based eating or offsetting air travel by supporting environmental nonprofits, share about it and encourage others to do the same in an approachable and engaging way.

"Runners have a strong community, and that can lead to collective action. It doesn't matter so much that we're runners specifically; what's important is that we are a large group of people who are deeply committed to a shared interest," says Dakota Jones. "Because we have this really important thing (to us) in common, we have a major incentive to work together on how to protect this thing. Obviously, climate change is going to screw up way more than just running, but running is the thing that brings us together and can serve as a springboard for action that will protect many other things."

A primary way to engage in collective action is as a citizen. Getting involved—whether it's through voting, volunteering, or organizing locally—has enormous potential for impact. We elect politicians who set policies that serve the public who voted for them. Much of our community's energy and climate policy is set by our state and local representatives and the staff they appoint.

Often, environmental-justice initiatives are small and hyperlocal, and they may not even identify explicitly as "environmental justice." We must educate ourselves about the issues that matter in our communities—whether it's water quality, sanitation, air quality, protection for LGBTQ+ folks, housing access, public transportation, recreation infrastructure, or mineral extraction. We can get connected with a group in the area that's engaged on that issue. If time is really limited, we can offer financial support or amplify their message and work in our spheres of influence.

Jones recommends looking for preexisting groups to join as opposed to starting our own. "There is almost certainly a climate or environmental organization in your region, no matter where you are, and the best thing you can do is reach out to them and offer to volunteer. They will teach you and guide you, and if you're really committed you will soon move to a leadership position. If there is not an organization that works for your goals, or you have a specific problem you wish to address, then find other people who are concerned about this and start taking action. Organize a river cleanup, march to your state senator's office, campaign about zoning laws outside the grocery store—whatever the issue is, doing the action is not enough; you have to organize other people to join you around the action. That's how you amplify the messaging and make individual actions into collective ones. And if there's not an organization already doing what you know needs to be done, then you need to have the courage to stand up and take charge. It's scary and it's hard. It's also the right thing to do, and if you don't, then who will?"

As runners, we should push for policy that funds the creation of new parks and open spaces through legislation. A lot of this happens at the local level, so finding out who these people are is as important as knowing who's in congress. State, county, and even city and local governments are largely responsible for the creation of new open spaces and land management, though this varies by region in the United States.

Participating in local elections, though less flashy than big presidential votes, is consequential for improving access to trails and open spaces at the local level. It's important to pay attention to specific candidate positions rather than mere party affiliation; representatives from both sides of the aisle can help fund, create, and expand trail, sidewalk, and park access.

> It's important to pay attention to specific candidate positions rather than mere party affiliation; representatives from both sides of the aisle can help fund, create, and expand trail, sidewalk, and park access.

Supporting and electing representatives from historically underrepresented groups ensures they have a seat at the table when decisions are being made about their well-being and access to recreation opportunities. To help guide better decision-making, local environmental groups will typically endorse candidates and break down specific issues for more in-depth guidance. The League of Conservation Voters and Protect Our Winters release fantastic, environmentally focused voting guides each election cycle. Ballotpedia also provides nonpartisan breakdowns of local candidates and issues.

"One of the biggest challenges is moving from information overwhelm, to understanding and knowledge, and, finally, to meaningful action. It can be especially frustrating if you're trying to figure things out on your own and then, based on what you learn, when you don't feel like you have agency or efficacy," says Thasiah. "The best advice, I think, is this: Find a solid, reputable environmental organization that summarizes what you need to know and provides you with pathways of action. Then, with your activism, keep your sense of humor, fight for what you desire, and make as many friends as you can along the way. Celebrate every win; learn from every loss."

We know we can push through discomfort. We know we get things done. It is time we directed some of that energy, motivation, and heart toward making our running community a better place for all of us.

While many of these suggestions may seem too intimidating or too intense for right now, start where you are and build up. Tina always thought a climate protest was too confrontational, but, over time, her confidence grew and her determination to take meaningful action strengthened. When an opportunity arose, she suddenly found herself in downtown St. Louis waving a sign and shouting climate information as loud as she could. Even if the public-facing actions seem too far out of your comfort zone now, practice with friends, family, and your local neighborhood. Most organized groups begin as friends coming together to speak up about something that matters to them; change can happen for you too.

ACTION STEPS

- Look at the people you admire and channel their courage to speak up about a topic that matters to you. If you are struggling to figure out what that is, pay attention to what issue viscerally affects your body and that is the topic you care about most.

- On your runs, look around. What do you see? What changes need to be made in your area to make outdoor recreation better for everyone?

- Consider the prominent elements of environmental racism where you live. How can you draw people in from affected communities to involve them in decisions being made?

- Talk to Indigenous leaders in your community about acknowledging their historic and current stewardship of the lands you run on.

- Push for policy funds to be used toward the creation of new parks rather than improving parks that are already in good condition.

- Donate to BIPOC-led organizations over better-funded, more established environmental groups.

- Urge land managers to engage and attract a more diverse array of visitors.

- Push for improved tribal consultation and expand comanagement opportunities as well as supporting LANDBACK initiatives that return lands to their original stewards.

- Consider how you can positively contribute to the community beyond your neighborhood, especially if you live in an affluent neighborhood.

- Find the overlap between what you are good at and what you love to do—that is where your energy should be directed.

- Volunteer with environmental groups in your area.

- Join a preexisting climate group instead of creating something new.

PART III | SUSTAIN YOUR PLANET

11 | Encourage Sustainable Events

There is enough to think about (or should we say obsess about?) on race day without adding climate concerns or the sustainability rating we would give our local event. We already have too much going on in our brains. In those final few hours before a race, time slows down. The mind is overrun with potential disaster situations that could derail our race. We know there is nothing we can do to control most outside factors (no matter how many times we check the weather!), but as adrenaline rushes through our body and our senses are on high alert, our brain is on the lookout for danger. Remote problems like the effects of climate change feel distant and unimportant in that moment.

An issue like climate change is big and complicated; therefore, the solutions are going to be big and complicated too. That said, there are several things that we can do to make a big impact. This chapter will break down how race directors can make changes, how brands can be more proactive, and how everything can fall into place once we, the participants, take the first step to speak up. We don't have to use precious race-day energy on sustainability, but we will explain how race day is one of the best ways the running industry can pivot to make positive change. Let's get to it.

Behave Responsibly

When it comes to our climate impact on race day, behaving responsibly generally means planning ahead as best we can up to race day, and then it falls to the race directors. We don't need to live like Greta Thunberg or carry our own stainless steel, reusable water bottle with us in a road race to make a difference—although we should be sure to dispose of our products responsibly.

Fernanda Maciel, women's winner of the 2009 TDS Ultra-Trail du Mont-Blanc, powerfully brought this point home in a bonus episode of the *Running Realized* podcast, which was a collaboration with the United Nations Office for the Coordination of Humanitarian Affairs (OCHA). She saw the impact of visitors when she completed one of her White Flow projects in Aconquija National Park. Fernanda's White Flow projects are iconic runs in some of the most beautiful and dangerous locations around the world, undertaken with the goal of promoting environmental and social issues. "You have so many visitors on this mountain that the exhibition companies in Aconquija remove 22,000 kg (48,000 lb) of rubbish from the base camp per season, which comprises just three months of the year," says Maciel. "There is a crazy amount of rubbish that visitors generate and leave on the mountain. It would be simple enough for visitors to bring a strong bag, and then carry their rubbish down to the entrance of the park. But, no, the visitors come and get tired from altitude sickness, and they cannot bring it down. Then I ask you: Why do you climb; why do you go for the mountains if you are not able to bring a bag, if you are not able to leave no trace? The first rule that I learned on the mountain was to leave no trace."

Courtesy of T.J. David.

Wherever our runs take us, as much as possible, we want to try to take our waste back with us to dispose of responsibly at home.

This leads to thinking about our own waste accumulation. The packaging that remains from our fueling may seem insignificant when we look at our overall consumption, but when it is combined with others' waste, the volume is staggering. Road and track running amasses a far greater amount of accumulated waste than trail events. If the average runner consumes four to six fueling items over 26.2 miles, the streets of New York City could be littered with 300,000 fueling packets on the day of their annual marathon! Road running and track events do, however, have event management teams in place to process the waste, with volunteers and staff ensuring that the removal process is as effective as possible.

> Even though running events account for the tiniest fraction of a percentage of the environmental problems we're facing, targeting them for change is a good use of time and energy because they represent a collective way of thinking that must rapidly shift.

Trail runners carry most of what they need with them, and it is easier to keep waste packaging in packs to be disposed of responsibly after the race. Packing our fuel and taking it back home gives us the opportunity to decide where it ends up. TerraCycle, whose mission is eliminating the idea of waste, allows businesses, governments, and individuals to redirect their trash out of landfills and incinerators, and they will recycle nutrition packets. TerraCycle has a partnership with GU Energy Labs, and together they recycle all brands of performance nutrition packaging. All consumers need to do is to create an account, collect the packages, print out a prepaid label, and ship the packets to them to be recycled. There are also TerraCycle drop-off points all over the world, making it even easier to recycle your nutrition packages.

Even though running events account for the tiniest fraction of a percentage of the environmental problems we're facing, targeting them for change is a good use of time and energy because they represent a collective way of thinking that must rapidly shift. The Council for Responsible Sport is doing a lot of the work for race directors by providing a certification program that offers a framework to help assess and certify their events' environmental impacts. This includes planning and communications, procurement, resource management, access, equity, and community legacy. According to the Council for Responsible Sport, their vision is "a world where responsibly produced sports events are the norm and its mission is to provide objective, independent verification of the socially and environmentally responsible work event organizers are doing to make a difference in their communities. A responsible event is one that undertakes a holistic assessment of the ways the event affects people, generates economic activity, and uses raw materials and energy that affect local ecosystems and Earth's broader ecology" (Villalobos 2020).

A lot of sustainable changes will require individual runners to speak up and ask for them, but the Council for Responsible Sport is making it easier for race management organizations to make some of them on their own. While the most important factor will always be eliminating impact wherever possible, alternate options and solutions are ready for most of the biggest climate-contributing human activities; we just have to make it clear that we want them.

Understand Carbon Impact

Before we discuss carbon offsets and how runners can make a difference, it is important to provide some background. In 2015, at the UN Climate Change Conference (COP21) in Paris, world leaders came to a historic agreement that they would, according to the United Nations, "substantially reduce global greenhouse gas emissions to limit the global temperature increase in this century to 2 degrees Celsius while pursuing efforts to limit the increase even further to 1.5 degrees." According to the information about the Paris Agreement on the website of the United Nations (2022), all 193 countries that belong to the United Nations joined the Paris agreement on that day. It is important to mention that 1.5 degrees Celsius of warming is considered the maximum global rise in temperature conservatively estimated to avoid the worst of the catastrophic effects of climate change. Net zero means the emissions being taken out of the atmosphere balance the amount of carbon emissions we are contributing to the atmosphere.

Dr. Hoesung Lee, chair of the Intergovernmental Panel on Climate Change, and Dr. Fatih Birol, executive director of the International Energy Agency, stated that "analysis by the Intergovernmental Panel on Climate Change (IPCC) clearly shows us that global emissions need to be reduced to net zero within the next few decades to avoid a dangerous increase in global temperatures." But there is good news: "We already have affordable, reliable technologies that can put the peak in global emissions behind us and start the drive down to net zero. The spectacular rise of renewable technologies like solar panels and wind turbines in recent years has shown us what is possible. Deployed quickly and on a major scale, the clean energy technologies we have at our disposal right now can bring about the kind of decline in energy-related emissions that would put the world on track for our longer-term climate goals" (Lee and Birol 2020).

Rapid decarbonization is the most important tactic to reach net-zero emissions, but this is where carbon offsets can play a part in positive change while systemic changes are being implemented. ClimateCare, a certified B corporation that helps brands, NGOs, and governments continue their journey to net zero, defines carbon offsetting as "an internationally recognised way to take responsibility for unavoidable carbon emissions." *Unavoidable* is the key word here. According to ClimateCare, "to offset your emissions you must purchase the equivalent volume of carbon credits (independently verified emissions reductions) to compensate for them. The payments you make to purchase these carbon credits (carbon finance) is what makes the emissions reductions projects which created them financially viable and sustainable" (Climate Impact Partners, n.d.).

Carbon offsetting means businesses or individuals calculate how much carbon they have put out into the atmosphere for an activity, event, or their collective contribution on a yearly basis (as a household or business). Companies like ClimateCare and Cool Effect partner with environmental and conservation projects around the world. Using a carbon offset means balancing the number of emissions you put in with the carbon you are preventing from entering the atmosphere or removing from the atmosphere through the money you are investing into climate-related projects. Races like the Chicago Marathon partner with offsetting nonprofits like Cool Effect so they can provide runners with the opportunity to offset the average emissions created for a runner entering the race. For the 2022 Chicago Marathon, that was $14.62 per runner, and participants could do so from their participant account or at the expo (Bank of America Chicago Marathon, n.d.).

It is one thing for individuals to reduce their own global emissions, but the rest of the running industry has a responsibility to do their part too.

Offsetting travel emissions via ClimateCare, Cool Effect, Native, Sustainable Travel International, or one of the other carbon offset companies (we share multiple options at the end of this chapter) helps in a few ways. It also provides the opportunity to offset carbon emissions for other areas of life and add up our total carbon footprint. When we see the amount of carbon we are responsible for putting into the atmosphere, it can be a shock but will make it easier to flex your pro-environmental muscle and provide the motivation required to make the uncomfortable outreach to brands to ask them when they will implement more sustainable practices.

While offsetting carbon from our races should be the norm and using carbon calculators is important, carbon offsets are being misused by corporations. Many of the biggest offenders, corporations in the 100 companies responsible for 71 percent of global emissions, can use the relatively low cost to offset their carbon emissions and carry on with harmful and dangerous business practices as usual while claiming they are carbon neutral—conveniently ignoring the word *unavoidable* in the definition of carbon offsetting: "an internationally recognised way to take responsibility for unavoidable carbon emissions." This allows major corporations to take themselves off the hook without actually making any of the changes needed to make an impact. Likewise, as individuals, we cannot rely solely on carbon offsets to negate a reckless and self-serving approach to our lives either.

Push for Group Effort

It is one thing for individuals to reduce their own global emissions, but the rest of the running industry has a responsibility to do their part too. Running events occur in hundreds of cities around the world every weekend. While this is a drop in the bucket compared to the global carbon emissions, the impact of races is not to be underestimated, especially as systemic changes occur when individuals come together to speak up about an important issue. Runners are often leaders in the outdoor and fitness space and beyond. If we nudge running events to find ways to reduce their impact, other events will follow.

It is unlikely that you are a race director, but if you are, great! There is plenty to utilize in this chapter. But for anyone else, we still have a role. When we ask race directors what they are doing to be more sustainable and request changes without judgment, it matters. Race directors want to provide the best experience for their runners, and if they know it's important to us, change can happen quickly. If the Chicago Marathon can become sustainable, smaller races can shift toward that too. The following ideas provide many potential ways we can help races make change, so determine which ones jump out at you and start asking!

Use Carbon Calculators

Adding a carbon footprint calculator into the registration process to allow runners to offset their travel-related emissions is a simple starting point. While offsetting carbon is relatively inexpensive, it may increase as other systemic changes become more cost effective. Carbon offsets are one way that individuals can get us closer to net-zero emissions, but, as always, rapid decarbonization through reducing our reliance on fossil fuels is the priority.

According to the Global Footprint Network, a research organization that is changing how the world manages its natural resources and responds to climate change, "the carbon footprint is currently 60 percent of humanity's overall ecological footprint and its most rapidly growing component. Humanity's carbon footprint has increased 11-fold since 1961. Reducing humanity's carbon footprint is the most essential step we can take to end overshoot and live within the means of our planet" (Global Footprint Network, n.d.).

It is hard to deny the impact humans have had on our planet's biodiversity. We see it on our runs, as nature, once left untouched, is cleared to make room for more humans living in bigger and bigger houses. *National Geographic* confirms these observations: "About 2,000 years ago, 80 percent of Western Europe was forested; today the figure is 34 percent. In North America, about half of the forests in the eastern part of the continent were cut down from the 1600s to the 1870s for timber and agriculture. China has lost great expanses of its forests over the past 4,000 years and now just over 20 percent of it is forested" (2019). But it is not just deforestation and house building; in addition to harming our planet in a multitude of ways that are currently detrimental, we are putting feedback loops into place that will drastically accelerate the harm and destruction.

> Just because we like medals, shirts, or single-use bottles after a race does not mean that we should keep taking them, race after race, year after year.

While regenerative agriculture, retrofitting buildings, and implementing renewables into our energy sector does not fall to race directors to figure out, they can work to eliminate or minimize demand for wasteful products in our sector.

Reduce Consumption

The simplest way to start is by eliminating the unnecessary. Just because we like medals, shirts, or single-use bottles after a race does not mean that we should keep taking them, race after race, year after year. Now is the time to examine what we are consuming before, during, and after a race and consider how it could be done differently. Race directors can work on assessing each element of putting on a race to ask, "Is this integral to the success of the event? Does this item generate waste? Is there a more sustainable option?"

Big, corporate race event companies have bulldozed their way into the space with huge budgets and irresistible swag to entice runners to their events over the small, locally owned races. Rather than trying to compete with those races by matching them in material goods (which is impossible for small, locally run businesses), is there another way that races in your area can add some special touches to stand out and make your events unique to your location? If you have ideas for your race directors, let them know! We know this is easier said than done. The event market is extremely competitive, and it can feel like the only way to entice runners is by offering more and more swag. Many race directors know that the textile and apparel industry is a big contributor to carbon emissions and water pollution but feel at a loss as to what to do instead. An estimated 2.5 billion tons of greenhouse gases are emitted annually, which is the direct result of the production and sale of the textile and apparel industry. Textile and apparel emissions amount to 2.465 billion tons of CO_2e per year, and the percentage of global emissions from this sector is currently at 7.25 percent but is expected to be 9.5 percent by 2030 (cKinetics 2021).

Sandy Gutierrez

Making clothing choices that consider the impact of materials and make durability a priority is one big way to reduce our consumption.

Learn About Precycling

As races work to reduce their carbon emissions, precycling needs to be an important step to make it easier on race-day staff and volunteers, runners, and, of course, our home. Republic Services, a waste and recycling service, says, "Precycling is about reducing your impact on what goes into the waste stream by purchasing and using items that are unpackaged, reusable or recycled. It has also been referred to as a low-waste lifestyle" (Republic Services 2020). This means as individuals we should bring our own fueling and conveniences to races and say, "No thank you, I don't need it," to the swag and single-use products. Brands, organizations, and businesses need to hear it. Race directors need to set aside time before race day to create a recycling plan for bulk materials and packaging. As race day closes in, there is a lot going on for event organizers. Placing someone in charge of sustainability (and volunteers if needed) will mean that initiatives and work invested don't get lost in the stress of prerace chaos. If you are able, volunteering for this role could be a huge help to your local race director.

Making Smaller Races More Attractive

While most races began as a place for competitive runners to chase down a big goal they had been working toward for months or even years, the landscape has changed. As running events become more inclusive (which is a good thing!), more races have appeared on the scene to appeal to various subsets of the general running population, who are there for reasons beyond personal bests. While there are now more organizations to compete against, there are also more runners to appeal to.

Getting a head start on sustainability can be a way for a race to stand out among the other races scrambling to figure out how to reduce their impact, particularly if there is a way to give back to the communities the race course travels through. The Around the Crown 10K in Charlotte is one such example; the race has defined itself through its commitment to sustainability and addressing environmental racism. Events that heed this advice may suddenly find that they are very appealing to runners, including those from communities who had previously felt ignored by these running companies. Bigger organizations struggle to change strategy quickly and are at a disadvantage. Research has found that 71 percent of millennials, 67 percent of Generation Z, and 63 percent of Generation X said that climate should be a top priority to ensure a sustainable planet for future generations (Tyson, Kennedy, and Funk 2021).

While large brands, businesses, and organizations have additional resources and funding, being smaller means being more nimble and able to change course without waiting for approval from 180 different people. That said, if the Chicago Marathon has been able to take steps to make their events more sustainable, there is a blueprint for smaller races to use through the Sustainability Guidebook that Chicago Event Management (CEM) created to help other events prioritize environmental impact (2021).

Additionally, for race directors who love hosting competitive races, at the elite level there has been a shift away from big corporate multi-events, toward the simplicity of racing fast for the sake of racing fast. There are opportunities to create those races for competitive runners, regardless of level, just as there are opportunities to create social experiences that are not about time at all. Focusing on a narrow niche through connection with a dedicated and passionate group, rather than trying to appeal to everyone, might be the way forward.

Having multiple recycling bins clearly marked in easy-to-reach places for runners and volunteers on race day is a must. If food is available (runners love bananas!), having a place to compost leftover food waste can have a bigger impact than we might think. In 2021, the Environmental Protection Agency (EPA) reported that 35 percent of the U.S. food supply is wasted every year, enough calories to feed more than 150 million people annually. The report also noted that "globally, food loss and waste represent 8 percent of anthropogenic greenhouse gas emissions," a number that can be reduced with composting (Jaglo, Kenny, and Stephenson

2021). Composting can turn race-day food waste into soil that helps grow plants and flowers in our towns and cities. Connecting with a company that collects food surplus before race day can provide a meaningful way for races to support the local community. Working with Food Rescue US, UKHarvest food rescue, and other similar charities ensures leftover bananas and other food items are transported to social service agencies serving the food insecure. This reduces food waste, a key contributor to global emissions. And donating surplus is an important and appreciated step to take.

For race events, diverting as much waste material away from landfills as possible is a priority. Chicago Event Management (CEM) has ensured that all their events, including the Chicago Marathon, use cups made from bamboo that break down in commercial compost. They separate their plastic water bottles to be upcycled into apparel like the T-shirts that they give out, which are made from 100-percent postconsumer recycled materials. In addition to reducing waste, using recycled polyester reduces carbon emissions by up to 30 percent compared to virgin (new) polyester. CEM also participates in the Blankets to Boards program through Heatsheets. The recyclable, lightweight blankets are given out at the finish, and after runners hand them in to designated zero-waste stations, they are combined with sawdust and turned into park benches that are eventually donated to neighborhoods along the marathon route.

While we understand the allure and sentimental value that swag items can provide to participants, offering the option of opting out for a lower registration fee or donating to a nonprofit is a must moving forward. Reaching out to the local race director to ask for this option can result in change. Suggesting that race directors consider Trees Not Tees is a way to take this one step further. Trees Not Tees is a fantastic company that plants a tree for every registrant who opts out of a T-shirt at associated races. This is an easy win for race directors, participants, and our planet alike. Adding an opt-out for participants during race registration can mean trees planted in the parks and neighborhoods your race traverses through.

As we move into the next era of racing, we need to consider how to safely reuse, upcycle, or dispose of our race bibs. The overwhelming majority of race bibs are immediately thrown in the trash after use (likely along with their pins). Most bibs are made of Tyvek, a plastic known for its durability and resistance to breakdown—great for sweaty runners during races but not so great for the environment or the landfill it lives in for hundreds of years. Tyvek is not currently widely recycled, but there have been pushes to change this. When it comes to pins, remembering to bring your own pins is another simple step to reduce your consumption. Apparel brand Tracksmith came up with a smart way to encourage runners to reuse pins by providing four gold pins with every Van Cortlandt racing singlet sold and a dedicated patch in one corner for the pins to reside between races.

Elitefeats has changed the game of race timing, scoring, online registration, and event marketing by mailing race bibs directly to participants (with the bib as the envelope itself). By doing this, they reduce the footprint associated with participants driving to pick up their bib and a significant amount of paper for the race directors to have printed for volunteers. Going paperless, especially in 2023 and beyond, is a realistic expectation.

Advancing beyond these early steps could mean providing virtual goodie bags instead of physical ones, or at least offering useful reusable items or swag from previous years over brand-new single-use options. Most of the items provided in plastic bags from race finish lines are thrown away or lost. Instead, provide virtual coupons, discount codes, and other runner-related freebies for later use.

When it comes to planning ahead, it can be very difficult for race organizers to predict exactly how many of each item to order, but considering how unneeded items will be disposed of is a necessary step. It is important for race directors to think about postevent waste before the exhaustion of event weekend hits. By considering it early, it is easier to seek out sustainable options while the enthusiasm is there to make thoughtful considerations.

More Portable Toilets, Please!

Yes, we're talking about the uncomfortable topic of human waste. One of the absolute worst parts of race day is having to stand in line for 20 minutes to use a portable toilet right before a race begins. As the start time gets closer, runners often seek alternative places to go, which is not ideal for the local surroundings. Adding more portable toilets to aid stations or anywhere people congregate not only eliminates the health risk to other humans (when runners find alternate places to relieve themselves) but also helps to support our ecosystem. Portable toilet use on race day reduces the use of municipal water, with the average toilet flush using up to 1.6 gallons of water. One-hundred-percent postconsumer waste toilet paper can also reduce the environmental impact of the event. Ensuring there are enough accessible portable toilets to support athletes with disabilities is also important, as well as providing gender-neutral toilets and changing facilities.

Ensure Access and Equity

Beyond the environmental viewpoint on sustainability, for races to survive and thrive in the years to come, they need to be welcoming to everyone who runs or is running-curious. There are runners who do not feel that the current racing scene is a safe space for them—and for good reason. While the running community is seen by some as welcoming, we have work to do. Bringing in runners from all backgrounds and experiences, rather than appealing to a small subset of the population, not only helps race organizers broaden their world view but will also create better events. Races where runners feel comfortable to be themselves means runners who come back year after year, bringing more friends each time.

Chris Mosier, activist and founder of the website TransAthlete, believes in the power of inclusivity to change the world, and he advocates for equity for all groups, especially trans people: "Running is universal. It doesn't matter your age, race, gender identity, hometown, or faith—we can bring communities together through running. People come to running to be a part of a group of like-minded folks—after all, they could do it alone, but they are choosing to sign up for your event. We must create training and racing environments that openly welcome and embrace runners from all backgrounds, identities, and abilities. Many people turn to running to escape, if only for a short time, the rest of their lives. Every person should have access to running."

How does a race director know if their event is considered welcoming? According to Mosier, "Race directors and training group leaders can know if they are doing a good job by looking around first: Does everyone at your event look the same? What does your leadership team look like? While we can't know each part of every person's identity, we can make efforts to openly include all runners, both in running our races and in the teams that put those races on."

Once again, while we are not all race directors, one of the best things that we can do is encourage race directors to make changes by showing them we are prepared to take time out of our day to speak up on behalf of those who are not represented.

Think about previous racing events you have been to, or look around at your next local race. Who isn't showing up? We need to be able to identify who might constitute an underrepresented and underserved population in our community before we can begin the work to include them. This means considering what barriers might be preventing them from participating. It could be language, the absence of categories that speak to runners' gender identity or disability, lack of equipment or gear, the expense of registration fees, lack of transportation or public transportation to get to the race, and, last but not least, safety and feelings of acceptance. It is difficult to determine which factors are preventing inclusion, especially if many come into play, but adding a Runner Requests section on event registration pages may offer more insight. Including diverse images in promotional materials makes runners feel that their feedback will be welcomed, but this is not just a box to check that will make runners feel welcome on its own. As visually impaired and blind runners rely on guides to support them during races, free entry for guides and ease of sign-up are small but important steps to making the community feel that their participation matters.

Consider the Community Impact

For most of us, races do not pass through our neighborhoods or affect any part of our day beyond road closures and a little extra traffic. The impact of running events on the local communities races do traverse through is rarely given any thought. Considering the race from the viewpoint of area residents can give a whole new perspective on an event that we previously considered to be great for everyone. Even better, listening to someone who lives in the area helps to paint a picture of how that race event affects them, for better or worse. Once we know of their frustrations, we can advocate for them. Tourism encourages growth and helps acquire wealth, but it can hurt residents and, by extension, the environment.

People around Aspen, Colorado, know this all too well. As housing becomes less affordable in Aspen, workers are pushed further down the valley. Over 80 percent of Aspen's workforce has a 30-minute commute to town, which, despite public transit, is a huge environmental issue. In many Colorado towns, housing and urban planning is one of the top three environmental arenas for action. Being aware of local issues, and patronizing businesses that support sustainable community development, is a more meaningful and potent action than carrying our own straws and utensils.

Connecting with race directors on behalf of our communities through email, social media, or letter writing can help them consider overlooked aspects of their event. For those who have connections to sponsors—either local, corporate, or somewhere in between—we can build relationships on behalf of community groups for causes that directly support them.

How to Approach a Race Director

As participants with dollars to spend, we can inform race directors about what is important to us before we sign up for their events. Reaching out to a race or event director may be intimidating, but through email we can easily contact race organizers without having to psych ourselves up to speak to them directly. If you do have the opportunity to speak to a race director in person during a relaxed moment (do not bring these topics up 30 minutes prior to a race!), that is most effective and means tone does not get lost in communication. Race directors are doing their best, and bringing events together in a cost-effective manner is no easy feat. It is important to go into any conversation with their humanity at the forefront. Even if they initially react with irritation, our feedback matters. We all have experienced the feeling that nothing we do is ever good enough, and with so many individual opinions being voiced, race directors can feel this too. Be supportive but firm. All runners deserve the opportunity to enjoy races, and our planet deserves to be treated with respect.

A lot of the changes suggested in this chapter are for race organizers, race directors, and running brands, but they need to know what is a priority for their participants, customers, and community. Unless we let them know that sustainability, inclusion, and community are important, how can they know? While sending an email or reaching out directly may be the item on your to-do list that gets buried (we know that well!), taking the time to do so feels good—much better than checking off any other item on your to-do list. You are helping to be the change you wish to see. Even if nothing changes for a while, you have planted a seed—a seed that could change the lives of future runners for years to come.

ACTION STEPS

For this chapter, we have split this section up into what individual runners can do and what race directors can do. If you are an individual runner, choose which areas you feel are most realistic for your local races to change, then combine that with what you are passionate about.

Individual Runners

- Bring fuel to races whenever possible and, if the race allows, bring a reusable silicone cup to limit the use of paper (or bamboo) cups.
- Whenever possible, take your gel packets, nutrition, and snack packages home with you to add to a TerraCycle collection box. Create a TerraCycle account to mail your used packages to be recycled, or find a drop-off point near you on the TerraCycle website.
- Offset your carbon emissions from travel to races.
- At the finish line, only take food items or products that you need. Just because it is there, that doesn't mean you need to take it. Demand this year affects supply next year.
- Connect with people in communities affected by races; ask what they wish they could change. Inform race directors of those impacts, and offer to support in making changes.
- Reach out to local race directors and offer suggestions for making a race more inclusive to all runners.

Race Directors

- Read through "The Practical Guide to Hosting Radically Responsible Events" from the Council for Responsible Sport and implement elements that are realistic.
- Build an offset calculator and feedback box into registration.
- Consider the planning, execution, and reflection of the race in its entirety by considering what changes can be made to reduce waste.
- Reconsider the sourcing and delivery of medals, awards, T-shirts, and single-use items. Is there a more meaningful way to celebrate runners? Could these be optional items or created in a more sustainable way?
- Start precycling: Consider what bulk items will need to be recycled, organize a food donation service for leftover food, and plan composting options for food waste.
- Ensure there are enough portable toilets for the runners.
- Think about what can be done to ensure the race is welcoming to every runner.
- Consider how the race affects the hosting community. Is there a way to show appreciation for using their land or give back resources?

12 | Be an Eco-Conscious Traveler

Even the most eco-conscious among us have some guilt around travel. Whether it is personal, business, or for racing, travel has the potential to exponentially increase our annual emissions. Many runners avoid contact with environmentalists for fear they will judge them for flying and make them promise to never fly to a race again. Not these environmentalists. That isn't what we are here to do.

Yes, reducing our carbon footprint will always involve a discussion about limiting our travel, especially on planes, but it does not mean never traveling to a race again or only signing up for races within 50 miles of your home. One thing most of us can agree on is that living "sustainably" is not as simple as it sounds. Traveling can be stressful at the best of times. We leave our comfort zone to immerse ourselves in a place where everything is new. As runners, we like to control as many aspects of our lives as possible, which can make staying in a new city stressful. Adding the stress of making environmentally conscious choices when there aren't any available can make us feel like terrible human beings, even though it is not our fault.

The most powerful companies in the world employ master manipulators who make us doubt every decision we make in our lives. They work hard to convince us that they are doing their part to save the planet by throwing around impressive eco-friendly words, finding shortcuts to claim they are carbon neutral, and making big promises on their tree-covered webpage pledges—all of which is *greenwashing*, which we'll talk about more in the next chapter. Despite this, they do very little to reduce their contribution to the climate crisis. This sends the message that if we as a human race fail to avoid the catastrophic devastation of climate change, it is our fault. They portray the message that large organizations have already done their part.

There is an approach to sustainability that doesn't leave us feeling like our efforts are hopeless. This method helps us assess our life choices, progressing toward a sustainable way of living without leaving us overwhelmed. It is a practice that allows us to train without giving up everything we know and love about exploring the world through our sport. It is time to start developing our pro-environmental lens.

Develop a Pro-Environmental Lens

In Tina's podcast with Knox Robinson, *Running Realized*, episode 7 of season 1 is entitled "The Sustainable Road Race." It focuses on the environmental impact of races and how we can do better. We only have to look at the ground around a water station at one of the major marathons, pay attention to the mountain of trash bags left behind after a race, or think about the number of flights that were taken by tens of thousands of participants to realize that while runners are infrastructure-light compared to some sports, we definitely have an impact.

Shelley Villalobos, former executive director for the Council for Responsible Sport, gave a powerful testimonial about runners and their impact within that episode of *Running Realized*. She shared the importance of runners building a pro-environmental lens, defined as "a pair of glasses, metaphorical, that help us get beyond unconscious consumption and into relationship with our own impact in the world and what we want it to be" (2021).

Within this chapter, our intention is not to persuade you to scratch your dream-goal race off your lifetime bucket list but to help you develop a pro-environmental lens. This allows us to make thoughtful decisions about which elements of our life are most important. Considering the impact that our fun weekend has on others, and using the power of our voice and dollars, we can make change happen. While this can feel too big or too unwieldy as individuals, we can drive change if we are brave enough to speak up.

Villalobos knows the internal discomfort and shame associated with becoming more environmentally conscious. There are plenty of books documenting the stages of climate change behaviors and how they affect our mental health as we progress through them. Dr. Margaret Klein Salamon's book, *Facing the Climate Emergency: How to Transform Yourself With Climate Truth*, can assist in embracing the emotions associated with accepting that climate change is here, right now. Emotions like fear, anger, grief, and guilt can be used to drive action and make change.

Villalobos recognizes that the best way to create change within our own lives is to continually and gradually modify our behaviors. Runners go through an evolution as we train and become better versions of ourselves. As our health and fitness improves, we start to look at the world with a different viewpoint. We pay attention to the health of others and the health of our planet. Villalobos has found that those who live an active lifestyle tend to have a positive attitude toward reducing the impacts of climate change and developing their pro-environmental lens. Once we are aware of this journey of growth and acknowledge the impact we have as individuals as well as collectively, we will take action. Doing so helps us process the guilt and shame we have for actions we have little opportunity to change. Villalobos says, "We can realize instead that every single action in our life has varying levels of impact. Being alive means you have an impact, but we have this really cool ability to choose and be creative and to shape the future. We can start to incorporate that into our decision-making as we go, in an ongoing way as a practice. If we do that, we won't be able to help but to demand and create a more ecologically oriented society." She also believes we are already moving in the right direction. We have work to do, and there is no finish line to this race, but change at the individual level is happening, and those in power are starting to notice. Once it gains enough momentum, changes will come fast and that is where we can come together collectively to figure out this climate challenge.

Often, we are left feeling hopeless, burdened by our own inadequacy when we think we are not doing enough. Or we believe that nothing we do will ever be enough to change the course of our future, with billions of people around the globe unable to agree on the smallest detail, let alone a course-correct for our world. Rather than pushing those feelings away, we can make a conscious decision to step up—maybe not literally, through protesting at the steps of our government buildings (although if you want to attend a climate rally, that goes a long way too!), but through a conscious effort to continually develop our pro-environmental lens. As Villalobos puts it, "Imagine if we put the same amount of thought and effort into climate-change solutions as we do into our training." If we can channel some of the energy from the gritty, determined, committed source of our training drive toward environmental action, not only would we be helping our beloved planet begin to heal, but we would also make our running adventures even more enjoyable. While we do not know if we have passed the point of no return, resilience is a key trait we need as runners and human beings as we navigate the effects of climate change.

> If we can channel some of the energy from the gritty, determined, committed source of our training drive toward environmental action, not only would we be helping our beloved planet begin to heal, but we would also make our running adventures even more enjoyable.

Explore Close to Home

While we aren't asking you to only participate in running events close to home, the reality is, most of us do not make the most of what we have. We tend to get stuck on our familiar routes, parks, and places, even if other exciting opportunities are just beyond those loops we know so well. Signing up for races in our area is one way to check out some of the best running environments, especially in trail running. Race directors put a lot of time and energy into their races; they want to make them the best experience they can for runners, which means they scope out the best spots to have runners traverse through. After all, races are heavily reliant on word of mouth to grow, and when runners share their race photos on social media or positive experience with others, it helps attract runners in the coming years.

It can be motivating and fun to work through a lifetime bucket list of races all over the country (or world), but it can also be rewarding to run every race in our area. It is also easier to be successful when we race locally, because it does not require a big financial investment, time off work, or days spent away from family. It can be enjoyable to experience every distance, variation, and level of silliness that we feel a desire to try. That could mean completing as many local races as possible within a year (if we can afford the associated expenses) or using local races to fill in the gaps between occasional big trips. It is important to include the bigger races that our city or town hosts, even if they may not seem as glamorous as some of the races we have done elsewhere. For most of us, local races will not involve 50,000 runners covering distinct boroughs like in the New York City Marathon, or the stunning beauty of running through the French Alps for Ultra-Trail du Mont-Blanc (UTMB), but they will have their own magic and offer something more effective at helping us perform well: hometown advantage.

For many runners, the most memorable and cherished races end up being hometown races—and for good reason. We know the streets; we feel safe and comfortable and can dedicate all our energy to the race rather than dedicating energy to process new stimuli. We know the heart and spirit of our town, and, most importantly, the course is lined with people we know and love. People who have seen and paid attention to the sacrifices we made to be in that moment and who have chosen to get up early on their day off to cheer us on. People who love us regardless of the outcome and will still be there to lend support, because they know that it means something to us. They care because we care. That energy drives us forward and becomes a bright spot in our race, even through tough stretches.

By selecting local races, we can sleep soundly (or at least better than in a new place) in our own beds, perhaps sleep in a little bit longer, and have the satisfaction of being home and showered (maybe sneaking in a nap if we are lucky) within a few hours. It places a lot less strain on our body and mind, our finances, and our planet.

Beyond the potential benefits to performance, running local races means we are supporting the local community. We demonstrate our appreciation for the race directors who work hard to provide events. Our cities can use the participant numbers and customer satisfaction ratings in their grant applications or for funding other outdoor recreation events. Races can even help heal a place that has experienced a traumatic event. Having a big turnout to a local event can indicate the strength of the community as a whole and can be a means of moving forward. Boston showed us the power of healing as a community in 2014, one year after the terrorist attack that occurred during the 2013 Boston Marathon, killing 3 people and injuring over 200 more. The city of Boston, along with the running community, rallied around the race with the slogan "Boston Strong" to show the power of healing by running (History.com 2019).

It can feel like our single entry does not mean much, and, yes, race entries can be expensive. There is no doubt that racing, and especially racing often, is a privilege—one not available to every runner. If we can help local races thrive, especially if they are competing against giant race organizations, we can demonstrate that our local community matters more than big, flashy events, and that feels good (even before we step on the race course).

Investigate Air Travel Options

Being a climate activist, or simply recognizing the need to reduce our climate impact, does not mean the end of flying to races. It is important that whenever possible we drive

Exploring races close to home gives us the opportunity to check out the best running our area has to offer.

or take public transport to races, especially those that require similar travel time once we add up the drive to the airport, check in, wait for departure, fly, deplane, and travel to our destination. Driving provides more freedom to stop and stretch, get food, and avoid soul-destroying flight delays.

That said, air travel is a part of life for many runners, and that is okay. By shaming or publicly humiliating activist runners who do take flights, we play directly into the hands of the companies that work so hard to make us feel it is all about individual action, as opposed to their larger-scale harmful practices.

Whenever possible, take a direct flight to the destination, which emits less greenhouse gas. If a connecting flight is required or is significantly less expensive, if time and finances allow, consider extending your layover to explore that city. This could eliminate separate subsequent flights for a future trip.

Once you reach the main hub in your destination, explore public transport within that area rather than booking a taxi or using a rideshare app. Public transportation options may be limited in your local area, but if the race you're traveling to is in a bigger city, using public transport can be a simple switch that builds your pro-environmental lens. While it adds an extra step, in most cases, once you get used to a system, it becomes easier and easier. Most of the time it is just habit to jump in an Uber, but breaking that habit quickly changes your view of a city, especially if you can use ebikes or scooters to explore the city in a new and fun way. The American Public Transport Association reports, "Public transportation with its overarching effects on land use, is estimated to reduce CO_2 emissions by 37 million metric tons annually" (2008). And, yes, 37 million metric tons annually does matter.

If public transportation feels like a hassle that could affect your performance, think again. Consider the choices of some of the top ultra-athletes. Kilian Jornet, winner of many of the most prestigious ultra races in the world, has committed to reducing his air travel by choosing to utilize public transportation to go to events (as well as exploring what is around him). Xavier Thévenard, three-time winner of the UTMB, no longer flies and has committed to doing the races around him instead of traveling. British professional ultrarunner Damian Hall discovered that traveling via public transport is not as awkward as you might think. When he traveled to UTMB by train rather than plane, he calculated that the carbon emissions from his trip were reduced from 190 kg to 55 kg; it only took two more hours, and he found it more enjoyable and comfortable. The downside is that the cost was more than double, so until prices come down for some types of transportation, there is unfortunately an additional expense. However, the more we utilize public transport, the more infrastructure will be added to make it more cost efficient.

Ride sharing with other runners, when possible, is another good practice. It cuts down on emissions and reduces costs because of the shared expense, and it also adds to the experience. Since we are all headed to the same place, excited and nervous for what race day can bring, talking through our emotions about the event with other runners and being vulnerable through sharing fears and doubts helps us process the investment we have made in the race and recognize that we have value regardless of what happens on race day. Besides, runners are great at reminding one another to stay hydrated and eat often before the race! Travel to the event can then become a part of the memorable experience, rather than about just race day itself, heightening it and allowing us to deepen friendships along the way.

Choose Where to Sleep

It is not easy to determine which hotels or other lodging options take sustainability seriously. We live in a world where buzzwords remove all meaning from the original intention, and sustainability-focused words are no exception. We may be able to use "green hotels" in our online search or find hotels with a certification, but it is difficult to know what exactly they are doing to follow through with that claim.

Shelley Villalobos half-jokes that in an ideal world we would be looking for hotels that use renewable energy sources, conserve water, have organic and plant-based continental breakfasts, and recycle. We know that not only are these hotels extremely hard to find, but they are significantly more expensive than other options. Finding a hotel that prioritizes its impact on Mother Earth is nowhere near as simple as it seems it should be. Once again, we can use our voice by reaching out to hotels we frequent to let them know our preferences and to give them the opportunity to make those changes. It also works the other way; positive comments on the sustainability initiatives at a hotel as you check out may inspire them to do more of the same. As with everything related to environmental action, talking about it matters. Your voice matters.

In the meantime, here are a few tips for finding hotels that are committed to sustainability. Hotels and apartments that make it a priority often prominently display their commitment, backing it up with the action they have taken, rather than wishy-washy statements. If a hotel is a member of 1% for the Planet, this means that they donate 1 percent of their revenue to environmental nonprofits and organizations. We can also look at the relationship the hotel has with the city it is based in. If it uses local foods in its restaurant or partners with local businesses and uses their products in the hotel itself, these are signs that they take sustainability seriously.

Sustainable Travel Packing List

We've planned a trip and want to make more sustainable choices while we are away. What can we do to make our out-of-town race vacation more environmentally friendly?

We've assembled a list of some things to add to our packing list. They'll help avoid some of the more wasteful aspects of travel and probably save us some money too!

- Reusable water bottle
- Reusable cutlery (fork and spoon)
- Reusable straw
- Reusable chopsticks
- Cloth napkins
- Coffee mug
- Trail mix and other snacks
- Tupperware or other containers
- Dish soap (if traveling for more than a few days)
- Soap and container
- Shampoo and conditioner
- Toothpaste and mouthwash
- Laundry bags
- Period underwear
- Reusable bag for shopping

And if we are racing, we should bring these:

- Safety pins for bib
- Heat sheet for before and after the race
- Water bottle and electrolytes for race

When it comes to our own impact on the hotel, turning off lights and temperature controls when we leave the room are easy actions to take, and we can also be sure to pack items that in the past we may have relied on hotels to provide.

Eat on the Go

When it comes to eating throughout your stay, try to select restaurants that are either plant-based or have plenty of plant-based options. Restaurants that are known for working with local farms and using organic ingredients are likely to have compostable packaging and try to minimize their environmental impact. Look for places that donate their remaining food to food banks or shelters, supporting the community and minimizing waste. If you have children, be sure to bring along their water bottles (along with your own!) rather than using plastic cups at restaurants. Bring a travel-sized container of dish soap to easily wash your utensils and water bottles.

If you return to your room to eat, be sure to wash out plastic containers with soap before putting them in the recycling bin. It is estimated that only 9 percent of plastic ever made since the 1950s has been recycled (with 12% being incinerated and 79% ending up in a landfill). It is also estimated that roughly 12 billion metric tons of plastic waste—weighing more than 36,000 Empire State Buildings—will be in landfills or the natural environment by 2050 (Geyer et al. 2017). Yuck.

One major reason for the low recycling rate is because when plastic is contaminated by food or anything else, it is thrown into a landfill or ends up in the ocean. For many municipalities, any recycling in plastic bags, any plastic that still has food on it, plastic cups with straws still inside, or plastic that has something unrecyclable still attached will almost certainly be thrown into the trash. This is why we could have easily found Tina climbing inside commercial trash cans

Sandy Gutierrez

We want to take steps to be environmentally conscious with our decisions, but we also don't want to hold ourselves to a standard of perfection. By doing so, we are setting ourselves up to fail.

when she worked with the sustainability team at the Chicago Marathon in 2022. One contaminated item can change the trajectory of an entire bin. The same rules apply to our at-home recycling too. We should check our local recycling policy to see if washing recyclables with soap and removing any items that cannot be recycled (yes, even if they have the triangle logo) is required in our area. Single-stream and dual-stream recycling have different rules, so be sure to check local recycling guidelines. And most plastic bags for produce or anything made from a soft plastic usually has to be taken to a store; sending them to the recycling facility through your at-home pickup will cause problems for the sorting center.

Tina's Thoughts

When I first began to understand that climate change was happening now—that this was not some far-off potential future that could affect my grandkids but was happening right now and is the greatest challenge humanity has ever faced—I started to feel stress about every decision I made.

When I traveled, I would take as much as I could with me, even though it weighed down my suitcase and made things awkward. I would whip up a batch of muffins for the trip, make my own trail mix, and pack extra containers for my leftovers. I made sure I told every carryout restaurant that I did not want utensils and felt anger well up inside me if they put them in my bag anyway. I found myself staring at plastic packaging in the airport as I envisioned it floating around in the ocean in a few months, all for the sake of having a few fruits and vegetables in my juice or smoothie. If I had a six-hour flight delay at the airport, I would spend an hour of that time walking back and forth between the options, trying to decide which one had the least impact associated with it. I spent my runs obsessing over the amount of trash I could see exploding out of trash cans, cursing the recycling items thrown in there that could have had a potential second life.

Traveling can bring climate guilt to the forefront of our minds, and it certainly did for me. I recognized that a lot of the swirling emotions I felt during travel were due to guilt over my own carbon impact. I had learned that my contribution to one round-trip flight like New York to Los Angeles or New York to London added 2,000 kg of CO_2 into the atmosphere per flight. To put that into perspective, 1.5 billion people in the world do not use that much emissions in a year, according to Climate Watch (2022), a group that offers open data, visualizations, and analysis to help policymakers, researchers, and other stakeholders gather insights on countries' climate progress. In many ways, knowing that information took away the joy of traveling. I would feel anxiety in the buildup to a trip, feeling like a fraud knowing that I was a climate activist, yet here I was, flying for work, which was, in the grand scheme of things, quite unimportant. Or at least it felt that way.

For that reason, while traveling still weighs on my mind for the carbon footprint of travel and hotels, it motivated me to find ways to make small changes. I began carbon offsetting my trips and became a member of 1% for the Planet to donate to environmental nonprofits. It forced me to be creative in reducing my impact in other ways

(continued)

Tina's Thoughts (*continued*)

when I am traveling. Now when I travel, I do a better job of limiting the amount of waste being sent to a landfill than I am able to do at home. Once I got used to carrying reusable items and limiting single-use items by packing for my own personal needs, it was really about my packaging consumption through food. I found that searching for vegetarian restaurants in the area, even before I became a vegetarian, became a way to find places that matched my environmental stance. While not every city has places with vegetarian options, and not every city understands what steps need to be taken to reduce our food waste, we can continue to ask about it when we travel.

Most of all, I learned to treat myself with grace. While I can stand up and speak out about the changes that need to be made, I also need to take care of my own mental health and prevent burnout. One of the ways I do this is by traveling and surrounding myself with others who view the world similarly to the way I do. I recognize there is privilege in that and, for me, work and self-care combine into one. Being a climate activist doesn't mean never traveling again; it means being thoughtful with my travel. I can do that, and so can you.

Does it feel uncomfortable to ask a hotel or restaurant what they are doing to improve their sustainability or reduce their impact on the environment? Absolutely, but ultimately, businesses want to survive and thrive. By asking, we are letting them know that this issue is important to us, and if they hear even a few of those requests, it may be enough for them to seriously consider what they can do to be part of the solution.

Even passionate climate activists still want to be able to explore the world, want to run as fast as we can, and can get fed up with all the extra steps we have to take to do everything and anything. It can be overwhelming and exhausting. We hope this chapter has shown that we do not have to be perfect—none of us will be or even can be—but we can all do better, together. By talking about it within our circles, and by getting used to bringing it up in conversation to continue building our pro-environmental lens, we will move our communities in the right direction. The neighbor effect is a powerful motivator, and by being a leader in our community, we can change this world for the better. We know it's possible.

ACTION STEPS

- Confidently build your pro-environmental lens: Look for small ways to reduce your impact.
- Create a local lifetime bucket list and begin working through it by exploring nearby parks, forests, and outdoor spaces.
- Limit air travel to races. Drive or take public transportation when it is an option, especially if the time involvement is similar.
- Travel with other runners to heighten the experience and reduce your carbon footprint.
- Whenever possible, select hotels or accommodations that use renewable energy sources, conserve water, have organic and plant-based continental breakfast, and recycle.
- Contact hotels that you frequent to let them know of your preferences toward sustainability; encourage them to join 1% for the Planet.
- Bring reusable items and food from home to limit the plastic packaging from purchased goods.
- Clean plastic containers with soap before placing them in the recycling bin of the hotel or lodging accommodations.
- Select restaurants that offer compostable packaging, have plant-based options, and use local, organic ingredients.

13 | Consume With Care

We buy for many reasons. We might buy a coffee for a midday pick-me-up, or a snack to tamp down the 3 p.m. tummy rumblings. We buy groceries to fill the fridge for a gathering the next day, and we stock up on gels for an upcoming race. Often, we purchase for less tangible reasons, and savvy advertisers are hip to the psychologies that drive our purchasing habits. Do we really need the newest colorway in this running shoe, or are we buying it to satisfy an emotional need? Do we really need this beet supplement, or are we buying it because an admired athlete is hawking it on Instagram?

It can be hard to know the difference. In the moment, we might convince ourselves that we do need it—that our old running shoe *has* lost some of its tread, that it will lose more, and that before we know it, we could be injured, so it's better to play it safe and get another pair. Just in case. Besides, that product made our favorite athlete fast; surely it will make us fast too. We rationalize.

Sometimes it's not even our own shopping habits. Well-intentioned loved ones may purchase items that are thoughtful and sweet yet unnecessary. What do we say to that? Do we risk hurting them and tell them "no, thank you"? Or do we graciously accept, continuing the cycle of consumerism but secretly donating or passing on the item the first chance we get? Or do we simply accept their purchases to keep the peace?

Living in a Western society, especially in the United States, means endless holidays, events, and celebrations. We can refuse to participate or find creative ways to celebrate sustainably, but as people who have done that for years and faced the disapproving glares for "ruining" a special day, it is exhausting. Many special occasions require that we bring gifts or purchase food, most of which ends up in the trash or tossed aside. It can be suffocating to think about the sheer volume of waste the average person creates. As we move into this chapter, we will be diving into consumerism and how our world has been shaped by big corporations to make us believe that purchasing makes our problems go away. We have been conditioned to get a hit of feel-good endorphins (not unlike a runner's high) when we purchase, and most items are disposable or break quickly, so we return for more. This chapter might make us look at the Western world differently, but it will also reduce feelings of exhaustion and claustrophobia as we pull away from what once felt like activities we "had" to participate in.

Break From Ad Manipulation

Once we are aware of the influence ads have on us, it can make us feel physically sick. No one likes to be manipulated. We like to think we are perceptive enough to know when someone is selling us something for the sake of consumerism. Unfortunately, they know exactly what to say to exploit our weaknesses and bypass our common sense. Athletes are simply trying to continue doing what they love, and endorsing products allows them to do that. Should we hold that against them? No. As two athletes who have worked with brands ourselves, we feel this deeply. However, it is important to remember that we will never see the full picture: A pair of shoes or an energy gel might be a component of running a personal best, but it will never be the difference between success and failure.

No one likes to be manipulated, and we'd like to think we are perceptive enough to know when someone is selling us something for the sake of consumerism. Unfortunately, they know exactly what to say to exploit our weaknesses and bypass our common sense.

There's a phenomenon called the *third-person effect* in which people believe that they might not be influenced by media or advertising but that others are (Salwen and Dupagne 1999). In fact, studies show that people who believe themselves to be invulnerable to messaging are, in fact, the most likely to fall prey to that same persuasion.

We've been trained and indoctrinated by a culture that projects our primary identity as that of consumer. Think about how much advertising we've seen today alone: online and on every billboard, small screen, big screen, park bench, and public bus. In the middle of writing this chapter, Zoë noticed a National Forest sign bedecked with branded stickers, obscuring the entryway to public lands with logos and slogans.

It can be tough to know what to do with this information. Billions of dollars are spent on creating hooks or alluring items that make us feel like we cannot live without them. This is the way things have always been—at least in the consciousness of most people alive today. Older generations may remember barely having enough money to put food on the table when they were a child. That scarcity often makes them want to give their loved ones everything they lacked. But how do we find a balance between endless excess and denying ourselves new things when we really need them?

Most of what we can control is our own habits and behaviors, and often the best way we can make change is to live by example and to talk about why we make those choices when the opportunity presents itself. No one likes being told what to do, and lecturing friends and family about their spending habits is not the way to encourage change. Trust us; we have tried!

Investigating the *why* behind our purchases can help us consume less, shop in line with our environmental values, and ease up on our spending. The truth is that we don't need the latest and greatest in running tech to compete at a high level. Companies tap into the image and influence of top elites to sell their products because it sends the implicit message that to run, train, look, and compete like them, we need to buy whatever they're selling, and we must buy it now.

> Investigating the *why* behind our purchases can help us consume less, shop in line with our environmental values, and ease up on our spending.

Before clicking that Buy button, ask yourself: Do I need this? What requirement is it meeting? Do I actually need a new T-shirt branded with this year's race date, or am I buying it to satisfy an emotional need or because I am nervous for the race and want to feel like I belong? Do I need connection, something that would be helped by a long chat with a friend rather than an online purchase?

While it sounds easy to stop and think before buying, it is not as easy in practice. We get sucked down rabbit holes as brands tap into our deepest insecurities and put desired items in front of us before we even recognize what's happening. How could Instagram possibly know that the lines in Tina's forehead were an insecurity and then put "frownies" wrinkle patches in her feed?

So, what can we do?

Put app limits on your social media.

This serves as a reminder that time spent on social media should help us to feel good and, if it doesn't, we are wasting our limited time for something that makes us feel bad. When you feel the urge to purchase something, instead use your phone to reach out to a friend you haven't talked to in a while. Being reminded that we have people who care about us, even if we haven't connected in months or years, is one way to snap ourselves out of chasing the rush of purchasing. Meaningful connection is much more powerful and lasts longer. Tina is a big fan of sending voice memos through WhatsApp or iMessage, which gives friends and family the opportunity to reply at their own convenience and lets them hear the voice, mannerisms, and personality of their loved one, deepening that connection without the back and forth of trying to schedule a chat.

Aim to pause before you act.

Make a rule to wait 24 hours or more before making a purchase. If you want it bad enough, you will wait for it. Corey Simpson, a Patagonia spokesperson, recommends slowing down before buying: "Buying feels good, for a moment. We've been preconditioned to keep up with the modern trends, feed our shopping highs, and prop up an apparel industry that contributes up to 10 percent of the pollution driving the climate crisis. But it doesn't have to be this way. We all have the power to change the way clothes are made. When you need something, we recommend buying used, repairing what you wear out, and demanding recycled,

Fair Trade, and organic. The best thing we can do for the planet is cut down on consumption and get more use out of stuff we already own."

It can be hard to see how the apparel and fashion industry contributes such a massive percentage of what drives the effects of climate change. Apparel seems so harmless and feels so important; we can't live without clothes! But the industry relies on our getting sucked into purchasing things, only to push new items every season. Aim to select pieces that are simple and classic, are not likely to go out of fashion, and can be used for many years. And ask yourself: Do I really need something new? Can I buy it used? Do I even need it at all?

"I appreciate brands that build a product not only to last from a durability standpoint but that is classic in design and therefore durable through changing trends. The emotional or psychological durability of a piece of apparel is just as important; it means you're not going to feel tired of that shirt or short in a season; it was designed to be timeless and worn, passed down to future generations. Okay—that's not always possible with run apparel . . . we beat our stuff up pretty well sometimes, but consider that for jackets, fleece, packs, etc. Caring about the environment can come through in your purchasing—where you put your dollars is what you're supporting indirectly or sometimes directly," says Jess Rogers, global product lead for trail running and hiking at Patagonia.

Rogers, an outdoor athlete and mother, knows all about the lure of buying new. But as someone committed to outfitting herself and her family in a way that aligns with her environmental ethics, she tries to get most stuff used: "'The more you know, the less you need.' Yvon Chouinard (founder and former CEO of Patagonia) has said that many times, and it always resonates with me when I'm building product or thinking about buying something new—whether it's apparel, footwear, or gear."

There are very few novel technologies and advancements that runners really *need*. Even though you see elite runners promoting products often, you may be surprised that many of these athletes eschew all but the simplest watches and shoes. They are often provided free apparel and products, which is one of the big perks of their hard work and talent, but be wary of well-written social media posts and ads that make a product seem too good to be true. An athlete may not use every single item they endorse as much as it appears. A runner may endorse a product as a way to support themselves in a sport that pays very little for running fast—which is not a bad thing, but we shouldn't let a slick ad or testimonial convince us that we need something if we don't.

The less we believe we are influenced by this type of messaging, the more likely we are to make decisions because of it. A little self-awareness and a check-in with yourself during the consumer decision-making process goes a long way. We're all familiar with the tricks that companies use to ply us into buying new things: *This shoe has a new, streamlined upper* (read: it's the same shoe). *This watch has an updated function* (one you'll probably never use). *This hat or shoe or headband is now Bluetooth compatible.* Companies have even tapped into our increasingly sustainable desires, luring us with appeals that satisfy our environmental values on a superficial level. Hollow assertions that a product is green or sustainable can seem suspect at best and deceitful at worst. These off-base claims allow us to feel like we're doing something good while encouraging us to consume and shop at the same level as before. All of it stems from a strategy to continue the cycle of purchasing. You need a laundry bag for your travel? No, a plastic bag won't do; how about this $19.99 laundry bag from our store? Why bother with washing a cloth napkin when you can purchase disposable ones and throw them away?

Zoë's Thoughts

I'm on lunch break, scrolling through Instagram. A brightly colored image of a female runner striding confidently in a cute, color-coordinated outfit catches my eye. My thumb lingers over the seductive image, and a navy bar appears at the bottom, beckoning me to *Shop Now*.

I want to! I want to shop now! I want to be like this woman in the photo, smiling and fit, whose shoes match her shorts and whose sports bra is coordinated with her socks. I can hardly even get my socks to match each other! Maybe if I add one more sports bra to my pile, or one more cute top to my wardrobe, I'd also be fast, happy, confident, and strong.

Almost automatically, I click the bar. I'm transported away from the app to an online store before I realize I've fallen into the same trap yet again. Was I really about to buy something because I was bored? Not because I actually desired or needed a new bra (or hat or pair of shoes) but because on a superficial level, buying something feels buoying in the moment, like a quick-hit self-esteem fix or cure for momentary boredom?

Panicked, I exit out of every window on my phone and kick myself for my near slip. *Not today.*

Beware of Greenwashing

If your social media feeds look anything like ours, they're full of brightly colored advertisements for "earth-friendly" workout tops, "eco-friendly" leggings made from 10 percent recycled ocean plastic, "circular" shoes that you can recycle, and "sustainable" apparel for every athletic pursuit imaginable. These ads represent what would be a sea change in the apparel industry. But how true are the environmental claims? Much of it is *greenwashing*, which happens when companies spread misleading or false sustainability claims or overemphasize bad faith attempts at eco-initiatives. As companies get hip to consumers' desire to shop in a more environmentally friendly way, some have distorted those desires in a bad faith attempt to get business.

Greenwashing, a term coined by environmentalist Jay Westerveld in 1986 in response to the hypocrisy of superficial environmental credentials, isn't new. It has led to a precipitous drop in consumer trust in companies' environmental claims. While we push for greater transparency,

> As companies get hip to consumers' desire to shop in a more environmentally friendly way, some have distorted those desires in a bad faith attempt to get business.

accountability, and regulation of the most offensive industries (energy, agriculture, or, for us, running gear and apparel), we can also shop a little bit smarter when we know what to look out for when it comes to greenwashing.

When considering environmental and sustainability claims from a company, be on the lookout for signs that something isn't quite adding up.

Look out for hidden trade-offs.

When a company suggests that a product is green based on one environmental attribute, always check the recycling math, says Simpson: "When it comes to recycled goods, keep your eye out for misleading percentages. 'Fifty percent more recycled material' sounds great until you find out the product only contained 1 percent recycled material in the first place."

Think about a pair of running shoes in which the laces are made from some recycled components; it's a small part of the shoe, particularly if no attention is paid to other important parts of the product and manufacturing like energy, water use, and carbon emissions. A recycled eyelet does not a green shoe make!

"It's all about knowing your numbers," says Jad Finck, VP of innovation at Allbirds. "If you want to make a difference with your dollars, pick brands that give you facts about their environmental footprints. Get beyond the pretty pictures and buzzwords. Allbirds quantifies the full carbon footprint of everything they make and puts that number right on the product for customers to see. Just like checking the calories of the food you buy at the grocery store, knowing your numbers is the first real step to making better choices."

Be leery of claims.

Watch for claims that cannot be substantiated by easily accessible or supporting information, ideally with third-party certification and verification. For example, if you see a rain jacket claiming that it "uses less water," you should wonder, "Less than what? Compared to what?" If there's not enough context given to support the claim, it might be a greenwashing red flag. Companies pledging 1 percent for the planet or doing the work to get a B Corp certification are generally good companies to support with your purchasing dollars.

Question vague claims.

Poorly defined words like *green* and *eco-friendly* can be misinterpreted or misleading to consumers. If the company doesn't show their work with proper data and third-party certification (the difference between "environmentally friendly" and "organically grown" cotton is huge—one has an actual definition and is verifiable), being "environmentally friendly" is about as meaningful as being "unicorn approved." If you see the phrase "chemical-free," *run.* Nothing is free from chemicals. Water is a chemical.

Ask questions about products that claim to be the lesser of two evils.

Such a claim risks distracting consumers from the greater environmental impact of a category as a whole, like gas-powered cars or insecticides. The "greenest" gas car still isn't very green, and we should always be skeptical of advertising that lets us off the hook for buying the least bad option. (You're not, but our time and energy would still be best spent advocating for change within that category.)

Be aware of irrelevant environmental claims that are technically true but unimportant or unhelpful.

Some claims can be outright falsehoods. Markets are paying attention to the fact that consumers are increasingly interested in more ethically and sustainably produced gear, but companies are preying on our best and worst impulses. We all want to feel like we're helping and not making things worse. It would be great if we could shop our way out of the environmental crisis, but we can't.

For now, the best we can do is advocate for regulations that make greenwashing harder and hold companies accountable for their environmental impacts. Each purchase is a small opportunity to vote with our consumer dollar, and every day is an opportunity to assess the impacts of our consumption.

Tina's Thoughts

In May 2022, I had the opportunity to talk to Romesh Patel, the director of materials at Allbirds. Eager to talk to someone about a topic I was very passionate about (and, if I am honest, trying to impress him), I asked Patel how close they were to a circular shoe. I had heard, read, and thought circular shoes (in which every part can be broken down and remade into something else) were the end goal. Patel patiently waited for me to finish my attempt to bowl him over with my knowledge before responding, "We aren't making one yet." *Uh what?!*

Patel went on to explain that circular shoes were not a reality right now. Ultimately, all materials that went into that shoe would end up in a landfill, even if they could be used in something else first. If an item was made circular, that's great, but with all the materials and parts that went into making a shoe, they would need to be sent to the same place to be broken down and made into something else. He explained that a company can only control the carbon footprint to build that shoe. Once the shoe leaves their hands, the carbon footprint continues to rise. If a shoe is express-shipped to a consumer through a third party, there is a massive increase in carbon footprint through flying that shoe to its destination. There is no control over where the shoe is taken by the consumer and what indirect impact it will have in that time. Once the shoe has ended its life with that consumer, a new carbon "clock" starts again. The shoe has to be sent back, in many cases around the globe, usually as an individual item. Even if the items were collected in bulk, they'd still need to be shipped back to some manufacturing regions.

Now factor in cleaning, sorting, reprocessing, and ultimately reformulating that same material, and we likely have a much higher carbon footprint than when we started. Virgin materials also need to be added to give that material its second life, producing more damaging materials. Then there is the additional manufacturing and delivery of that new product from production to its new location. Having a fully recyclable shoe could be a reality, but the biggest challenge is not materials but rather logistics. More specifically, logistics married with sustainability. *(continued)*

Tina's Thoughts *(continued)*

Carbon is not inherently bad. All living things are made of carbon. When we think of carbon in the context of our impact, we are referring to carbon dioxide in the form of a gas, released into the atmosphere, which, in excess amounts, leads to global warming. The carbon trapped in a shoe that ultimately goes into a landfill does not sound like an ideal solution, but it is far better than any added CO_2 released into the atmosphere in an attempt to remake a shoe out of older shoes. Ultimately all those steps have added carbon into our atmosphere, and the product will still end up in the landfill after that step. Patel proposed that the best thing to do is to minimize the carbon footprint going into the shoe in the first place.

Makes sense to me. Consider me humbled.

Photo courtesy of Allbirds, 2022.

Tina hosting an Allbirds event, shortly before Romesh Patel (standing on Tina's left) enlightened her to what the future of sustainability really looked like.

Let Your Money Do the Talking

While it can feel like our individual consumer impact is very small when large corporations own so much of the world, the money we spend does matter. Bennett Grimes, senior product manager at REI, has seen this in his various roles working in the running shoe space. When a major brand spends an extra $3 per shoe because they use sustainable materials, something they do not have to do, they raise the price to maintain their profit margin. When consumers purchase that product, accepting the additional cost, it sends the brand a message that consumers care about this—not just through words, but through action—and, in turn, the brand will then be prepared to spend more money investing in additional ways to produce their shoes sustainably.

When consumers say they care about the environment but don't spend the money to purchase that item that costs slightly more, it sends a conflicting message to the brand: one that says that the lowest cost is still most important. Of course, that leads to the biggest problem of all: Due to the unequal distribution of wealth, many consumers are unable to afford to add a few dollars to the cost of anything. But those consumers who do have the ability to spend a few extra dollars help to lower the cost for everyone, while more efficient methods are realized to drive down the cost of production. Some brands are coming out with a shoe that does not have the price increase but is sustainably made. Will consumers purchase a more sustainable shoe if it is the same price? Only time will tell (we hope the answer is yes; you have the power to prove that). Now that big brands are putting sustainable options out there, it is important to vote with our dollars. It can feel like selecting a pair of shoes made of 50 percent recycled materials does not matter, but it does.

When consumers say they care about the environment but don't spend the money to purchase that item that costs slightly more, it sends a conflicting message to the brand: one that says that the lowest cost is still most important.

Consider the shoes we buy for running. Regardless of ability, runners want to be able to perform the best they can. There is no doubt that shoes have changed the game in recent years. As the major brands duked it out to bring out the best carbon-plated shoe as quickly as possible, the environmental damage began to pile up. Not only are the shoes made of pure fossil fuels that take a long time to break down in landfills, but they only last about 100 miles and break down in the box as they sit on the shelf waiting to be purchased.

This is not to cause shame if you have purchased the newest and sleekest shoes available, but we do want to make everyone aware that while running in shoes that maximize potential is important, there is an associated cost that needs to be considered. If running is a hobby, something we do in our free time, having the latest and greatest is not something that should make or break our relationship with running. Being a sustainable runner means a lifelong relationship with the sport and a commitment to running that goes beyond performance.

Sustainably made alternatives are available, and the technology is continuing to improve. Allbirds and Adidas partnered in 2022 to create Futurecraft Footprint, a shoe with a carbon footprint of only 2.94 kg. A 2013 MIT study by Randall Kirchain and Elsa Olivetti found that the average pair of running shoes generates around 13.6 kg of CO_2, the equivalent of keeping a 100-watt lightbulb on for one week.

Brands like Allbirds are pushing running brands to show their carbon footprint number, as a way for consumers to see who is truly committed to sustainability, rather than just using empty words. It's working; Asics is coming out with a shoe whose carbon number is the lowest ever. For Allbirds, displaying the carbon number on each and every product is a way to hold themselves accountable and to get it as low as possible for each product. They have gone so far as to create a lifecycle assessment calculator and a manual with instructions on how to use it. The calculator, manual, and carbon footprint labels that they use on their products are all available to download for free on their website. The calculator helps brands "calculate the Carbon Footprint of our products, identify hotspots, and drive emissions reductions." A 2017 report by the Ellen MacArthur Foundation, a charity whose goal is to accelerate transition to a circular economy, found that the percentage of global carbon emissions by the global fashion industry is anticipated to be 26 percent by 2050 if we continue on the path we are on. It is estimated that 35 percent of all microplastics in the ocean come from washing clothes with polyester or other synthetic materials. Microplastics never biodegrade, but they can easily enter our bodies, the damage of which we will find out in the decades to come. Spending resources figuring out an alternative to synthetic materials that shed microplastic could be a bold statement that shoe and apparel brands can make to show that they are committed to change, not just using persuasive words.

It is also important to make it clear to our favorite brands that we want them to move in this direction. We can reach out on social media to ask when they are adding their carbon number to their products or website, send them a letter to request that they prioritize sustainability first, talk about brands and sustainability as often as possible in club or group settings, and ask about it at the local running store.

Consider What Is Really Necessary

In their roles as a professional gear tester for *Trail Runner* magazine and as a sponsored runner, Zoë and Tina have seen running gear fads and phases come and go. Minimalist shoes. Maximalist shoes. Carbon shoes. Every year, gear companies hawk some new innovation. One of the biggest investments we can make is in quality, durable gear. Even if a rain jacket or a pair of shoes is manufactured in a sustainable way, it's not doing much good for the earth if it's flimsy, is ineffective, and ends up quickly in a landfill.

"According to a 2019 McKinsey report, apparel purchases have increased by 60 percent over the past 15 years, while the average lifespan of each garment decreased by half. Our criteria for the best product rests on function, repairability, and, foremost, durability. Among the most direct ways we can limit ecological impacts is with goods that last for generations or can be recycled so the materials in them remain in use. Making the best product matters for saving the planet," says Corey Simpson.

Here's a list of the gear that we actually need.

- *Shoes.* A good pair of shoes is the best investment we can make. Footwear isn't a good place to cut corners; inadequate or inappropriate shoes can lead to myriad running injuries. For a reasonable pair of daily drivers, the typical cost is $120 to $150.
- *Watch.* Electronics are expensive and hard to dispose of in an environmentally friendly way. The best thing to do is to buy a watch—any watch—and use it until it absolutely dies. Bonus points if we can find a manufacturer that will replace parts such as buttons, the charging apparatus, or the band so that we can use it for as long as possible. We should resist the urge to buy a Dragon 37000 just because it has some fancy new feature that might not ever be used. We must be realistic about the features we need and why.

- *Sports bra.* Healthy breasts make a healthy runner. In some studies, the nipple has been shown to accelerate from 0 to 60 faster than a Ferrari because of the oscillations that breasts make while running. Women should invest in a good sports bra that currently fits well and that feels comfortable and supportive. Air drying bras helps them last longer, so those babies should be kept out of the dryer!
- *Shell.* A good shell will help get us outside in the grimmest conditions. Treating it with Nikwax helps the waterproofing last longer.

Runners are tough on clothing and shoes. We sweat in them for hours on end; put them through various weather scenarios; and then aggressively wash them to remove the grime, dirt, and, yes, the stink. Or we leave our mud-caked shoes for weeks before finally making the time to clean them (or appreciating some fresh snow to do the work for us). We need running clothes and shoes to do what we love without destroying our bodies in the process (we can be guilty of doing enough of that anyway!). But, as much as possible, we want to minimize new purchases. Zoë purchases almost all her clothes secondhand (except for shoes and socks). There are plenty of places to access those items in good condition to take them for a second round of adventures.

Wash, Rinse, Repeat

Taking care of our gear is essential too. Rather than purchasing new items with each season, we should take care of our clothes as best we can to ensure they live a long and happy life. Taking a few extra moments to wash our hydration vests, air out wet or muddy shoes, and properly clean our apparel can make them last much longer. Even clothes with anti-odor properties, rad as they are, still need to be properly cared for.

"What customers often forget is to simply wash their product," says Jess Rogers, global product lead for trail running and hiking at Patagonia. "Yes, it's durable, but your sweat, dirt, and blood can cause microorganisms to collect on garments and slowly break down the integrity of the materials. Following the wash and care instructions is super important. For example, our Patagonia Houdini jacket has a PFC-free DWR (durable water repellent) finish on it. Part of the care instructions are to wash *and* dry the jacket. Many times, folks tell me they hang dry their Houdini or they're afraid to throw it in the dryer, but the heat from the dryer is what reinvigorates the DWR chemistry on the jacket. If you wash but don't dry it, you might be disappointed in its performance. Similarly, it's okay to wash puffy jackets; please wash your tights and your shorts. Just remember to follow the instructions!"

Houdini jackets aside, putting most running clothes in the dryer drastically reduces the life, and they break down sooner. Air drying outside when it is warm (and hanging running clothes on a rack inside when it is not) reduces energy usage and makes most items last longer. Once again, reading the label is important to ensure your running clothes live their longest and best life.

Earth-Friendly Laundering Tips for Apparel Care

- The biggest mistake many folks make is using too much detergent, especially on smelly, sweaty clothes. Using extra detergent doesn't clean our clothes better; it just leaves a residue that may trap odors in clothes.
- Elastic clothing doesn't like the heat. Air dry your stretchiest togs!
- Wash similar textures together. Don't launder jeans with soft shirts; the friction can cause extra wear and tear.
- Consider a bag or filter to catch microplastics, which are small plastic pieces that shed from our clothes and are harmful to our ocean and aquatic life.

Normalizing multiple-day use of clothing—yes, even running clothes—reduces impact too. For extended long runs or on exceptionally hot days, the sniff test may be needed. Put sweaty clothes outside to dry, then take in a big whiff. You may discover they need to go immediately into the laundry basket, but most of the time, items can be worn at least twice, drastically reducing water usage and doubling their lifespan.

When it comes to which detergent to use, we have to be honest: We don't have the perfect answer. Our running clothes take quite a beating with excessive sweat, friction, dirt, and our favorite anti-chafing product. To deal with that again a few days later, they need to get clean—really clean. There has been a lot of debate about whether to use a detergent that is powerful but contributes damaging effects to the environment or whether to use a plant-based detergent that is less effective. Many of the large-corporation detergents are produced in sacrifice zones that expose residents to toxic chemicals and other environmental threats. Sacrifice zones are fence line communities where residents—usually low-income families and people of color—live in proximity to polluting industries (Climate Reality Project, 2021).

One alternative is to use plant-based detergents that use natural ingredients that are environmentally safe but may require a second wash to rid our running clothes of odor and grime. Tina uses Puracy, which does a great job of getting even the stinkiest running clothes clean and is made from organic and plant-based ingredients.

Another neglected consideration is to regularly clean your washing machine and wipe the drum clean after each use. Make sure not to overfill it, but also remember that washing only a few items at a time is a waste of water.

Become an Activist Consumer

We can think about our choices as a consumer by breaking down the ethical versus activist consumer framework. This is simply a tool we can add to our pro-environmental lens, and it takes pressure off to feel better about our purchases.

A Company Striving to Make a Difference

Jess Rogers is tasked with overseeing the team that designs and builds new products at Patagonia, and she spends a lot of time thinking about how each step of that process affects the environment and about where she can lessen that impact while educating and outfitting consumers.

"A lot goes into building a new product—including the mental energy of challenging the *why*; what is the problem we're trying to solve, who is it for, why do they need it, what makes it different?" says Rogers. "If we can't answer those questions clearly, we shouldn't be building it. There is a lot of stuff out there; working in the apparel industry, we contribute to a massive amount of waste, so before building something new, I always want to make sure it's something that will last for more than just a few seasons. A successful product is one that can be timeless and relevant, durable, comfortable, empowering or exciting to the user, inclusive and accessible, and also is built in a way that it can easily be recycled or passed on at end of life. All of the apparel in the Patagonia trail running line uses recycled materials and is built in a fair trade factory; that was a milestone we hit in 2020 and now is a baseline standard for any new products going forward.

"I think the customer appreciates that; buying sustainably made products has become more and more important in their lives. Another element that is super important to me through the product creation process is how we think about including more diverse voices, body types, abilities, etc. Saving our home planet is Patagonia's mission statement; we can't do that just thinking about sustainable materials—the social justice and human side is equally important if we truly want to reduce our impact. How we educate; where we show up; who's involved in building, testing, selling our product being more representative of the communities we serve; and building product for everyone on the trail is a big part of what keeps me going."

Unfortunately, even the greenest consumption is still consumption. Even if a company promises to plant a tree or recycle a water bottle for every purchase we make, we shouldn't be tricked into thinking we're actually doing something good. (Anytime a company gives you warm fuzzies with some vague environmental claim, especially about planting trees, that should raise a red flag.)

Patagonia founder Yvon Chouinard sums up this conflict succinctly in his book *The Responsible Company*: "No human economic activity is yet sustainable. Everything we do at work, unless you happen to sell organic seeds or night-soil compost, hurts the environment more than it gives back."

Ethical consumers buy into the idea that individual choices are the most important and primary driver of change. They believe that consumers are at fault for the bad ethical throughlines that inform systems of supply and demand. They think consumers can shop their way to equality, sustainability, and justice through moderating their own decisions. They're easily swayed by dubious certifications they don't fully understand and might buy anything that has a stamp of approval, no matter how superficially vetted that certification might be. They believe that the best way to gain transparency from companies is to buy from "good" companies, and they tend to pursue narrow changes through private means as opposed to collective action or political organization.

Sound familiar? There is no judgment here. We have fallen into this mindset ourselves and likely will again. Many of the big corporations spend millions (or billions) funneling as many people down this path as possible. It takes our eyes off of them and keeps us busy as we frantically obsess over how our small decisions are hurting the planet. This is a surefire way to expend a lot of energy with little to gain.

"First impressions don't always tell the full story," says Rogers. "Taking the time to learn about where you're putting your dollars and what you're supporting when you buy into a brand is really important." Rogers created a list of questions to research about companies we are considering purchasing from. These questions can be applied worldwide because most of the certifications are globally accepted:

- Do they use sustainable materials?
- What sustainable initiatives are they supporting?
- Do they have a fair trade certification?
- Do they have a B Corp certification?
- Are they members of an environmental giveback, giving part of their profits to a nonprofit dedicated to climate solutions, like 1% for the Planet?
- What does their end-of-life recycling look like?
- Do they upcycle their products or put thought into how to lower the CO_2 created in making and distributing the product?

While this list can be a lot, after looking into a few companies, you will quickly learn the markets and industry that have specific certifications and learn the questions that are applicable. We don't need to know about end-of-life recycling for our bananas or apples, and it's unlikely our new washing machine will be fair trade certified. Once you do this a few times, it will become easier to see the patterns to identify greenwashing and find the ones genuinely doing the work.

Rogers reminds us to "stay away from fast fashion brands and chains that are constantly churning out new products and making those new products more and more technical and detailed. The more bells and whistles and extra colors, logos, and features a product has, the higher the carbon footprint and therefore the less of a priority sustainability is to that brand. While higher-quality items may cost more, it's generally for a good reason; it has been designed to be more durable, last longer, and, in many cases, it now uses sustainably sourced materials as well."

In trying to do the right thing, ethical consumers might have a closet full of clothes from "sustainable" companies and be easily swayed by shiny advertisements on social media or TV that tout a company's sustainability without much data or third-party validation to back up those claims. The fact that there are organic sports drinks is a good running example of how trending words like *sustainability* or *organic* can be cheapened when there is no regulation as to its meaning in a global market. Ethical consumers believe that, ultimately, it's up to individual consumer choices, rather than broad-scale political organization and regulatory pressure, to regulate the market. They might blame others for making different consumer choices that don't fit into their worldview as opposed to taking a broad view and trying to examine why that person might be making their consumer decisions.

This could look like someone who buys sustainable running clothes but doesn't look into the environmental values of their elected representatives or who shies away from doing advocacy work for fear of "getting too political." They might use an "environmentally friendly" credit card but not push for regulation of the financial industry (a known megadriver of climate change).

Tina's Thoughts

I have always had an environmentally leaning perspective. My family raised me to limit waste, keep the door closed to prevent wasted energy from leaving the living room, and be thoughtful with purchases. *FernGully* was a movie my sister and I watched often, and I would cry every time I watched the video for "Earth Song" by Michael Jackson, which I did repeatedly. As I moved toward motherhood, I started to think about this more often. The more I read and learned, the more I noticed the anxiety and guilt growing in me. As I added more steps to acknowledge how my actions affected the environment, I started feeling more stressed, not less. I began to feel anger toward others for not considering how their decisions were affecting the planet. In many ways, I resented their ignorance and wished I could go back to that. Environmental concerns started to fill my mind.

I was going out of my way to avoid adding waste to our landfill—selecting a hot drink in the middle of summer at my local coffee shop because I could use a reusable mug, double checking with a restaurant when I ordered takeout so that they did not give me utensils or extras, and picking up bottles and trash I could recycle or throw away myself. I would purchase "all natural" everything and pace the aisles of the store as I tried to figure out which item was the most environmentally friendly. There was something that felt wrong about the big-box stores having a picture of a tree on their products and claiming it was sustainable. I could be led to believe they were trying, but were they? Or was I being manipulated? The frustration in me continued to build. I would be seething mad when the local restaurant gave me utensils anyway. I argued with the greeter at the entrance of Whole Foods when they wouldn't let me bring in my reusable bags after the reusable bag ban had been dropped during the pandemic. If I forgot to take my reusable bottle, I would not drink for hours on end in the summer rather than purchase a plastic one. It was starting to overtake my life and everyone I cared about. Keeping an open mind, I continued to read and learn, and it became clear that my efforts, no matter how hard I tried or how many people I convinced to do the same, were futile. Individual changes matter, yes, but what matters more is the systemic, political decisions that we would all much rather ignore. I wish it were the case that each of us collectively making changes in our own lives would successfully address the climate emergency. Unfortunately, though, that is not the case; we need to be activist consumers if we really want to make change.

Again, if this feels aimed at you, there is no need to feel guilty or dumb. There has been a master class in manipulation at play by many of the most powerful companies in the world to turn us into these consumers. We are not aware that it is happening, which means we try to do what we can to control what we can control, so we feel like we are doing something, even if we know deep down it is futile.

Activist consumers believe that companies have a responsibility to society. They understand that markets should be tamed by a democracy and that smart regulation tends to benefit consumers and society when well executed. Activist consumers try to change markets and society systematically so that the public benefits, rather than just their bottom line as consumers. They believe they can gain knowledge of supply chains and hold corporations and governments accountable through direct action like reaching out to companies, writing letters, making calls, and, yes, sending tweets. Activist consumers usually work up to boycotts, strikes, and protests (but we do not have to go that far!).

Above all, activist consumers try to pursue social change through public means like political action rather than small, consumption-based "solutions." And we should all approach our consumption a bit more like activists. That means consuming less, enacting change outside of markets, and, when consumption is inevitable, being savvy about what we buy.

Most of us, especially those who identify as female, have been raised to keep our heads down and follow the rules. Making waves, participating in boycotts, strikes, and protests may seem like a lot to take on—and, if so, we can begin with smaller actions. We can start by talking to our neighbors one-on-one when they ask us a question about a choice we are making to live a more sustainable life. Or we can send a letter to our favorite brand to let them know they can do better. We can work our way up, and once we attend our first activist event and are surrounded by others who care deeply about the same things we do, doing more will seem easier to do.

This chapter can be hard hitting. It might bring up feelings that are hard to accept or address. When Zoë and Tina were first alerted to how they have been manipulated, they felt enraged. The reality is it will happen again. Yet once we start taking action, the climate anxiety starts to dissipate. We feel like we are doing something real: change that we might not even see within our lifetime, but we know deep down we are making meaningful change. Even if the others we influence are a small circle of friends in our neighborhood. Think globally; act locally. We don't need to do everything tomorrow—just something today. We can start honing our pro-environmental lens and paying attention to our decision-making today, and we can bring a friend along for our activist consumer journey.

ACTION STEPS

- Investigate the *why* behind your purchases. What do you really need?
- Practice slowing down before you buy. Wait a week and see if you still want or need that item.
- Words like *green*, *sustainable*, and *natural* have lost their meaning through giant corporations using them for minimal changes. Be aware.
- Have the hard conversation with loved ones about their purchases for you that you don't need. Let them know how important it is to you and that you would much rather spend time with them over having more items. When you are given unwanted gifts, pass them on via a Buy Nothing group or Facebook marketplace.
- Be aware of the third-person effect—the more you think you are not getting sucked into marketing efforts, the more likely you are!
- Reach out to a friend you haven't spoken to in a while if you are feeling an urge to purchase something—you might be lonely.
- Choose quality over quantity when purchasing running clothes. Choose items that are durable, simple, and timeless.
- Consider that the more features, items, colors, and details an item has, the higher the carbon footprint.
- Take care of your running gear. Wash your hydration vests and bottles immediately upon returning home, and clean muddy shoes promptly.
- Properly wash and take care of running clothes and, unless stated on the label, air dry your running clothes.
- Limit detergent use for your clothes. Using more detergent does not mean cleaner clothes, but it does mean the washing machine is more likely to break down. Consider Puracy if you want to try plant-based detergent.
- Work toward being an activist consumer instead of an ethical consumer.
- Be on the lookout for greenwashing, especially by big corporations.
- Look for carbon numbers on clothing and shoes. If a company you love doesn't display them, ask what it is. Step one for reducing impact is to know your starting point!

14 | Reduce, Reuse, Recycle

The exact source of the *reduce, reuse, recycle* marketing campaign and statement is unknown, but it is widely considered to have originated from a speech by Wisconsin Senator Gaylord Nelson on the first Earth Day in 1970 (Wisconsin Historical Society and Nelson Institute for Environmental Studies n.d.). It has been seared into the minds of millions of folks all over the world as a simple approach to reduce carbon footprint.

The *reduce, reuse, recycle* slogan has been around for quite some time, but, unfortunately, the least important word seems to be the one most people use to show their "commitment" to the environment: *recycle*. How did the third word become the only word? A 2015 investigation revealed that a senior scientist at one of the world's largest oil companies, ExxonMobil, concluded in 1977 that the use of fossil fuels would warm the planet (Supran 2017). In a meeting with the management committee at Exxon, James F. Black stated, "In the first place, there is general scientific agreement that the most likely manner in which mankind is influencing the global climate is through carbon dioxide release from the burning of fossil fuels" (Banerjee et al. 2015). Over the coming years, he continued to talk about the effects of 1, 2, 3, and even 10 degrees of warming, and how it would harm humanity.

In 1977. Let's just let that sink in for a moment.

As of this book's publication, it has been 46 years since humans discovered our behaviors cause devastating side effects to our planet. Almost a half-century later, emissions are going up, not down. That was partially the impetus for this book. While the running community is smaller than other groups, and we likely don't have executives at one of the 100 most powerful companies, our voices matter; we matter.

As we come into the final chapters, it is time to settle in for the tough conversations—the harsh realities humanity needs to face. There is hope, and there is a lot of optimism, especially within the climate activism community, but we have to take our heads out of the sand and listen. We have to do the one thing we would pay any amount of money to avoid doing: Speak up even when it means having awkward, uncomfortable conversations.

Is it fair? Absolutely not. Should we feel irritation that we have to clean up a mess we didn't create and had no choice in the world we are inheriting? For sure. Do we have to make sacrifices in our own lives, knowing that the mighty and powerful will continue to change nothing and to create more impact? Unfortunately, yes. Will we have to spend our hard-earned money on showing that sustainability matters? Yep. And, yes, frankly, it sucks.

Part of addressing climate change is allowing ourselves to feel these emotions, whatever they may be. We might feel anger toward previous generations for leaving us in this situation, or anguish because it seems hopeless. How are we ever going to figure this out, when the few people with power have so many resources and can pay mind-boggling amounts to keep things exactly as they are? We might also grieve the future we are losing. By accepting that climate change is here and now, we have to let go of what could have been our future. But if we allow ourselves to see the love, beauty, and strength of others in the fight with us, we can make a difference in what matters most. We can simultaneously feel crushed by seeing another centenarian tree come down to make way for another giant house while at the same time appreciating warm sun on our face as we sit and listen to the birds on a spring morning.

Tina in St. Louis at her first climate protest. While it was scary to show up, standing shoulder-to-shoulder with others who were just as passionate made it empowering and enjoyable.

We have a lot of work to do; by this point in the book you know this, and the only way we will be able to do this work is to counter it with everyday moments of joy: taking simple moments of pleasure and appreciating them, even if the world seems like it is on fire (or even if it is). If we close our hearts to all emotion, we will find ourselves in a place of doom. We can continue to listen and learn, while also taking care of our bodies and minds.

So let's keep going.

Reduce What You Use

Back to *reduce, reuse, recycle*. There is a reason the phrase is in the order it is and why recycling is last. Reducing our consumption to the best of our ability should always be the first step. As we build our pro-environmental lens, we must be on the lookout for ways to cut back and to use our dollars to send a message that we do not need as much or that there is an alternative we prefer.

The single most important thing we can do as runners is to simply buy less gear and apparel. A 2014 report found that the average consumer bought 60 percent more clothing than they did in 2000, and that it lasted half as long (World Resources Institute). The 2022 U.S. consumer spending report found that "consumers—in particular, younger generations—say that their choices are at least somewhat influenced by environmental, social, and governance (ESG) factors" (Alldredge et al. 2022). They concluded that "in general, younger consumers prioritize authenticity and social issues such as diversity, equity, and inclusion, whereas older consumers pay more attention to health and environmental issues."

> The single most important thing we can do as runners is to simply buy less gear and apparel.

Systemic changes will produce the most drastic emission reductions, but for our role as individuals, one major thing needs to change; we need to shift away from our convenience-first lifestyle and move toward reducing and reusing. That will require slowing down our pace of life (and therefore our use of resources) and being more intentional—two things that do not come easily to most of us. We can say no to more stuff, save money in the process, and use those savings toward our future or an adventure we've always dreamed about taking. Moving to a simpler life begins to feel good.

At our current rate, we are using 1.6 Earths every year, accumulating a huge ecological debt. What does this mean? Global Citizen, an action platform dedicated to achieving the end of extreme poverty, explains: "The Earth can regenerate its resources only so fast: a tree can grow so fast, a fish population can repopulate so fast and rivers can regain their water supply so fast. Every year, there is a limit beyond which the planet can't regenerate to stable levels. This measurement considers carbon emissions, cropland, fish stocks, the use of forests and timber and other resources. If this limit is surpassed in a given year, humanity goes into ecological debt" (McCarthy 2015).

Tina's Thoughts

"Mama! Another book!"

A few years ago, my daughter, Bailey, was sitting on my lap, looking up at me with her innocent eyes, requesting yet another book. I looked at the large pile of Berenstain Bears books passed down from my husband's family and flipped through them, looking for one that spoke to me. My jaw dropped when I noticed one titled *The Berenstain Bears Don't Pollute (Anymore)*. On the cover of this book, Papa Bear was marching alongside his kids, proudly holding a "Save the Earth" flag. As someone building a pro-environmental lens, it caught my attention. Books on sustainability and the environment weren't exactly regular topics for kids' books.

As I read the book, I began to feel inspired, hopeful. Yes! We should be teaching kids to respect and love Mother Earth. Yes! We should be teaching kids why dumping trash in rivers and lakes is catastrophic. Yes! We should be having competitions in classrooms to be the most environmentally friendly family. This book was speaking my language. I laughed at Papa Bear's familiar response to climate change: "Everything looks fine outside, what could possibly be wrong?" I nodded in agreement with Brother and Sister Bear as they considered the perspectives of the squirrels, ducks, and fish. The book addressed littering, pollution, ecology, conservation, and recycling in a manner appropriate for children. This was the kind of book I wanted to read to my daughter.

I knew a children's book was never going to address systemic issues within our society with complexity and nuance, but the final message was important and somewhat accurate. I thought to myself, "Hmm, I wonder when this was written?" and flipped to the front of the book.

My stomach dropped. 1991!

This book was written when I was three years old. Zoë wasn't even born yet. This message and these important practices had been public for over 30 years, and most of them still weren't being implemented or taken seriously. It felt like every American I knew had read at least one Berenstain Bear book in their life. How did the message not sink in? How were we in the third decade of the 21st century but the only message that stuck has been recycling plastic (a practice that is, in many ways, a myth)?

In 1991, these suggestions were somewhat adequate to address climate change. But now? Not even close. I felt sick. How have we been ignoring this problem for all these years, not only on the individual level, but on the systemic level too? As of 2011, 260 million copies of the Berenstain Bears books had been sold, in 23 languages (Loviglio 2011). Yet the messages in this book still seem controversial, and the suggestions woefully inadequate (while still being pushed as a solution).

Reuse Apparel and Running Gear

The average American produces more than 82 pounds of textile waste per year, of which 85 percent ends up in our nation's landfills (Sustain Your Style n.d.). It's also bad for water. According to research by Greenpeace (2016), most of those textiles (particularly athletic clothing) contain polyester, a fossil fuel by-product that releases two to three times more carbon emissions than cotton and doesn't break down in the oceans. In 2015 polyester production for textiles released about 706 billion kg (1.5 trillion pounds) of greenhouse gases—the equivalent of 185 coal-fired power plants' annual emissions. In many countries that produce garments, untreated wastewaters from textile factories are dumped right into rivers and can carry toxic substances like lead, mercury, and arsenic. This is harmful not only to wildlife but also to the millions of people who live near and depend on those waterways.

We need to give our purchased items as much love as we can, but it is not easy when most clothes are specifically designed to be cheap and to fall apart after just a few washes. According to the Environmental Protection Agency Office of Solid Waste, Americans throw away more than 81 pounds of clothing and textiles per person per year, and rubber, leather, and textiles represent about 9 percent of the municipal solid waste (Environmental Protection Agency, 2016).

Learning to fix your own gear is a great way to extend its lifetime. Adhesive patches can work wonders on down and shells, and even those of us with inexpert hands can wield a needle with enough efficiency to keep some shorts together. If an outside layer starts to feel leaky, slap some Nikwax on it to improve waterproofing. For DIYers, ifixit.com has incredible tutorials on how to repair a variety of technical apparel and running gear. Consumers can bring Patagonia products that need more complicated fixes into a Patagonia store or can send them to Patagonia's Repair Center in Reno, Nevada, one of the largest apparel repair facilities in the United States. REI offers a range of repairs too; from fabric to footwear, REI connects us with a repair person or cobbler to fit our needs.

Aside from choosing clothes and gear made in the European Union, Canada, and United States, where there are stricter environmental regulations, we can keep clothing out of landfills and reduce our environmental impact by buying used.

As secondhand apparel and gear become more mainstream, it's more accessible online than ever. You can get used gear at REI and Allbirds, and Patagonia's Worn Wear program lets you mail in old togs in exchange for store credit. Geartrade also has an amazing selection of outdoor-oriented products and apparel. Facebook Marketplace in and around mountain towns and outdoor hubs is also a great resource, with the added benefit that you can often pick stuff up in person rather than paying to have it shipped (again, reducing emissions). Poshmark isn't specifically outdoor-oriented, but you can score some sweet deals on great running apparel there. GotSneakers, a recycling and redistributing enterprise that compensates runners to mail in old running shoes, also offers the largest selection of used running shoes on their SneakerCycle website. One caution: While you can find low-mileage shoes secondhand, always look for a photo of the tread to assess wear; if you see any indicator these have been worn, avoid these for running. There are some things that are best to buy new; running shoes, socks, and underwear are those things.

Every little bit counts, and when it comes to the apparel industry, we have a long way to go. Though we're never going to thrift our way out of the environmental crisis, we love rocking our secondhand style while holding our government and corporations to account. And not only is shopping secondhand more sustainable, it's also significantly more affordable and even fun. Where else are you going to get a neon green ski shell from the spring 1986 collection?

In British Columbia, Internet and TV network TELUS sponsored Canada's first ever Circular Economy Month in October 2022. The awareness campaign, aimed at reducing waste and consumption, helped to educate and encourage Canadians to move, repair, recycle, or upcycle their old phones and tablets, instead of sending them to a landfill, and to reduce electronic waste (TELUS Communications Inc. 2022).

WEEE (Waste, Electrical and Electronic Equipment) Ireland is a nonprofit that has been working hard to divert electronic waste away from landfills. In 2021, they collected 18.7 million electrical waste items. They also recovered "127,000 fridges and 205,000 TVs and monitors, as well as over 2.3 million lightbulbs in a total takeback of 38,464 tonnes—57% of the average goods sold over a three-year period" (Waste, Electrical and Electronic Equipment Ireland 2022). Refrigerators can be especially harmful for the environment, with the release of damaging chemicals, if not disposed of correctly. There is a reason Project Drawdown, the world's leading resource for climate solutions, referred to refrigerant management as the number one climate solution to address (Hawken 2017).

Buy Nothing groups on Facebook or similar community groups are a great way to pass along gently used (or never used) items. We can also pick up items we need rather than purchasing them new. This symbiosis strengthens our communities, which is critical to our future. Humans have a deep, instinctual desire to work together and feel like we belong.

> We all have a role to play, but the first step is to change our perspective on consumerism and how much we need to purchase, especially new.

These examples, along with the many others provided in the book, are ways in which communities and businesses, big and small, can work collectively to make change happen. We all have a role to play, but the first step is to change our perspective on consumerism and how much we need to purchase, especially new. This message has been around for decades, but we are at the point where we can no longer ignore it. The future of humanity is on the line.

Reuse Plastics

A 2015 article in the *Journal of Science* calculated that 275 million metric tons of plastic waste were generated in 192 coastal countries in 2010, with 4.8 to 12.7 million metric tons entering the ocean (Jambeck et al. 2015). Let's think about that for a moment. A metric ton is a million grams, and 275 million metric tons is . . . a lot, and that number is only expected to increase. Plastic has also been found at the top of Mount Everest, in the deepest parts of the ocean, and at both the North and South Poles. There are also microplastics in our bodies (Senathirajah 2021). A recent study suggests that people are consuming about 2,000 tiny pieces of plastic every week, which add up to around five grams of

Zoë's Thoughts

Although I'm a professional gear tester who puts the latest, greatest, and techiest gear through the ringer in my day job, most of my personal gear is used or secondhand. Gear companies are eternally touting cutting-edge technologies to wick sweat and tape seams; however, the best gear I've used is also some of the oldest.

The habit started when I was a broke graduate student living in Boulder, and I started perusing thrift shops and garage sales, looking for secondhand ice tools and running shoes. The average Boulder rummage sale rivals some better suburban REIs, so I was amazed at the quantity and quality of gear I was able to purchase. I've purchased everything from shorts to shells to hydration packs secondhand.

My advice is to ignore the marketing hype. Ignore the holiday rush. These are fabrications from an industry that thrives on us feeling like we need the best new shoe or the lightest jacket to excel. There is no single shirt or shell or pair of shorts that we need to run better or travel lighter. So you might as well buy it used. By reducing the overall impact produced by the rest of my closet, I rest a little easier when I can't always opt out of the gear-industrial complex.

A lot of times the best gear is the stuff we already have. And the more times we can circulate those things (reduce, reuse!), the better. While it can be obnoxious to try to find the exact thing we want in our size and preferred color, easy consumerism is exactly what got us into this mess in the first place. The more mindful we are about our consumption habits, the better.

---

plastic a week, the weight of a credit card (University of Newcastle Australia 2019). These microplastics in our system will only continue to increase as our plastic consumption increases. Plastic is made from fossil fuels and will be the chief focus for oil companies if renewable energy becomes the primary source of fuel in the years to come. In 2019, the Center for International Environmental Law released an in-depth report that found 850 million metric tons of greenhouse gases will be added to the atmosphere in 2019 alone (Hamilton and Feat et al. 2019). That is the equivalent of the emissions of 189 five-hundred-megawatt coal power plants.

Finding ways to reuse everyday items, especially single-use plastics, is an important step toward reducing consumption. Once you actually step back and see all the single-use items you go through in a day, it will be hard to go back to a place where you don't. And it's not only about purchasing items for long-term use but also trying to maximize use out of the single-use plastics we have little choice over. Rather than going to storage shops to buy expensive boxes to store our safety pins from races, use old yogurt tubs; instead of throwing away a takeout container, use it to bring your prerace meal along; instead of purchasing containers to store holiday decorations, use boxes from a previous delivery; instead of purchasing plastic bags for sandwiches and snacks, use tortilla or bread bags; or instead of purchasing oatmeal from Starbucks, make your own and bring it in an applesauce jar. The options are endless.

Reuse Feminine Hygiene Products

Feminine hygiene products are a major contributor to waste accumulation in landfills. A 2022 exploratory study estimated that 15 million women in the United Kingdom menstruate over the span of 37.5 years, using approximately 3.3 billion units of single-use menstrual management products (pads and tampons) every year (Blair et al. 2022). Every year! They estimated that 28,114 tons of waste are generated annually from menstrual products, 26,903 tons of which are disposable. Menstrual cups, reusable pads, and period underwear can change that. It is important to select the appropriate product for you and your lifestyle. Unfortunately, this is not a situation where we can tell you "the best" menstrual cup for your body since we are all different. The website putacupinit.com has a quiz to answer questions about your body and will recommend a brand and style from the results. These can be sanitized or washed between uses, and once you switch to these items, you may wonder why you didn't make the shift sooner.

Tina's Thoughts

My period stopped when I was 19 years old. I finally got it back at age 28 and became pregnant immediately. I spent another three years in pregnancy and postpartum without a cycle. At age 33, I knew my body well from a training perspective and generally considered myself an intuitive person, but when it came to my hormonal body, I was clueless. I knew I didn't like tampons, and pads felt awkward and uncomfortable (plus they made me very self-conscious in my running clothes). With my environmental focus, I knew I wanted to figure out the better, more sustainable way to do this, but where to start?

As I pondered this, my friend Helen messaged about "period pants" being amazing in a group chat. I had no idea what that meant, but I was curious to learn more. Period pants are essentially underwear with a highly absorbent liner. I liked the look of Modibodi, but the price initially took me by surprise. It seemed like a big investment for something I wasn't confident I would like. But I trusted Helen's advice, and I went for it. When I put them on, I was shocked. They did not feel big and bulky like pads, and they didn't get stuck to my skin or require awkward changes in the bathroom; they felt like everyday underwear. I couldn't believe it. I was sold. I bought multiple pairs, including a few "active" pairs for exercise, and five years later I am still using those same pairs every month.

I did need one tweak though. On the first day of my period, I found the flow was a little too heavy to rely on the underwear alone, especially if it was a hot day. I love to wear shorts, like the Tracksmith Session Speed shorts, which are loose. I found the underwear mixed with sweat to leave a reddened patch on the under part of my running shorts, not something I wanted.

So, I added a menstrual cup to the mix. My sister Jess suggested the quiz at putacupinit.com to find one that worked for me. I loved that it recommended a brand of menstrual cup that was different from the one that she used and that in turn was different than the cup suggested to friends. I needed to size up after the birth of my second daughter, but if the cup is inserted correctly, I can wear it all day, barely noticing it is there. While the learning curve with menstrual cups is pretty steep and, to be honest, at times I felt embarrassed, like I wasn't able to do the simplest thing for my body, once I got the hang of it, it was easy.

I also tried reusable pads, but I didn't really like them. They felt big and bulky, especially compared to the ease of the period pants, and they made me more aware I was on my period, not less. As someone who was essentially a teenage girl in terms of experience in understanding my period, I was already self-conscious, and this made it much worse. I was glad I found what worked for me, and now I don't have to purchase anything new each month, I have my routine, and it works great!

Recycle Better

Aspirational recycling. Something we all do often. Something that contributes to the abysmally low recycling rate, and deep down, we know it. Rubicon, a digital marketplace for waste and recycling, explains aspirational recycling as "the action of feeling like something should be recyclable, so you throw it in the recycling bin under the assumption that if it's not, the individuals sorting through your recycling at the materials recovery facility (MRF) will simply take it out (2019)." Sounds logical, right? We thought so too. But as Rubicon goes on to explain, "While practices vary between cities and municipalities, more often than not if you perform aspirational recycling by placing something in your recycling bin that isn't recyclable, it will cause the whole load to be thrown out. This is recycling contamination, and it's a big problem for commercial and residential customers alike."

There is always going to be a limit to what we can do through recycling, and while it has become our go-to method of releasing ourselves from accountability, putting items of dubious recyclability into the system has very damaging effects. The problem is, we don't have better alternatives, even though they actually do exist. It can be argued that aspirational recycling, or even recycling in general, is worse for the environment than if it didn't exist. Recycling lets us off the hook to think we are doing something when in fact we are not. It gives us a way to deal with our anxiety for the future but actually takes our eyes off the real problem: the systems in place.

The plastic film surrounding DVDs, food items, and other sealed products is especially damaging to recycling facilities. When those items are thrown into a regular single- or dual-stream recycling bin (unless your local municipality specifically says these items are okay), they jam up the machinery, requiring that it be stopped and repaired before it can continue sorting. This costs the facility time, labor, and money to fix. It makes it even more difficult for the facility to stay afloat and be able to process our recycling.

Let's talk about what the word *recycling* actually means. Recycling is breaking something down and making it back into the exact same thing. Aluminum cans, if recycled correctly, can be melted down and turned back into other aluminum cans.

They can go through this process again and again—in theory forever. Glass can also be recycled in this way. The U.S. Environmental Protection Agency stated that 3.1 million tons of glass containers were recycled in 2018, a recycling rate of 31.3 percent. Not great, but according to the EPA, "Making new glass from recycled glass is typically cheaper than using raw materials." This is something to put energy into: making sure the glass we recycle is cleaned out fully, and lids removed. As

Recycling Around the World

While we have primarily focused on the United States for much of this chapter, recycling is approached differently in other countries. Their practices could make recycling better for the environment and break us out of our bad habits.

Sweden

Sweden is shifting the way they view waste disposal to transition away from recycling to reusing for their goal of becoming zero waste. For Swedes, sorting their waste into different bins (dual-stream) is a part of life. According to the Swedish Institute, 86 percent of bottles made of PET (polyethylene terephthalate, the most common type) and 87 percent of aluminum cans in the deposit system were recycled in 2020, and 54 percent of household waste and similar waste was turned into energy in 2020 (Sweden.se n.d.).

Canada

While Canada is not a leader in recycling rates, they have found creative ways to reduce waste and move toward a circular economy. They have installed cigarette butt recycling programs in many cities and parks throughout the country to collect this plastic litter (that also releases harmful chemicals). The cigarette butts are then sent off to TerraCycle to be sorted and separated into compost, recycling, and upcycling to become benches and picnic tables (Parks Canada 2022). Canadians must pay a tire recycling fee (TRF), a fee collected by a provincial tire stewardship organization to ensure that the tire will be managed responsibly at the end of its useful life. The tires are then mixed with other materials to create safe playground surfacing, supershred mulch, and delineator bases (Canadian Association of Tire Recycling Agencies, 2022).

Wales

Wales has become a world leader in recycling through specific initiatives targeting waste reduction. Their household recycling rates have skyrocketed from 5.2 percent in 1999 to 60.7 percent in 2019. Municipal (city, town, or district) recycling has risen a similar amount. Wales has a 99 percent household food waste collection rate since the Welsh government introduced funding to local authorities. The Welsh government recognizes the danger to our future in trying to ignore the problem and is making big changes to put this into action (Llywodraeth Cymru Welsh Government 2020).

always, check the rules and requirements for your location since they vary depending on the type of recycling collection. In single-stream recycling, also known as single-sort recycling or mixed recycling, all recycling items are put into the same bin or trash can to be sorted at an MRF. Most U.S. cities use single-stream recycling, and it has become economically viable through machine sorting. These MRFs can process hundreds of tons of recycling in a single day (St. Louis Public Radio 2015).

The majority of items we put in recycling bins are downcycled, which means they never reclaim the structure of the original product, and are made into something different. That does not mean we shouldn't recycle; it means there is a limit to what most recyclables are able to become. According to the U.S. Environmental Protection Agency, paper can be broken down five to seven times before the fibers become too short to bond into new paper (United States Environmental Protection Agency n.d.).

It looks bleak. This chapter went deep in the weeds, and if it is your first time reading about this, you are likely feeling the concern for our planet and our future in the pit of your stomach. We do. But here is the thing: There are a lot of people out there who are doing good work, incredible work actually; we shared some examples, but there are many others who are working hard to alter our path. Now is not the time to believe that we are doomed. We share this information to be honest that, yes, we are in the middle of a big mess—a mess that feels like it shouldn't be ours to figure out, but here we are. We have all made mistakes; that is part of being human, but making connections is also human: working together and figuring things out.

The information shared in this chapter may cause internal angst, especially when trying to explain the gravity of the situation to loved ones who are not ready to listen. Lead by example, share little things you learned, and try to open the door to a discussion about practices that really matter. We want to move the conversation away from recycling being the answer, and toward addressing the bigger, systemic changes that need to happen. You can use your role in your career and groups to ignite conversations with others in our community, but, as always, you need to start by listening. If you begin by preaching and throwing statistics, people will switch off. Anyone would. You have to listen—really listen—to their point of view and respond to their concerns with love and understanding before even thinking of offering an alternative perspective.

A third of this book is about community because when we begin with our local community, we have the power to implement changes that can then be duplicated by other communities. We are not in a sprint; we are running an ultra: a Courtney Dauwalter, may-not-ever-end type of ultra that will require a long-term, patient approach. At times people are not going to be ready to hear what we have to say, even if we have really listened and genuinely empathized with their point of view. This is maddening and means we need someone with whom we trust to talk about these issues. Like-minded friends, especially ones who have read this book, may be a good place to start, as well as others throughout the running community.

ACTION STEPS

- Accept your feelings about the future, whatever they may be. It is okay to feel grief for the future you have lost or anger toward the situation. By acknowledging rather than suppressing these emotions, you can work through them and move forward.

- Reduce your consumption whenever possible. Use Buy Nothing groups and share between friends.

- Set a challenge to reuse each packaging item at least once. Remember, you don't have to be a zero-waste master who fills only a mason jar of waste each week, but it is about reusing things whenever you can.

- Rethink your running clothes by choosing quality over quantity, even if they're a little more expensive. Higher-quality clothes last longer and look (and feel) better, and they will be able to withstand multiple workouts before needing a wash, which reduces time and water spent on washing.

- Revamp your feminine hygiene stock. Find the right personal menstrual cup and try period underwear or reusable pads instead of disposable ones.

- Stop aspirational recycling. If you are unsure if it can be recycled, throw it in the trash.

- Talk to loved ones and friends about climate change as often as possible, but remember to listen first, and pause the conversation to cool off if needed.

15 | Eat and Drink Responsibly

Think about everything you've eaten today. The almond, oat, or cow's milk you poured over your cereal. The blueberries you mixed into your yogurt, the arugula and salmon salad, and even the chocolate bar you had for dessert.

Now, think about what it took to get each of those products from the field or stream they came from and into our mouth. Where were they grown? How were they raised? How were they harvested, transported, stored, shipped, washed, displayed, hydrated, and purchased? What kind of soil did they grow in? What kind of water did they live in? Who caught or harvested them? Where were they picked, and by whom?

Whew. It can be overwhelming to consider the numerous climate factors that contribute to the foods you eat. The science behind food's climate footprint is confusing, and the problem of climate change overwhelming. But taking just a few simple steps to alter your eating habits can have a big impact. Roughly one-third of global greenhouse gas emissions come from food production, and about half of that comes from animal agriculture (Xu et al. 2021). Food production also taps about 70 percent of usable freshwater and occupies 40 percent of global land (Owen 2005). And it's not just about what you eat, but what you don't eat (and throw out!) as well.

According to a 2020 study published in the journal *Nature Communications*, food production is the largest factor threatening species with extinction, contributing to deforestation, desertification, eutrophication (an excess of nutrients in water due to runoff), coastal damage, and degradation of reefs and marine ecosystems (Howard et al. 2020). Agriculture isn't just a driver of climate change but is also a victim of its shifting conditions as the climate grows less stable and increasingly unpredictable. As Jonathan Safran Foer wrote in his book *We Are the Weather*, "Changing how we eat will not be enough, on its own, to save the planet, but we cannot save the planet without changing how we eat" (Foer 2020).

Global food systems as they exist today may not be sustainable, but there is hope because three times a day (or more—runners are hungry!), we athletes can rethink this relationship to the planet, starting with what's on our plate. Experts have identified two fairly simple actions as being some of the most impactful actions individuals can take. Minimizing food waste and reducing consumption of animal products are healthy and cost-effective measures accessible to most runners. In many cases, the actions we need to take are small and unsexy: composting a bit more here, buying a bit less there, writing lists, and planning ahead.

"The good news is that a lot of things that are good for the planet are good for athletes too," says Kylee Van Horn, a registered dietitian nutritionist who specializes in working with endurance athletes. In this chapter, we are going to talk through what fueling as an environmentally conscious runner looks like: addressing our relationship to food, and how that affects our dietary choices; reducing our intake of meat (notice we did not say cutting it out completely; the world doesn't need to be 100 percent vegan for it to matter!); and fueling our runs with more thought and intention. Once again, community is at the heart of these changes, and whether it is shopping local or advocating for climate action through breaking down stigmas, we have a lot to learn. But, thankfully, most of these actions only need a little change to make a big difference.

Growing your own fruits and vegetables, even if only a few, can increase your appreciation of the gift of fresh food.

Zoë's Thoughts

Content Warning: disordered eating and eating disorders. This is a personal story, and it may not resonate with everyone. If you struggle or are in recovery, take care of yourself.

I grew up in northern Arkansas, working on my family's apple orchard. My earliest memories include running around the orchard, climbing trees, and eating apples that were the epitome of fresh. From an early age, I had a unique glimpse into what an ideal relationship with food could look like. For me, it was working side by side with my grandpa at the farmers market, chatting with folks, and helping them pick the perfect type of apple. My dad, a professor who specialized in researching sustainable and organic crop development, let me follow him around on his research farm, picking berries, weighing root balls, and falling in love with food as a meaningful way of engaging on climate action. At age 17, I swore off meat and became a vegetarian.

That relationship with food soured as I grew older. My body changed in ways I wasn't comfortable with, and a bent toward perfectionism in college manifested in anxiety, depression, and an eating disorder. Eating disorders can manifest differently for everyone, and mine was associated with a drive to be seen as the perfect student, so I overcommitted myself academically, which led to feeling exhausted and overwhelmed. I coped with those feelings by using exercise to avoid negative feelings (exercise bulimia) and setting strict but arbitrary boundaries around the perceived healthiness of certain foods (known as orthorexia). Rather than athletic performance, my restriction was driven by anxiety around academic achievement. In my experience, eating disorders have a way of sinking their teeth into our biggest vulnerabilities.

Food, which had once been a healthy point of connection for my family and friends, became a source of anxiety and fear. I started telling people I was vegan as a way of wriggling out of social eating situations or to avoid eating something I didn't think was healthy enough. I passed on entire food groups, like dairy, or anything too processed. But this fear was based on a perception of myself rather than the actual nutritional value of a food. While there are perfectly good reasons to omit foods from our diet (allergies, sensitivity, dislike), I skipped them out of fear. What started as an empowering dietary choice to eschew animal products got twisted up in mental illness and distorted by my inability to reconcile the two. My days were dominated by rules I set for myself around food that made connecting with others a challenge and made healthy, sustainable training and functioning on a day-to-day basis nearly impossible.

Thankfully, I had a dear friend who convinced (read: forced) me to get help. He dragged me to our college's counseling office and sat with me while I waited for my first appointment. After years of hard work, therapy, and support, I identify as proudly in recovery. I don't know that I'll ever be fully recovered, but letting go of an idealized process or end point has been healing for me.

I still eat in a way that aligns with my environmental values, but I no longer adhere to any particular "diet," or stick to hard-and-fast rules. Rigid rules and labels don't work for my brain, which is likely to fall into traps of perfectionism or black-and-white thinking.

But I do strive to guide my nutrition choices out of love for my planet and people, even if that means not following strict guidelines. For several months, I lived and

(continued)

Tina's Thoughts (*continued*)

reported in rural communities in the Alaskan bush. Fresh food was expensive ($9 for a bunch of bananas, $3 for a single apple) and tough to obtain, so, while I don't normally eat animal products, I enjoyed caribou tacos and moose stroganoff. Being flexible allowed me to better connect with the communities I was in and was actually more climate-friendly too. An elk steak prepared lovingly by the hunter who killed it beats a crappy, three-dollar convenience-store apple any day.

Now I think about eating as a way of fueling my training and my climate work. To show up fully for the causes I care about, I need to be fueled and connected. I need to be able to bond with friends and family over shared meals, to fully inhabit my life and work without worrying about what I'm eating. I'm not interested in putting a strict label on my diet; I'm more interested in making decisions that reflect my own core values. For me, this more flexible, situationally dependent framework helps me reconnect with my love of food and make independent decisions about how I can use that relationship to express my love for our planet, farmworkers, and animals.

Food is a tough subject for many. It's personal and political—a function of race, class, and socioeconomic privilege. For working parents, just getting three square meals on the table a day is stressful enough without agonizing over the carbon footprint of a particular brand of black beans. As a southerner, many of the foods that bring back the most joyful family memories are stigmatized or overlooked by the wellness-industrial complex. (Whaddup collard greens? I see you. You will always be better than kale.) I get it. I'm not here to tell you how or what to eat but to give you power and permission to make tough nutrition decisions in a way that resonates with your life and your core values. That can and should look different for every athlete and every activist. If saving the world begins at breakfast, caring for yourself starts there too.

And if you're not there yet, I recommend reaching out to a mental health professional or other specialist who works with athletes and eating disorders or disordered eating. This stuff is tough, but working through it is so rewarding.

Waste Not

According to one study, if food waste were a country, it would be the third-largest emitter of greenhouse gases behind China and the United States (Hanson et. al. 2015). Another study by Project Drawdown, a multidisciplinary coalition of experts on climate-change solutions, ranks food-waste reduction as the single most impactful climate action we can take (Project Drawdown 2019). Some studies show that as much as 11 percent of greenhouse gas emissions could be eliminated if food waste were brought to zero (Spiegel 2019).

In the United States, according to the National Resources Defense Council, upward of 40 percent of food produced each year is wasted (2012). While some food is wasted as part of agricultural processes and throughout the supply chain, consumers are responsible for the majority of food waste. The United States Environmental Protection Agency (EPA) estimates 28 percent of the planet's agricultural land is used to grow food that ends up in the garbage. Food waste is the single largest solid-waste component of America's landfills—an estimated 80 billion pounds—and emissions from it are equivalent to the greenhouse-gas output of 33 million cars (EPA n.d.). This is an environmental and food justice disaster.

Even the best-intentioned among us have overordered at a restaurant or bought too much at the grocery store. Sometimes, our athletic ambition is only rivaled by our voracious appetites when we're on the hunt for postrun food. We add a few extra items to our grocery cart without a plan for their use, or we get an extra appetizer at the restaurant (artichoke dip!) and can't finish our main course. Maybe we take it home, intending to eat it the next day, but it gets pushed to the back of the fridge, lost until we discover it a week later, sad and defeated.

"Everyone can minimize the amount of food they waste," says Emily Olsen, a trail runner and director of the Cloud City Conservation Center, an environmental and food-justice nonprofit based in Leadville, Colorado. "If you want to make a difference at the intersection of climate and social justice, just eating the food we buy is it."

Van Horn urges runners to start thinking ahead about their shopping and meal planning habits. Haphazardly making a shopping list or going to the grocery store without a plan can cause you to overbuy things like produce or even things that are not needed (such as repeat items that you may already have in the house), which can be avoided by doing a cursory pantry and fridge check.

"If you do overbuy, think about ways to prolong the life of the food you may have excess of," says Van Horn. "For instance, if you bought too much bread, put it in the freezer or if it is going bad, make croutons out of it. For produce, blanch/freeze or dehydrate it to be able to use in soups or smoothies later."

Leftovers are a climate-conscious and economically conscious way to eat. Extend leftovers by adding rice or tofu, depending on your carbohydrate or protein needs. Turn last night's pizza into tomorrow's breakfast. Bam! Climate action.

The absolute last-ditch effort: Compost it. Compost is a great way to reduce the amount of food waste that you send to the landfill, and it can be used in your home garden. Find out if there is a compost option in your community (some even have subsidized or sliding-scale payment options) to divert some of your household waste. It's fun to know that your coffee grounds, paper towels, and orange peels can go on to feed a garden and give life to something new.

Cut Down on Meat

A study at the World Resources Institute (WRI) calculated the greenhouse gas emissions associated with producing a gram of edible protein of various foods (Hanson et al. 2015). Foods like beans, fish, nuts, and eggs have the lowest impact. Poultry, pork, milk, and cheese have medium-size impacts. Far and away the biggest impacts (just in terms of greenhouse gas emissions—we're not even accounting for habitat loss, land use, or other external costs) are associated with beef, lamb, and goat. According to the WRI, the planetary impact of Americans' meat and dairy consumption accounts for nearly 90 percent of all the land used to produce food and 85 percent of diet-related greenhouse gas emissions (Ranganathan 2016). Basically, we need a whole lotta land to feed and produce the meat we eat, and we are quickly running out of land that can (or should) sustain livestock.

The average American eats about 185 pounds of meat a year, which is about eight ounces per day. But, USDA's 2020 dietary guidelines recommend under half that—3.7 ounces—which comes out to around 84 pounds per year. Eating the recommended amount would mean halving current meat consumption.

"Reducing meat consumption reduces both our carbon emissions and our agricultural footprint," says Peter Newton, professor of environmental sciences at the University of Colorado Boulder and an accomplished trail runner (Rom 2021). According to a 2016 study published in the Proceedings of the National Academy of Sciences of the United States of America, projected global greenhouse emissions could be reduced as much as 70 percent if everyone on earth adopted a vegan diet, and 63 percent for a vegetarian diet (Springmann et. al. 2016). "From purely an environmental perspective (i.e., ignoring human health and animal welfare for a minute) most of the problem could be solved without anyone needing to become vegan. Rather, a dramatic reduction in meat consumption would suffice," says Newton.

Being vegan or vegetarian isn't nearly as tough as it once was. Gone are the days of carob chips (a truly hideous chocolate alternative) and inedible, soggy tofu. There are multiple plant-based meal services, and nearly every grocery store is stocked with fun, plant-based alternatives to taco meat and chicken nuggets. If living without burgers or pulled pork nachos feels like too big an ask, you can let yourself have them on special occasions. Since Tina became a vegetarian in 2020, she has enjoyed a few burgers and fish tacos with zero guilt. Being vegetarian or vegan does not have to mean never again. Enough people making a lot of imperfect decisions and committing to action will have more impact than throwing up our hands at the thought of never eating another cheesesteak. According to a 2015 study by the journal *Frontiers in Nutrition*, a diet that is vegetarian five days a week and includes meat just two days a week would reduce greenhouse-gas emissions and water and land use by about 45 percent (Ruini et al. 2015). Eating organic, grass-fed, free-range beef doesn't let you off the hook either. Meat is still a heavy emitter, no matter how it's raised.

Van Horn recommends that athletes interested in transitioning to a plant-based diet start small: "If you are wanting to transition to a more plant-based diet, yet you lead a busy lifestyle and are training a lot, consider transitioning to a couple of days per week that meet your plant-based expectations so you can see how well it fits. Keep in mind that dietary changes should never feel like a burden or cause you mental stress that affects the rest of your life. For instance, if you are traveling and there are no vegan options, yet you are hungry, flexibility could be beneficial in this social situation to allow yourself to take in some sort of nutrition." She recommends runners who want to reduce their meat consumption start with eliminating meat at one or two meals a day, rather than going, excuse the pun, whole hog right away. Meat can be seen as a treat rather than a dietary default.

For athletes concerned about getting enough protein, Van Horn is a huge fan of lentils, which contain twice the protein of most beans per serving. "It's all about balance," says Van Horn. Protein recommendations for athletes range from 98 grams of protein a day for casual competitors to 176 grams for serious endurance athletes, depending on weight. "You can still get plenty of protein while minimizing meat," says Van Horn. Beans, while less protein-rich than lentils, still pack a punch depending on the variety. Soybeans, split peas, and white beans are some of the highest in protein per serving.

Fueling Your Runs

Fueling your runs while reducing waste and seeking out plant-based options may seem like it requires a lot more mental energy than you have to spare, but once you find the low-emission sustenance that works well for you, it will be easier to make tweaks as alternatives become available. Finding eco-friendly chews and gels is difficult, and wrappers from those products can add up. Even if you do recycle them with the GU TerraCycle program, that process still involves burning carbon. Nutrition brands are working hard behind the scenes to figure out how to create compostable packaging, but this is not an easy ask when the package has to preserve the food inside and handle rough (often sweaty) treatment in our packs and pockets, but still break down after use.

For ultra and trail runners, maple syrup and honey are good food options that don't require at-home prep. You can use a refillable flask for these sweet options (or for homemade mashed potatoes). Van Horn also recommends making a gel-like mixture of mashed sweet potatoes, salt, and a drizzle of maple syrup. Foods like mini-muffins or cookies are easy to make and fairly portable fuel as well.

If filling a flask with honey or mashed potatoes or trying to fuel an entire ultra with syrup doesn't sound appealing, choose nutrition products from companies with a demonstrated commitment to environmental values. Clif Bar & Company is part of the Ellen MacArthur Foundation Global Commitment, which pledges to help create a world in which plastic never becomes waste or pollution. They are committed to creating more eco-friendly packaging and driving education by using the How2Recycle label on their packaging. Other brands like GU Energy Labs are doing their part by improving their production process. They produce 95 percent of their energy needs from solar panels installed at their headquarters, use nontoxic cleaning products, and have reduced their water usage by 20 percent (GU Energy Labs n.d.). It's not perfect, but it's a start.

Get Local

Another way we can reduce the carbon footprint of our food is to buy local and in season. Buying in season helps support long-term environmental health and supports small businesses and healthier soil. Healthy soil absorbs more carbon, retains more water, and reduces harmful runoff from crops.

Zoë's Thoughts

When I was a teenager working at the farmers market in Fayetteville, Arkansas, the community and market managers came together to figure out how to make fresh, locally produced food more accessible. Farmers markets may feel like a welcoming space to those of us inclined to spend an entire Saturday walking around with an NPR tote bag full of kale, but the cost and culture are prohibitive to many folks.

The Fayetteville farmers market started to make fresh produce more accessible by incentivizing and destigmatizing SNAP (Supplemental Nutrition Assistance Program, colloquially called "food stamps") usage at the market. First, the market installed machines that looked like ATMs that would let folks use their EBT (Electronic Benefits Transfer) cards to turn SNAP or WIC (Women, Infants, and Children) credits into wooden tokens that could be used as cash around the market. Since many farmers didn't have technology that would process SNAP or EBT cards, minimizing the friction between people who wanted to use their SNAP benefits and farmers who wanted to sell produce was key. Using the wooden tokens helped minimize some of the shame and stigma associated with receiving government assistance, and farmers would be reimbursed with the cash equivalent after market.

Market managers used data from the machines to determine that many people tended to come to the farmers market later, after peak hours. So they worked with regional public transportation to add buses at times when folks needed them most. They also identified that many SNAP users preferred less crowded days to visit, preferring the midweek Wednesday market to the more busy Saturday option, and added buses to and from the market at those times as well. The farmers market also worked to print and distribute educational resources, like recipe cards and buying advice in Spanish, Hmong, and Marshallese. Knowing what food is in season, and how to cook culturally appropriate and relatively easy meals, helped incentivize market participation as well.

The program was so successful in its first years that the Walmart Foundation provided a matching grant that would let consumers "double their dollars" so that when they cashed out 10 dollars' worth of benefits with their EBT card, they would get the equivalent of $20 to use at the market. In addition to incentivizing the purchasing of fresh food, it minimized the cost barrier and put money directly into the local economy in farmers' pockets.

I share this story because it illustrates some of the many barriers that prevent people from being able to participate in the nutrition and climate decisions we make every day. While making sure we do our best to eat in a way that aligns with our climate values is important, the benefit is negligible if we fail to address, through comprehensive policy change and solutions, the socioeconomic barriers that limit the ability for others to do the same. If we truly care about eating in a way that's good for the planet, we need to do everything possible to make sure everyone in our community has the same access to food and that food systems are reconstructed to align with our environmental values. Saving the world might start at breakfast, but failure to engage with food justice as a driver of climate change means our efforts will fall short in communities where they are needed most.

Mariah Foley, Zoë's frequent running partner and agricultural manager of the Aspen Center for Environmental Studies, says, "If you can buy directly from local farms, it helps the farmers capture a higher profit. In turn, this goes to support environmentally sustainable farming practices that create a healthier soil profile." Plus, money spent locally will circulate in the local economy, leading to a healthier, sustainable economy. Economic sustainability can help support environmental sustainability.

Like any run, climate action starts with a lot of small steps. Committing to reducing food waste where we can and cutting out red meat while reducing animal products are the most impactful climate choices an individual can make. It doesn't have to be perfect to count, and a few simple adjustments can go a long way. Emphasize plant-based proteins. Stop wasting food. Get creative in the kitchen. Stop worrying about having the "perfect" diet. We can still eat for performance while minimizing our carbon footprint.

"Your health is linked to the health of your neighbors, your community, and your planet. And that's powerful," says Olsen.

Saving the planet begins at breakfast. Let's do this.

ACTION STEPS

- Plan ahead and prepare to reduce food waste.
- Start with small changes. Rather than going vegan right out of the gate, try cutting out animal products for most meals each day or for at least a few days of the week.
- Remember that it's entirely possible to get enough protein and nutrients on a plant-based or planet-centered diet.
- Reconsider your fueling options. Can you switch out some of your packaged products for whole foods carried in reusable sandwich bags or fuel packs?
- Shop locally as much as possible.
- Food justice is an important part of climate action; consider what lesson you can take from the example we shared about the Fayetteville farmers market.

EPILOGUE

It might feel overwhelming.

All the possible ways we could be more sustainable, thoughtful, intentional, better humans—it feels impossible, like nothing we do will ever be enough. The more we open our eyes and hearts to do better, the more we realize how little we have actually done.

But just like the sport we love, it is about breaking it down: one step at a time, one day at a time, small changes that add up. In the same way that we become comfortable talking about our runs as part of what moves us toward becoming our best selves, when we begin speaking up in small ways to improve the future of our community and world, we become more proficient at it (and more confident!).

No one's perfect, and trying to be something we're not risks disconnecting us from the relationships that got us into this work in the first place. Perfection is not the goal: Under our current social and economic systems, it's just not possible. Squabbling over the impact of shoes or gel wrappers obfuscates the real work that needs to be done. The need to demonstrate some perceived climate action "perfection" just falls into the ideological traps that perpetuate climate inaction. We're embedded in a world that fossil fuel has made, and we are here to help you do your best, while moving toward the most fulfilling and effective action possible.

This book has not been written with the intention of making you feel greedy and ungrateful and selfish; we will leave that to the fossil fuel companies that are desperately trying to shift blame. We are actually going for quite the opposite. We are asking for change, but all of us make mistakes, and we won't get it right every time. Doomsday language will continue to be pushed into our consciousness when it comes to the future of our planet. It is placed there intentionally, and we get stuck on it because our brains are hardwired to be on the lookout for danger. But that gloomy view is also present in the running world through well-intentioned comments about protecting our knees or about people losing their lives, for one reason or another, while running.

The more we are curious about how interconnected we all are as humans, and as living organisms—part of an inconceivably intricate and beautiful planetary, and even universal, system—the better off we will be. The key is finding your place in this journey toward sustainable living. For Zoë and Tina, that role is using their platforms to help spread the message that we can have a better, healthier, and more sustainable relationship with ourselves, those we interact with, and our home.

Your path forward will look different. You bring an entirely different (and equally necessary) array of talents, connections, abilities, and passions to the table. We can't do this without *you*.

While it can feel like mighty movements of hundreds of thousands of people are the only way to make change, the reality is that everything starts off small. Greta Thunberg's global impact began with her sole act of sitting outside parliament in Sweden on a Friday. The Black Lives Matter movement began with a few courageous women—Alicia Garza, Patrisse Cullors, and Ayo Tometi—who created the hashtag #BlackLivesMatter following the acquittal of George Zimmerman for shooting and killing Trayvon Martin.

Act locally; think globally. It is the combined efforts of all those local changes that builds into something global. It is the employee who suggests to their boss that the department switch to digital notes for a meeting instead of endless pages of printed notes. It is the party host who asks guests to bring a plate and silverware to avoid plastic alternatives. It is the foodie who shares a delicious vegan entree with friends who had no idea vegan food could taste this good. Seeds are being planted with every decision we make. We may never sit under the shade of those trees, but what matters is that we're out here sowing our hearts out.

While we can wish that we could flip a switch to make everyone think about becoming sustainable humans, the reality is that we have the opportunity to build ourselves into the people we want to become, one decision at a time. Every time we make a choice, we have the opportunity to inspire someone else to do the same. It happens every time we choose to rest from running when we know our body needs to fight off an infection. It happens when we choose to donate our time to volunteering or give advice to a new runner who has mustered the courage to show up to a group run for the first time. It happens when we send an email to our local race director, asking if they would consider offering a no-shirt option by working with a nonprofit like Trees for Tees.

You matter. Your choices matter. Your decisions matter. It can feel like they don't. But just as an ocean is made up of droplets, and together those droplets make something beautiful, powerful, and strong, we can come together with our own unique gifts to amount to something really special.

We believe in you. Let's start this ultramarathon together, one step at a time.

BIBLIOGRAPHY

Allbirds. n.d. "Don't Hide Your Pollution. Label It." Accessed October 23, 2022. www. allbirds.com/pages/carbon-footprint-calculator.

Alldredge, K., T. Charm, E. Falardeau, and K. Robinson. 2022. "How US Consumers Are Feeling, Shopping, and Spending—And What It Means for Companies." *McKinsey & Company.* May 4, 2022. www.mckinsey.com/capabilities/growth-marketing-and-sales/our-insights/how-us-consumers-are-feeling-shopping-and-spending-and-what-it-means-for-companies.

Allied Market Research. 2021. "Weight Loss and Weight Management Diet Market by Product Type (Better-for-you, Meal Replacement, Weight Loss Supplement, Green Tea, and Low-Calorie Sweeteners) and Sales Channel (Hypermarket/Supermarket, Specialty Stores, Pharmacies, Online Channels, and Others): Global Opportunity Analysis and Industry Forecast, 2021–2027." Last modified May 2021. www.alliedmarketresearch.com/weight-loss-management-diet-market.

American Public Transport Association. 2008. "Public Transportation Reduces Greenhouse Gases and Conserves Energy." American Public Transport Association . February 2008. www.apta.com/wpcontent/uploads/Resources/resources/reportsandpublications/Documents/greenhouse_brochure.pdf.

Aral, S., and C. Nicolaides. 2017. "Exercise Contagion in a Global Social Network." *Nature Communications* 8:14753. https://doi.org/10.1038/ncomms14753.

Asics Corporation. 2020. "New Study Explores the World's New-Found Love of Running." Last modified June 9, 2020. https://corp.asics.com/en/press/article/2020-06-09-1.

Association for Size Diversity and Health. n.d. "Haes® Principles." Accessed October 17, 2022. https://asdah.org/health-at-every-size-haes-approach.

Aubrey, A. 2011. "The Average American Ate (Literally) a Ton This Year." *National Public Radio.* December 31, 2011. www.npr.org/sections/thesalt/2011/12/31/144478009/the-average-american-ate-literally-a-ton-this-year.

Bacon, L., and L. Aphramor. 2011. "Weight Science: Evaluating the Evidence for a Paradigm Shift." *Nutrition Journal* 10:9. https://doi.org/10.1186/1475-2891-10-9.

Bain, P., T. Milfont, Y. Kashima, , M. Bilewicz, G. Doron, R.B. Garðarsdóttir, V.V. Gouveia, Y. Guan, L.-O. Johansson, C. Pasquali, et al. 2016. "Co-Benefits of Addressing Climate Change Can Motivate Action Around the World." *Nature Climate Change* 6: 154-157. https://doi.org/10.1038/nclimate2814.

Banerjee, N., L. Song, and D. Hasemyer. 2015. "Exxon's Own Research Confirmed Fossil Fuels' Role in Global Warming Decades Ago." *Inside Climate News.* November 16, 2015. https://insideclimatenews.org/news/16092015/exxons-own-research-confirmed-fossil-fuels-role-in-global-warming.

Ballew, M., A. Gustafson, P. Bergquist, M. Goldberg, S. Rosenthal, J. Kotcher, E. Maibach, and A. Leiserowitz. 2019. "Americans Underestimate How Many Others in the U.S. Think Global Warming Is Happening." Yale Program on Climate Communication. https://climatecommunication.yale.edu/publications/americans-underestimate-how-many-others-in-the-u-s-think-global-warming-is-happening.

Balsasalobre-Fernandez, C., G. Grivas, and J. Santos-Concejero. 2015. "The Effects of Strength Training on Running Economy in Highly Trained Runners: A Systematic Review With Meta-Analysis of Controlled Trials." *The Journal of Strength and Conditioning Research* 30(8). www.researchgate.net/publication/285588167.

Bank of America Chicago Marathon. n.d. "Carbon Offset: U.S." Cool Effect. https://organizations.hakuapp.com/organizations/9b4ada1d9a92ebcf8016/event_products/8060/?single_product=true.

Baptista, A.I. and A. Perovich. 2020. "Environmental Justice and Philanthropy: Challenges and Opportunities for Alignment." Building Equity & Alignment for Environmental Justice. Accessed October 27, 2022. https://bea4impact.org/our-work/landscape-assessment.

Barnes, M., P. Abhyankar, E. Dimova, and C. Best. 2020. "Associations Between Body Dissatisfaction and Self-Reported Anxiety and Depression in Otherwise Healthy Men: A Systematic Review and Meta-Analysis." *PLOS ONE* 15 (2): e0229268. https://doi.org/10.1371/journal.pone.0229268.

Basso, J.C., A. McHale, V. Ende, D.J. Oberlin, and W.A. Suzuki. 2019. "Brief, Daily Meditation Enhances Attention, Memory, Mood, and Emotional Regulation in Non-Experienced Meditators." *Behavioural Brain Research* 356:208-220. https://doi.org/10.1016/j.bbr.2018.08.023.

BBC. n.d. "Dunbar's Number: Why We Can Only Maintain 150 Relationships." Invisible Numbers. Accessed October 13, 2022. www.bbc.com/future/article/20191001-dunbars-number-why-we-can-only-maintain-150-relationships.

Berenstain, S., and J. Berenstain. 1991. *The Berenstain Bears Don't Pollute (Anymore)*. New York: Random House.

Blagrove RC, Howatson G, Hayes PR. Effects of Strength Training on the Physiological Determinants of Middle- and Long-Distance Running Performance: A Systematic Review. Sports Med. 2018 May;48(5):1117-1149. doi: 10.1007/s40279-017-0835-7. PMID: 29249083; PMCID: PMC5889786.

Blair, L.A.G., Y. Bajón-Fernández, and R. Villa. 2022. "An Exploratory Study of the Impact and Potential of Menstrual Hygiene Management Waste in the UK." *Cleaner Engineering and Technology* 7. https://doi.org/10.1016/j.clet.2022.100435.

Brad, R.A. 2015. "Overreaching/Overtraining." *ACSM's Health & Fitness Journal* 19 (2): 4-5. https://doi.org/10.1249/FIT.0000000000000100.

Bracy, A. 2021. *Mental Training for Ultrarunning*. Champaign, IL: Human Kinetics.

Brown, B. 2010. *The Gifts of Imperfection*. Center City, MN: Hazelden.

Brown, B. 2022. *Atlas Of The Heart*. New York: Random House.

Bullard, R.D., P. Mohai, R. Saha, and B. Wright. 2007. "Toxic Wastes and Race at Twenty 1987–2007." National Resource Defense Council. March 2007. www.nrdc.org/sites/default/files/toxic-wastes-and-race-at-twenty-1987-2007.pdf.

"burnout." n.d. *Merriam-Webster Collegiate Dictionary*. https://www.merriam-webster.com/dictionary/burnout.

Canadian Association of Tire Recycling Agencies. 2022. "Canada's Tire Recycling Fees." February 8, 2022. www.catraonline.ca/storage/files/shares/publications-en/Canada_TRFs_by_province_by_tire_type-8_Feb_2022.pdf.

Chen, K.W., C.C. Berger, E. Manheimer, D. Forde, J. Magidson, L. Dachman, and C.W. Lejuez. 2012. "Meditative Therapies for Reducing Anxiety: A Systematic Review and Meta-Analysis of Randomized Controlled Trials." *Depression and Anxiety* 29(7): 545-562. https://doi.org/10.1002/da.21964.

Chicago Event Management. 2021. "CEM Launches Sustainability Guidebook to Help Other Events Prioritize Environmental Impact." Chicago Event Management. September 15, 2021. https://cemevent.com/2021/09/15/cem-launches-sustainability-guidebook-to-help-other-events-prioritize-environmental-impact.

Chloe Maxmin. n.d. "About Chloe." Accessed October 20, 2022. https://firsttherethen-everywhere.wordpress.com/about-chloe.

Chouinard, Y., and V. Stanley. 2012. *The Responsible Company: What We've Learned From Patagonia's First 40 Years.* Patagonia Books.

Chu, J. 2013. "Footwear's (Carbon) Footprint." *MIT News.* May 22, 2013. https://news.mit.edu/2013/footwear-carbon-footprint-0522.

cKinetics Writers. 2021. "Blah Blah Briefing of the Textile and Apparel Sector: How the Sector Can Meet Its Climate Goals." *cKinetics.* www.ckinetics.com/climate/TextileSectorBlahBlah.

Claudio, L. 2007. "Waste Couture: Environmental Impact of the Clothing Industry." *Environmental Health Perspectives* 115 (9): A449-A454. https://doi.org/10.1289/ehp.115-a449.

Climate Impact Partners. n.d. "Carbon Offsetting." Accessed October 20, 2022. www.climatecare.org/calculator/carbon-offsetting.

Climate Reality Project. 2021. "Let's Talk About Sacrifice Zones." Last modified May 13, 2021. www.climaterealityproject.org/blog/lets-talk-about-sacrifice-zones.

Climate Watch. n.d. Accessed October 23, 2022. www.climatewatchdata.org/?source=caithistorical/Country%20GHG%20Emissions.

Cohen, S., W.J. Doyle, C.M. Alper., D. Janicki-Deverts, and R.B. Turner. 2009. "Sleep Habits and Susceptibility to the Common Cold." *Archives of Internal Medicine* 169 (1): 62-67. https://doi.org/10.1001/archinternmed.2008.505.

Cook, J., N. Oreskes, P.T. Doran, W.R.L. Anderegg, B. Verheggen, E.W. Maibach, J.S. Carlton, S. Lewandowsky, A.G. Skuce, and S.A. Green. 2016. "Consensus on Consensus: A Synthesis of Consensus Estimates on Human-Caused Global Warming." *Environmental Research Letters* 11 (4). https://doi.org/10.1088/1748-9326/11/4/048002.

Couronne, I. 2019. "Greta Thunberg's 'How Dare You?' A Major Moment for Climate Movement." Phys.org. Accessed October 27, 2022. https://phys.org/news/2019-09-greta-thunberg-major-moment-climate.html.

Dove. 2010. "The Real Truth About Beauty: Revisited." Last modified 2011. www.dove.com/my/stories/about-dove/our-research.html.

Downey, L. and B. Hawkins. 2008. "Race, Income, and Environmental Inequality in the United States." *Sociological Perspectives* 51 (4): 759-781. https://doi.org/10.1525/sop.2008.51.4.759.

Drew, D., and G. Yehounme. 2017. "The Apparel Industry's Environmental Impact in 6 Graphics." *World Resources Institute.* July 5, 2017. www.wri.org/insights/apparel-industrys-environmental-impact-6-graphics.

Effron, L. 2016. "Michael Jordan, Kobe Bryant's Meditation Coach on How to Be 'Flow Ready' and Get in the Zone." *ABC News,* April 6, 2016. https://abcnews.go.com/Health/michael-jordan-kobe-bryants-meditation-coach-flow-ready/story?id=38175801.

Ellen MacArthur Foundation. 2017. "A New Textiles Economy: Redesigning Fashion's Future." https://emf.thirdlight.com/link/2axvc7eob8zx-za4ule/@/preview/1?o.

Environmental Protection Agency. "Advancing Sustainable Materials Management: 2014 Fact Sheet." November 2016. www.epa.gov/sites/default/files/2016-11/documents/2014_smmfactsheet_508.pdf.

Environmental Protection Agency. 2016. "America's Food Waste Problem," April 22, 2016. www.epa.gov/sciencematters/americas-food-waste-problem.

Environmental Protection Agency. n.d. "Facts and Figures About Materials, Waste and Recycling: Glass: Material-Specific Data." Accessed March 30, 2022. www.epa.gov/facts-and-figures-about-materials-waste-and-recycling/glass-material-specific-data.

Environmental Protection Agency. n.d. "Sources of Greenhouse Emissions." www.epa.gov/ghgemissions/sources-greenhouse-gas-emissions.

Environmental Protection Agency. n.d. "Wastes: Resource Conservation: Common Wastes & Materials: Paper Recycling." Accessed March 30, 2022. https://archive.epa.gov/wastes/conserve/materials/paper/web/html/faqs.html.

Epstein, D. 2019. *Range: Why Generalists Triumph in a Specialized World.* New York: Riverhead Books.

Figueres, C., and T. Rivett-Carnac. 2020. *The Future We Choose: Solving the Climate Crisis.* New York: Alfred A. Knopf.

Fleischman, L. and M. Franklin. 2017. "Fumes Across the Fence-Line: The Health Impacts of Air Pollution From Oil & Gas Facilities on African American Communities." *NAACP.* November 2017. https://naacp.org/resources/fumes-across-fence-line-health-impacts-air-pollution-oil-gas-facilities-african-american.

Foer, J.S. 2020. *We Are the Weather: Saving the Planet Begins at Breakfast.* London: Penguin.

Food and Drug Administration. 2016. "FDA's Policy on Declaring Small Amounts of Nutrients and Dietary Ingredients on Nutrition Labels: Guidance for Industry." Last modified July 2016. www.fda.gov/media/98834/download.

Fortune Business Insights. 2021. "Cosmetics Market Size, Share & COVID-19 Impact Analysis, by Category (Hair Care, Skin Care, Makeup, and Others), by Gender (Men and Women),by Distribution Channel (Specialty Stores, Hypermarkets/Supermarkets, Online Channels, and Others), and Regional Forecasts." Last modified September 2021. www.fortunebusinessinsights.com/cosmetics-market-102614.

Geyer, R., J.R. Jambeck, and K. Lavender Law. 2017. "Production, Use, and Fate of All Plastics Ever Made." *Science Advances* 3:7. https://doi.org/10.1126/sciadv.1700782.

Gimlet Media. 2018. "Is Your Carbon Footprint BS?" March 18, 2021. In *How To Save A Planet*, podcast, 43:17. https://gimletmedia.com/shows/howtosaveaplanet/xjh53gn.

Gimlet Media. 2021. "Recycling! Is it BS?" January 21, 2021. In *How to Save a Planet*, podcast. https://gimletmedia.com/shows/howtosaveaplanet/brh3jeg.

Ginis, K.A., S.M. Burke, and L. Gauvin. 2006. "Exercising With Others Exacerbates the Negative Effects of Mirrored Environments on Sedentary Women's Feeling States." *Psychology and Health* 22:945-962. https://doi.org/10.1080/14768320601070571.

Global Footprint Network. n.d. "Climate Change." Accessed October 20, 2022. www.footprintnetwork.org/our-work/climate-change.

Good Times. 2021. "Running Experiences Huge Surge in Popularity During Pandemic." Last modified January 26, 2021. https://goodtimes.sc/cover-stories/running-surge-popularity-during-pandemic.

Green Sports Alliance. n.d. "Council for Responsible Sport Now Developing Responsible Sport Standard for Organizations." Accessed October 20, 2022. https://greensportsalliance.org/council-for-responsible-sport-now-developing-responsible-sport-standard-for-organizations.

Greenpeace. 2016. "Timeout for Fast Fashion." November 24, 2016. www.greenpeace.org/static/planet4-international-stateless/2018/01/6c356f9a-fact-sheet-timeout-for-fast-fashion.pdf.

Griffin, P. 2017. "The Carbon Majors Database: CDP Carbon Majors Report 2017." *The CDP*. July 2017. https://cdn.cdp.net/cdp-production/cms/reports/documents/000/002/327/ original/Carbon-Majors-Report-2017.pdf?1501833772.

GU Energy Labs. n.d. "Powered by the Sun." https://guenergy.com/blogs/product-deep-dive/powered-by-the-sun.

Hamilton, L.A., S. Feit, C. Muffett, S. Feit, M. Kelso, S. Malone Rubright, C. Bernhardt, Eric Schaeffer, D. Moon, J. Morris, et al. 2019. "Plastic and Climate: The Hidden Costs of a Plastic Planet." Center for International Environmental Law. www.ciel.org/wp-content/uploads/2019/05/Plastic-and-Climate-FINAL-2019.pdf.

Hannibal, K.E., and M.D. Bishop. 2014. "Chronic Stress, Cortisol Dysfunction, and Pain: A Psychoneuroendocrine Rationale for Stress Management in Pain Rehabilitation." *Journal of the American Physical Therapy Association* 94 (12): 1816-1825. https://doi.org/10.2522/ptj.20130597.

Hanson, C., B. Lipinski, J. Friedrich, and C. O'Connor. 2015. "What's Food Loss and Waste Got to Do With Climate Change? A Lot, Actually." World Resources Institute. December 11, 2015. www.wri.org/insights/whats-food-loss-and-waste-got-do-climate-change-lot-actually.

Harvard Business School. 2016. "The Ecological Impact of Feminine Hygiene Products." Last modified November 4, 2016. https://digital.hbs.edu/platform-rctom/submission/the-ecological-impact-of-feminine-hygiene-products.

Hasemyer, D. and Cushman, Jr., J.H. 2015. "Exxon Sowed Doubt About Climate Science for Decades by Stressing Uncertainty." *Inside Climate News*. October 22, 2015. https://insideclimatenews.org/news/22102015/Exxon-Sowed-Doubt-about-Climate-Science-for-Decades-by-Stressing-Uncertainty.

Hawken, P. 2017. *Drawdown*. New York: Penguin.

Hayhoe, K. 2018. "The Most Important Thing You Can Do to Fight Climate Change: Talk About It." TED video, 17:03. https://www.ted.com/talks/katharine_hayhoe_the_most_important_thing_you_can_do_to_fight_climate_change_talk_about_it?language=en

History.com. 2019. "Boston Marathon Bombing." June 7, 2019. www.history.com/topics/21st-century/boston-marathon-bombings.

Howard, C., C.H. Flather, and P.A. Stephens. 2020. "A Global Assessment of the Drivers of Threatened Terrestrial Species Richness." *Nature Communications* 11. https://doi.org/10.1038/s41467-020-14771-6.

Internal Displacement Monitoring Centre (IDMC). 2022. "Global Internal Displacement Database Data" Accessed, January 1, 2023. https://www.internal-displacement.org/database/displacement-data

Jaglo, K., S. Kenny, and J. Stephenson. 2021. "From Farm to Kitchen: The Environmental Impacts of U.S. Food Waste." November 2021. www.epa.gov/system/files/documents/2021-11/from-farm-to-kitchen-the-environmental-impacts-of-u.s.-food-waste_508-tagged.pdf.

Jambeck, J.R., R. Geyer, C. Wilcox, T.R. Siegler, M. Perryman, A. Andrady, R. Narayan, and K.L. Law. 2015. "Marine Pollution: Plastic Waste Inputs From Land Into the Ocean." *American Association for the Advancement of Science* 347 (6223): 768-771. https://doi.org/10.1126/science.1260352.

Kraemer, W.J., and N.A. Ratamess. 2005. "Hormonal Responses and Adaptations to Resistance Exercise and Training." *Sports Medicine* 35(4): 339-361. https://doi.org/10.2165/00007256-200535040-00004.

Kundera, M. 1999. The Unbearable Lightness Of Being (M. H. Heim, Trans.). London, UK: Faber & Faber.

Lastella, M., G.D. Roach, S.L. Halson, and C. Sargent. 2015. "Sleep/Wake Behaviours of Elite Athletes From Individual and Team Sports." *European Journal of Sport Science* 15(2): 94-100. https://doi.org/10.1080/17461391.2014.932016.

Lauersen, J.B., D.M. Bertelsen, and L.B. Andersen. 2014. "The Effectiveness of Exercise Interventions to Prevent Sports Injuries: A Systematic Review and Meta-Analysis of Randomised Controlled Trials." *British Journal of Sports Medicine* 48:871-877.

Lavender Smith, S. 2020. "Giving Back: Running and Outdoor Nonprofits You Can Support." *iRunFar.* November 29, 2020. www.irunfar.com/giving-back-running-and-outdoor-nonprofits-you-can-support.

Lee, H., and F. Birol. 2020. "Energy Is at the Heart of the Solution to the Climate Challenge." *Intergovernmental Panel on Climate Change.* July 31, 2020. www.ipcc.ch/2020/07/31/energy-climatechallenge.

Lehmann, M., C. Foster, and J. Keul. 1993. "Overtraining in Endurance Athletes: A Brief Review." *Medicine and Science in Sports and Exercise* 25 (7): 854-862. https://doi.org/10.1249/00005768-199307000-00015.

Llywodraeth Cymru Welsh Government. 2020. "How Wales Became a World Leader in Recycling." March 18, 2020. https://gov.wales/how-wales-became-world-leader-recycling.

Loria, K. 2018. "14 of The Biggest Sleep Myths Debunked." *The Independent.* Modified March 5, 2018. www.independent.co.uk/life-style/health-and-families/sleep-myths-debunked-coffee-tips-snoring-tired-dreams-a8240456.html.

Loviglio, J. 2011. "50 Years Along, Berenstain Bears a Family Affair." *Washington Times.* January 30, 2021. www.washingtontimes.com/news/2011/jan/30/50-years-along-berenstain-bears-a-family-affair.

Magness, S. (@Stevemagness). "Don't aim to be consistently great. Aim to be great at being consistent." Twitter, March 15, 2019. https://twitter.com/stevemagness/status/1106558669427232768?lang=en.

Mah, C.D., K.E. Mah, E.J. Kezirian, and W.C. Dement. 2011. "The Effects of Sleep Extension on the Athletic Performance of Collegiate Basketball Players." *Sleep* 34 (7): 943-950. https://doi.org/10.5665/SLEEP.1132.

Mahan III, J.E., W.J. Seo, J.S. Jordan, and D. Funk. 2014. "Exploring the Impact of Social Networking Sites on Running Involvement, Running Behavior, and Social Life Satisfaction." *Sport Management Review* 18 (2): 182-192. https://doi.org/10.1016/j.smr.2014.02.006.

Mann, T., A.J. Tomiyama, E. Westling, A.M. Lew, B. Samuels, and J. Chatman. 2007. "Medicare's Search for Effective Obesity Treatments: Diets Are Not the Answer." *The American Psychologist* 62 (3): 220-233. https://doi.org/10.1037/0003-066X.62.3.220.

McCarthy, J. 2015. "Humanity Consumes 1.6 Earths Each Year." *Global Citizen.* August 17, 2015. www.globalcitizen.org/en/content/humanity-consumes-16-earths-each-year.

McCarty, C., P.D. Killworth, H.R. Bernard, E.C. Johnsen, and G.A. Shelley. 2001. "Comparing Two Methods for Estimating Network Size." *Human Organization* 60 (1): 28. https://doi.org/10.17730/humo.60.1.efx5t9gjtgmga73y.

McFall-Johnsen, M. 2020. "These Facts Show How Unsustainable the Fashion Industry Is." *World Economic Forum.* January 31, 2020. www.weforum.org/agenda/2020/01/fashion-industry-carbon-unsustainable-environment-pollution.

Meschke, J. "Ultrarunner Rickey Gates runs San Francisco streets." Runner's World. Published December 19, 2018. https://www.runnersworld.com/runners-stories/a25628489/ultrarunner-rickey-gates-runs-san-francisco-streets/.

Milman, O. and F. Harvey. 2019. "US Is Hotbed of Climate Change Denial, Major Global Survey Finds." *Guardian*, May 18, 2019. www.theguardian.com/environment/2019/may/07/us-hotbed-climate-change-denial-international-poll.

Morgado, F. F., A.N. Campana, and M. Tavares. 2014. "Development and Validation of the Self-Acceptance Scale for Persons With Early Blindness: The SAS-EB." *PloS One* 9(9): e106848. https://doi.org/10.1371/journal.pone.0106848.

Moss, P. 2019. "The Waste of Aspirational Recycling." *Rubicon*. April 3 2019. https://www.rubicon.com/blog/aspirational-recycling/.

Muir, T., and K. Robinson. 2021. "Running and Climate Change with the United Nations Humanitarian Office." November 2, 2021. In *Running Realized*, podcast. https://runningforreal.com/running-realized-cop26/.

Muir, T., and K. Robinson. 2021. "The Sustainable Road Race." June 7, 2021. In *Running Realized*, podcast, 56:48. https://runningforreal.com/running-realized-episode-eight.

NASA. n.d. "Do Scientists Agree on Climate Change?" Accessed October 27, 2022. https://climate.nasa.gov/faq/17/do-scientists-agree-on-climate-change.

National Geographic Society. 2019. "Deforestation." *National Geographic*. July 16, 2019. www.nationalgeographic.org/encyclopedia/deforestation.

National Geographic Society. 2021. "Transportation and Climate Change." *National Geographic*. March 1, 2021. www.nationalgeographic.org/media/transportation-and-climate-change.

National Resources Defense Council. *Wasted: How America Is Losing Up to 40 Percent of Its Food From Farm to Fork to Landfill*. NRDC Issue Paper: August 2012. www.nrdc.org/sites/default/files/wasted-2017-report.pdf.

Native. n.d. "Calculate." Accessed October, 20, 2022. https://native.eco.

Nelson, K. 2022. "Reduce, Reuse, Recycle . . . Redefine? MSU Students Use Campus Waste for Atypical Fashion Design." *The State News*. October 10, 2022. https://statenews.com/article/2022/10/reduce-reuse-recycle-redefine?ct=content_open&cv=cbox_latest.

Outdoor Industry Association. 2021. "2021 Outdoor Participation Trends Report." June 21, 2022. https://outdoorindustry.org/resource/2021-outdoor-participation-trends-report.

Owen, J. 2005. "Farming Claims Almost Half of Earth's Land, New Maps Show." *National Geographic*. December 8, 2005. www.nationalgeographic.com/history/article/agriculture-food-crops-land.

Paavolainen, L., K. Häkkinen, I. Hämäläinen, A. Nummela, and H. Rusko. 1999. "Explosive-Strength Training Improves 5-Km Running Time by Improving Running Economy and Muscle Power." *Journal of Applied Physiology* 86(5): 1527-1533. https://doi.org/10.1152/jappl.1999.86.5.1527.

Parks Canada. 2022. "Parks Canada's First Cigarette Butt Recycling Program Launches in Rouge National Urban Park." October 7, 2022. www.pc.gc.ca/en/pn-np/on/rouge/info/nouvelles-news/2022terracycle.

Phillips, A.J.K., W.M. Clerx, C.S. O'Brien, A. Sano, L.K. Barger, R.W. Picard, S.W. Lockley, E.B. Klerman, and C.A. Czeisler. 2017. "Irregular Sleep/Wake Patterns Are Associated With Poorer Academic Performance and Delayed Circadian and Sleep/Wake Timing." *Scientific Reports* 7:3216. https://doi.org/10.1038/s41598-017-03171-4.

Plante, T.G., M. Madden, S. Mann, G. Lee, A. Hardesty, N. Gable, A. Terry, and G. Kaplow. 2010. "Effects of Perceived Fitness Level of Exercise Partner on Intensity of Exertion." *Journal Of Social Sciences* 6 (1): 50-54. www.psychologytoday.com/sites/default/files/attachments/34033/jssarticle.pdf.

Project Drawdown. n.d. "Table of Solutions." Accessed June 21, 2022. www.drawdown. org/solutions/table-of-solutions.

Ranganathan, J., D. Vennard, R. Waite, B. Lipinski, T. Searchinger and P. Dumas. 2016. "Shifting Diets for a Sustainable Food Future: Creating a Sustainable Food Future, Installment Eleven." World Resources Institute. www.wri.org/research/shifting-diets-sustainable-food-future.

Reichart, E., and D. Drew. 2019. "By the Numbers: The Economic, Social and Environmental Impacts of 'Fast Fashion'." *World Resources Institute*. January 10, 2019. www. wri.org/insights/numbers-economic-social-and-environmental-impacts-fast-fashion.

Republic Services. 2020. "What is Precycling?" February 3, 2020. https://www.republicservices.com/blog/what-precycling

Rohrer, J.M., D. Richter, M. Brümmer, G.G. Wagner, and S.C. Schmukle. 2018. "Successfully Striving for Happiness: Socially Engaged Pursuits Predict Increases in Life Satisfaction." *Psychological Science* 29 (8): 1291-1298. https://doi. org/10.1177/0956797618761660.

Rom, Zoe H. "An Athlete's Guide to Environmentally Friendly Eating." *Trail Runner Magazine*, 10 June 2021, https://www.trailrunnermag.com/people/environment-people/an-athletes-guide-to-environmentally-friendly-eating/.

Ruini, L. F., Ciati, R., Pratesi, C.A., Marino, M., Principato, L., and Vannuzzi, E. 2015. "Working Toward Healthy and Sustainable Diets: The 'Double Pyramid Model' Developed by the Barilla Center for Food and Nutrition to Raise Awareness About the Environmental and Nutritional Impact of Foods." *Frontiers in Nutrition,* 2. https:// doi.org/10.3389/fnut.2015.00009

Salwen, M.B., and M. Dupagne. 1999. "The Third-Person Effect: Perceptions of the Media's Influence and Immoral Consequences." *Communication Research* 26 (5): 523-549. https://doi.org/10.1177/009365099026005001.

Sargent, C., S. Halson, and G.D. Roach. 2014. "Sleep or Swim? Early-Morning Training Severely Restricts the Amount of Sleep Obtained by Elite Swimmers." *European Journal of Sport Science* 14 (1): S310-S315. https://doi.org/10.1080/17461391.2012.696711.

Saujani, R. 2022. "The Importance of Teaching Girls How to Successfully Fail." May 20, 2022. In *Running for Real*, produced by Tina Muir, podcast, 1:02. https://runningfor-real.com/reshma-saujani.

Senathirajah, K., S. Attwood, G. Bhagwat, M. Carbery, S. Wilson, and T. Palanisami. 2021. "Estimation of the Mass of Microplastics Ingested—A Pivotal First Step Towards Human Health Risk Assessment." *Journal Of Hazardous Materials* 404 (B): 124004. https://doi.org/10.1016/j.jhazmat.2020.124004.

Shetty, J. 2020. *Think Like a Monk: Train Your Mind for Peace and Purpose Every Day.* New York: Simon & Schuster.

Smith, J. 2020. "2020 Was a Crazy Running Year. Here's the Data to Prove It." *Runner's World*. Last modified December 30, 2020. www.runnersworld.com/news/a34949046/2020-year-in-running-data.

Spiegel, J.E. 2019. "Food Waste Has Crucial Climate Impacts." Yale Climate Connections. May 6, 2019. https://yaleclimateconnections.org/2019/05/food-waste-has-crucial-climate-impacts.

Springmann, M., Godfray, H.C.J., Rayner, M. and Scarborough, P. 2016. "Analysis and Valuation of the Health and Climate Change Cobenefits of Dietary Change." *Proceedings of the National Academy of Sciences of the United States of America*. March 21, 2016. https://doi.org/10.1073/pnas.1523119113.

St. Louis Public Radio. 2015. "Does Single-Stream Recycling Really Work? Yes! And No." March 8, 2015. https://news.stlpublicradio.org/health-science-environment/2015-03-08/does-single-stream-recycling-really-work-yes-and-no.

Stellingwerff, T., I.A. Heikura, R. Meeusen, S. Bermon, S. Seiler, M.L. Mountjoy, and L.M. Burke. 2021. "Overtraining Syndrome (OTS) and Relative Energy Deficiency in Sport (RED-S): Shared Pathways, Symptoms and Complexities." *Sports Medicine* 51:2251-2280. https://doi.org/10.1007/s40279-021-01491-0.

Stulberg, B. 2021. *The Practice of Groundedness: A Transformative Path to Success That Feeds—Not Crushes—Your Soul.* New York: Penguin Random House.

Supran, G., and N. Oreskes. 2017. "Assessing Exxonmobil's Climate Change Communications (1977–2014)." *Environmental Research Letters* 12. https://doi.org/10.1088/1748-9326/aa815f.

Sustain Your Style. n.d. "Fashion's Environmental Impacts." Accessed October 24, 2022. www.sustainyourstyle.org/en/environmental-impacts.

Sustainable Travel International. Terrapass. n.d. "Power Carbon Offsetting With Our Ready-to-Use Travel Carbon Footprint Calculator." Accessed October 20, 2022. https://sustainabletravel.org.

Swann, W.B., and M.D. Buhrmester. 2015. "Identity Fusion." *Current Directions in Psychological Science* 24 (1): 52-57. https://doi.org/10.1177/0963721414551363.

TELUS Communications. 2022. "Repair, Recycle and Upcycle: Join the Movement to Reduce Electronic Waste." *Global Newswire,* October 12, 2022. www.globenewswire.com/news-release/2022/10/12/2533090/0/en/Repair-recycle-and-upcycle-Join-the-movement-to-reduce-electronic-waste.html.

Terrapass. n.d. "Calculate." Accessed October 20, 2022. https://www.terrapass.com.

Tire Recycling Atlantic Canada Corporation. n.d. "Innovative Products From Recycled Tires." www.tracc.ca.

Tod, D., J. Hardy, and E. Oliver. 2011. "Effects of Self-Talk: A Systematic Review." *Journal of Sport and Exercise Psychology* 33 (5): 666-687. https://doi.org/10.1123/jsep.33.5.666.

Treece, K. 2021. "The 6 Best Carbon Offset Programs of 2022." *Treehugger.* March 1, 2022. www.treehugger.com/best-carbon-offset-programs-5076458.

Twenge, J.M., G.N. Martin, and W.K. Campbell. 2018. "Decreases in Psychological Well-Being Among American Adolescents After 2012 and Links to Screen Time During the Rise of Smartphone Technology." *Emotion* 18(6): 765-780. https://doi.org/10.1037/emo0000403.

Tyson, A., B. Kennedy, and C. Funk. 2021. "Gen Z, Millennials Stand Out for Climate Change Activism, Social Media Engagement With Issue." Pew Research Center. May 26, 2021. www.pewresearch.org/science/2021/05/26/gen-z-millennials-stand-out-for-climate-change-activism-social-media-engagement-with-issue.

United Nations. n.d. "For a Livable Climate: Net-Zero Commitments Must Be Backed By Credible Action." Accessed October 20, 2022. www.un.org/en/climatechange/net-zero-coalition.

United Nations. n.d. "The Paris Agreement" Accessed October 20, 2022. www.un.org/en/climatechange/paris-agreement.

University of Newcastle Australia. 2019. "Plastic Ingestion By People Could Be Equating to a Credit Card a Week." Last modified June 12, 2019. www.newcastle.edu.au/newsroom/featured/plastic-ingestion-by-people-could-be-equating-to-a-credit-card-a-week.

Villalobos, S. 2020. "A Practical Guide to Hosting Radically Responsible Events." Council for Responsible Sport. February 2020. https://www.councilforresponsiblesport.org/stories/2020/radicallyresponsible

Walker, M. 2017. *Why we sleep: unlocking the power of sleep and dreams.* Simon & Schuster Audio: New York, NY.

Walker, M. 2021. "Sleep Is Your Superpower." May 10, 2021. In *Rich Roll*, produced by Rich Roll, podcast, www.richroll.com/podcast/matthew-walker-600.

Wanderlust. "Bill McKibben: We Can Save the Planet If We Work Together." *Wanderlust*, 9 Mar. 2018, https://wanderlust.com/journal/bill-mckibben-we-can-save-the-planet-if-we-work-together/.

Waste, Electrical and Electronic Equipment Ireland. 2022. "E-waste Warning as Record Number of Electrical Items Recycled." June 20, 2022. www.weeeireland.ie/2022/06/20/e-waste-warning-as-record-number-of-electrical-items-recycled.

Wisconsin Historical Society and Nelson Institute for Environmental Studies. n.d. "Meet Gaylord Nelson: Founder of Earth Day." https://nelsonearthday.net/gaylord-nelson-founder-of-earth-day.

World Bank Writers. 2019. "How Much Do Our Wardrobes Cost to the Environment?" September, 23 2019. www.worldbank.org/en/news/feature/2019/09/23/costo-moda-medio-ambiente.

Xu, X., P. Sharma, S. Shu, T.-S. Lin, P. Ciais, F.N. Tubiello, P. Smith, N. Campbell, and A.K. Jain. "Global Greenhouse Gas Emissions From Animal-Based Foods Are Twice Those of Plant-Based Foods." *Nature Food* 2:724-32. https://doi.org/10.1038/s43016-021-00358-x.

Yeung, J.W.K., Z. Zhang, and T.Y. Kim. 2018. "Volunteering and Health Benefits in General Adults: Cumulative Effects and Forms." *BMC Public Health* 18 (1): 8. https://doi.org/10.1186/s12889-017-4561-8.

INDEX

ABOUT THE AUTHORS

Zoë Rom (left) and Tina Muir.

Originally from St. Albans, England, **Tina Muir** was a professional runner who represented Great Britain and Northern Ireland in a world championship. Now in St. Louis, Missouri, Muir founded her own business for runners, Running for Real, providing camaraderie and opportunity for growth. Her podcast, *Running for Real*, has amassed over five million downloads and was voted Best Fitness Podcast at the Sports Podcast Awards in 2021. It is a collective of conversations about running, the climate emergency, and social justice. Guests have included Rich Roll, Des Linden, David Epstein, Kara Goucher, and Michael Gervais. Muir also hosts a second podcast with Knox Robinson called *Running Realized*, noted as the "*Invisibilia* of running" by *Women's Running*.

Muir has published articles in *The Guardian*, *Runner's World*, *Self*, and *Women's Running* and released a self-published book in January 2019 that was featured on major running outlets as well as multiple podcasts. In 2021, she began collaborating with the United Nations and has been celebrated as one of the lead climate activists in the running space. Voted as one of the 17 women changing the world of running by *Women's Running* in 2017, she has inspired many others to speak out about their own passions.

Zoë Rom is the editor in chief at *Trail Runner* magazine; managing editor at *Women's Running;* and writer, host, and producer of the *DNF* podcast, which has been called the "*This American Life* of running podcasts" by *Los Angeles Review of Books*. In 2022, she joined a collective of athletes and writers (including Kara Goucher and other elite runners and podcast hosts) as part of Relay, which creates written content, podcasts, and videos that are offered through a Patreon subscription.

Rom is an award-winning journalist whose work has been featured in *Outside*, *Backpacker*, and *Trail Runner* magazines as well as on NPR's *Morning Edition* and *All Things Considered.* In 2019, she won the Colorado Broadcasters Association's award for Outstanding Feature Reporting. Her writing has also appeared in

Women's Running, Discover, REI Co-op Journal, and on *Threshold*, a Peabody-award-winning environmental podcast.

Rom is an elite trail runner with a master's degree in environmental journalism from the University of Colorado Boulder. She has covered sled dog racing in the Alaskan bush, arctic sea ice exploration in Norway, morel hunting in northern Arkansas, competitive alpaca racing in the Colorado Rockies, and much more. Her running accomplishments include first place at the Crested Butte 100K and Athens Big Fork Trail Marathon as well as two consecutive wins at the War Eagle 50K.